1299

MW00514363

SECRETS OF

SUCCESSFUL MARRIAGES

Matthew N. O. Sadiku, Ph.D.

Covenant Publishers
P. O. Box 26361
Philadelphia, PA 19141

Scripture quotations are from the Revised Standard Version of the Bible (RSV), copyrighted 1946, 1952, 1971 by the Division of Christian Education of the National Council of Churches of Christ in the U.S.A. Used by permission.

Scriptures quotations marked AB are from the Amplified Bible, copyright 1962, 1964, 1965 by Zondervan Publishing House.

Scriptures quotations marked KJV are from the King James Version of the Bible.

Scriptures quotations marked LB are from The Living Bible, copyright 1971 by Tyndale House Publisher, Wheaton, Illinois 60187.

Scriptures quotations marked NASB are from the New American Standard Bible, copyright 1960, 1962, 1963, 1968, 1971, 1972, 1973, 1975, 1977 THE LOCKMAN FOUNDATION.

Scriptures quotations marked NIV are from the New International Version of the Bible, copyright 1973, 1978, 1984 by International Bible Society.

Copyright © 1991 by Matthew N. O. Sadiku

All rights reserved

No part of this publication may be reproduced in any manner whatsoever without the prior written permission of the publisher except in the case of brief quatations embodied in books, critical articles, and reviews.

Book design and typesetting by Malcolm Litchfield

This book is composed in Adobe Garamond

Printed in the United States of America

Library of Congress Catalog Card Number: 90-085047

ISBN: 1-879420-00-7 Cloth

1-879420-01-5 Paper

To

Chris

who has been a blessing in every way!

ACKNOWLEDGMENTS

I am indebted to all colleagues who have contributed in this area and whose works I have drawn from. I owe special thanks to Dr. Ashiwel S. Undie, Rev. Hosea Anderson, and Ifeanyi Onyemaobim whose critical comments on the manuscipt enhanced its quality. I am deeply grateful to Steve Dunham, Dr. Obi Echewa, and Michelle Esbenshade for thorough editing. I greatly appreciate the sacrifices made by my wife, Chris, and our daughter, Ann, while I wrote this book.

CONTENTS

Part II: Social Secrets

INTRODUCTION

*The secret things belong to the LORD our God; but the things that
are revealed belong to us and to our children for ever,
that we may do all the words of this law*
Deuteronomy 29:29

This book is an exploration of the principles, secrets,
laws, or rules by which a marriage works. Most books
on marriage are based on counseling experiences. This book
gives you more than experiences; it gives you principles,
secrets, handles for a successful, happy marriage. Experience
tells you what works, but principles tell why it works. When
principles are understood, many things tend to take care of
themselves.

To everything in life, there is a secret or principle that must
be learned to know how that thing works. We all started life
as babies. Like savages, we knew nothing about language,
customs, religion, etc. That is partly why we go to school, to
learn the secrets of life—the principles of our language,
geography, mathematics, physics, biology, etc. There are
secrets, principles, rules in every aspect of life. For example,
there are secrets to doing well in school, to becoming rich, to
being an effective leader, and to winning a war. In the same

way, there are secrets that must be mastered for a marriage to be successful.

Principles are handles on life. It is common in life that a special key, secret or principle opens up many discoveries. Many breakthroughs in science and technology, for example, are due to discovery of principles. Like a ship (or anything else), your marriage is subject to principles or secrets that determine its success. If any of these principles is violated, you are in turbulence, destined to capsize. However, if you discover which principle you are violating and change your attitude and actions accordingly, your marriage will survive the storm.

A secret is something either concealed from others or not readily understood by them. The Bible talks about secrets. For example, Job's friend talked about the secrets of wisdom (Job 11:6) and Paul talked about the secret of contentment (Philippians 4:12).

The principles or secrets of a successful marriage ought to be learned prior to the time one gets married. The ultimate goal of going to school is to be able to function effectively in society—in a job situation, church, etc. So you go to school to learn the basics, the fundamental principles of life and you apply them later in life. By the same token, one should be familiar with the fundamentals of marriage before getting married. Otherwise you learn the principles the hard way and your spouse becomes the guinea pig you experiment with. However, it is never too late to learn. If you are already married, the sooner you know the principles, the better.

But, what is a successful marriage? It is not easy to describe a successful marriage. But just for the sake of definition, a marriage may be considered successful when the couple live together for the rest of their lives. No one marries with the intention of getting a divorce. The willingness to live with your spouse for life is expressed in your wedding vow. Therefore, one may regard your marriage as successful if you adjust to your spouse's lifestyle to the extent that the two of you can live together until death separates you. A successful marriage produces a successful, happy husband, wife, and children. It is a happy marriage. Having a successful marriage is a large part of what it means to succeed as a man or woman. As William Lyon Phelps excellently said:

Every man who is happy at home is a successful man, even if he has failed in everything else.

This is also true of every woman.

In the chapters to follow, I will share with you ten secrets or principles that will make your marriage work and be successful. There are places in the book where I will address you as an individual because there are certain things each individual must do to make one's marriage work. At other places, I will address you as a marriage couple because certain things must be done jointly to ensure success.

The book is meant to stimulate your thinking. The principles discussed serve as windows through which you look and see your role as a husband or a wife. They will transform for the better your personal life and consequently your marriage. They will help you develop a lasting and intimate relationship.

The principles set forth in this book have not only met the test in my own marriage, but in the marriage experience of others. These secrets come from God's Word. God reveals secrets to His people (Deuteronomy 29:29; Daniel 2:22,28,30; Amos 3:7). As the Author of life and the Institutor of marriage, He reveals the secrets of a happy, successful marriage. These are truths you can count on while building the marriage you dream of. They are wise and practical; they work. If you refuse to give heed to God's plan for your life, designed for your benefit, you will reap what you sow. But don't blame God if things fall apart in your marriage. If you pay close attention to His Word and obey it, you are guaranteed a successful marriage. Therefore, as you discover the secrets, believe in them and personalize them. The degree to which you believe in them and apply them determines the success of your marriage. Your willingness to accept God's Word and change your attitudes and actions will dictate the effect of this book on your life. The effort you put into applying the principles presented in the book will lead to rewarding results in your life and home.

As we come to the end of this introduction, keep this in mind as Secret Number 0:

> A key to success in anything in life is doing the right thing, at the right time, in the right way, and for the right reason.

But how do we know the right thing, the right time, the right way, and the right reason? In the rest of the book, I will show you how.

PART I

SPIRITUAL SECRETS

CHAPTER ONE

THE SECRET OF A CHRIST-CENTERED HOME

Apart from me, you can do nothing
John 15:5

A strong, happy, and successful family life doesn't just happen. It takes time and study, just like any other worthwhile endeavor. It is the result of careful planning, deliberate effort, determination, and growth. It involves proper adjustment to each other and incorporation of divine principles of marriage into a couple's daily living.

As shown in Figure 1.1, marriage is a triangular affair—God bringing together a man and woman. Life without God is futile; so is a marriage not centered on Christ. A Christian couple has the best possibilities for a happy, successful marriage because their marriage has a third person—Jesus Christ. It is He who provides meaning, guidance, and direction to their marriage. In fact, it is a contradiction of terms to think of a Christian marriage without Christ presiding over the marriage. If the man and woman are properly related in a personal way to God, they will most likely be properly related to each other. This is why both the husband

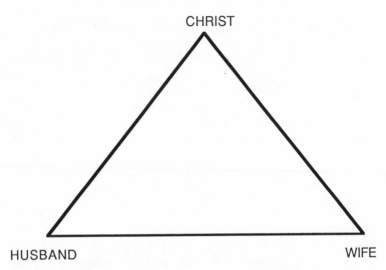

Fig. 1.1   Marriage is a triangular affair.

and wife should have accepted Jesus Christ as their Lord and Savior prior to their wedding. It is only when Christ is the Lord of your marriage that your home will abide in lasting peace and blessing. Jesus said:

Apart from me you can do nothing (John 15:5).

The wise man said,

A threefold cord is not quickly broken (Ecclesiastes 4:12).

It is needless to say that God instituted and ordained marriage. Marriage is not a human invention. It is a covenant relationship between a man and a woman established under God. The family belongs to God. He created it as the basic unit of society. He determined its structure, purpose, and goal. It is intended to be where we discover God in the framework of love and truth. Thus it is not your marriage, but His marriage; not your home, but His home; not your children, but His children.

For a happy and successful marriage, a couple must establish and maintain a Christ-centered home. Everything in your marriage relationship must be focused or centered around Christ. A family that is committed to Jesus Christ enjoys an enormous advantage over the family with no spiritual basis. To have a family committed to Christ involves three things:

- establishing a divine order,
- living according to divine will, and
- making Christ the focus.

Establishing a Divine Order

It is of paramount importance that a divine order, a chain of relationship, be maintained in a home. Without it, things will be out of order. Each member of the family, the husband and wife in particular, must maintain personal contact with the Lord. Each individual must set aside some time each day to have a personal devotion with God. Let God talk to you on a personal basis. It is through such personal effort in seeking God that you discover yourself and your mission in life. As Josh McDowell rightly put it:

The truest thing about you is what God says about you in His Word, the Bible. Your emotions, your culture, or your feelings cannot dictate who you are. If you allow them to, you can be misled easily.

The divine order for husband-wife relationship is plainly established in the Scriptures. Whenever we build our lives, our marriages, our homes on values and principles that are contradictory to the time-honored wisdom of God's Word, we are laying a foundation on sand, sowing the wind, and bound to reap the whirlwind.

The divine order is one of authority and responsibility. It is the human government God has established to curb human selfishness and lawlessness. God has established human government in the three spheres in which a person finds himself or herself: home, church, and society. That is why we are supposed to submit to the governing authorities in every realm.

> *For there is no authority except from God, and those that exist have been instituted by God. Therefore he who resists the authorities resists what God has appointed, and those who resist will incur judgment* (Romans 13:1,2).

At home, the divine order is clearly spelled out:

> *The head of every man is Christ, the head of a woman is her husband, and the head of Christ is God* (1 Corinthians 11:3).

> *Children, obey your parents in everything, for this pleases the Lord* (Colossians 3:20).

The divine order and design for the family is based on the principles of headship and submission. The order is illustrated in Figure 1.2. God is head over all. Jesus in terms of rank is under God. Of course the Holy Spirit is under Christ as far as rank is concerned, but here we are only using the examples

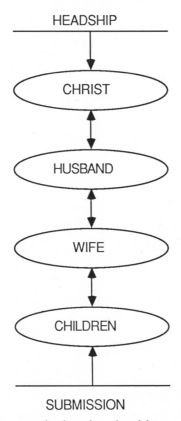

Fig. 1.2   Divine order based on headship and submission

of God and Jesus. The husband lives under the headship of Christ. Under the husband comes the wife and, under the wife, the children. Thus the divine order is clearly specified and any deviation leads only to disaster.

1. *For the Husband*

With the divine authority vested in a husband comes responsibility:

> *Husbands, love your wives, as Christ loved the church and gave Himself up for her ... Even so husbands should love their wives as their own bodies. He who loves his wife loves himself. For no man ever hates his own flesh, but nourishes and cherishes it, as Christ does the church* (Ephesians 5:25,28,29).

> *Husbands, love your wives, and do not be harsh with them* (Colossians 3:19).

Both the authority and responsibility of the husband are modeled upon Christ. Just as Christ's authority over the church was rooted in the sacrifice of Himself, the husband's authority is rooted in the sacrifice of himself. The most obvious expression of this is seen in the husband's support of the family.

Men often quote Ephesians 5:25 and demand that their wives submit to their authority. The same chapter that urges wives to submit also says:

> *Be subject to one another out of reverence for Christ* (Ephesians 5:21).

The submission, in a sense, is mutual. If a husband is not playing his role properly, he has no right to demand his wife's submission. It is an easy thing for a wife to submit to her husband when the husband himself is following Christ's example. Men should be heads and leaders at home. And leaders do not demand submission; they command it.

The husband is not just the head in terms of authority, he is the leader in spiritual matters. He is to minister to his wife and children. To be head of the family is to be committed to meeting their needs and supporting their interests. The husband is to hold standards, be exemplary in practicing the standards, and help his wife and children live by them.

2. *For the Wife*

To the wife, God has given the privilege to choose freely to submit to her husband just as Christ voluntarily chose to submit to the Father (Philippians 2:5-9). So the wife's role is put this way:

> *Wives, be subject to your husbands, as to the Lord. For the husband is the head of the wife as Christ is the head of the church, his body, and is Himself its Savior. As the church is subject to Christ, so let wives also be subject in everything to their husbands* (Ephesians 5:22-24).

> *Wives, be subject to your husbands, as is fitting in the Lord* (Colossians 3:18).

How much should the husband love his wife? How far can he go in the love business? As Christ loved the church. Christ's love is the yardstick, the standard of comparison. By this same token, the wife is expected to submit to her husband just as she would submit to the Lord. Paul added that her submission is the fitting or proper thing to do; it is in accordance with the divine order. Her submission should not be conceived as a passive role. Submission does not mean allowing your husband to make all the decisions. It does not make you inferior in any sense, just as Christ's submission to the Father does not rob Him of His equality with the Father (Philippians 2:5-11). God established this order as a means of social balance for her benefit and good, for her protection, and for the harmony of the home. He intends for a woman to be sheltered from some of the rough encounters of life. Remember, the submission is to *your own husband* (KJV), and that is the only man you are necessarily meant to submit to.

As a wife, you have a high calling, a great job to do. Your influence on your husband and the atmosphere you create for the people in your life are enormous. A gentle and quiet spirit dominating your life is one of the greatest accomplishments possible for you as a wife. It is of great value in the sight of God.

3. *For Children*

The divine order for children is that of obedience:

> *Children, obey your parents in everything, for this pleases the Lord* (Colossians 3:20).

> *Children, obey your parents in the Lord, for this is right. "Honor your father and mother" (this is the first commandment with a promise), "that it may be well with you and that you may live long on earth"* (Ephesians 6:1-3).

God's plan for children is for them to obey their parents. Every child starts life as a barbarian or a savage. He is completely ignorant and selfish. His parents are the first to contribute to his social, moral, and spiritual development. In this process of civilizing the child and teaching him self-discipline, the child must be obedient. Obedience is a basic law of spiritual and social life. God's authority often comes into our life through human authority, which is instituted and designed by God Himself to curb our excessiveness and lawlessness. If a child cannot obey his parents, how can he obey his school teachers, pastor, police, etc.? It is through submission and obedience to parents that children learn to submit to people in authority.

By way of motivation, Paul pointed out that obedience to parents is the first commandment with a promise attached to it: *that it may be well with you, and that you may live long on earth.* As with every command God gives, it is for our own good.

Living According to Divine Will

Marriage is like building a home. So you need to draw the plan, lay the foundation, construct the floors, and erect the roof. Marriage is also like weaving. You must decide on a pattern, the color, the textures, and the strength of the warp threads. In all of this, you desperately need wisdom.

As a Christian couple, you cannot afford to base your whole life and marriage on culture, customs or tradition; they will disappoint you because they are made by humans. You need Christ to give you wisdom and guidance in building a successful marriage.

Unless the LORD builds the house, those who build it labor in vain (Psalm 127:1).

In Matthew 7:24-27, the Lord gave a parable on two kinds of people who follow Him: the wise and the foolish. The man whose house collapsed is regarded as foolish, not because he did not lay the proper foundation. He built his house on "shifting sand," which represents human opinions, cultures, customs, and traditions as opposed to the principles of Christ. Remember that human opinions are subject to change, but that God's Word is certain and sure.

> *The law of the LORD is perfect, reviving the soul; the testimony of the LORD is sure, making wise the simple; the precepts of the LORD are right, rejoicing the heart; the commandment of the LORD is pure, enlightening the eyes* (Psalm 19:7,8).

For your marriage to be successful, you must let the doctrines of Christ, not traditions of men, prevail in all your decisions. He must be your Lord, not just your Savior. Everything you do must be centered, focused around Him. You must live according to His revealed will. To do this involves three things. You must:

- know God's Word, the Bible,
- believe His Word, and
- learn His will.

1. *Know God's Word, the Bible*

Doing the will of God is a sacred act in living. But it is hard to do God's will if we do not first know it. It takes cultivating the habit of reading and studying His Word on a daily, regular basis. It takes the discipline of studying the mind of God as revealed in His Word.

The secret things belong to the LORD our God; but the things that are revealed belong to us and to our children for ever, that we may do all the words of this law (Deuteronomy 29:29).

Through diligent study, we get to know God's revealed secrets, His principles, His mind. The Word of God is the compass for living. It is supreme in its authority, progressive in its revelation, complete in its manifestation, varied in its presentation, and alive and relevant in its applications.

Remember that your natural thoughts and ways of doing things are opposed to His thoughts and ways:

For my thoughts are not your thoughts, neither are your ways my ways, says the Lord. For as the heavens are higher than the earth, so are my ways, higher than your ways, and my thoughts than your thoughts (Isaiah 55:8,9).

Your thoughts are influenced by the world system. There are three major influences on a person's life: culture, education, and religion. One's mind has been programmed by these influences. Of the three influences, culture has the greatest impact. As A. T. Robertson says, "There is nothing more binding on the average person than social custom." Why? Because as a child, culture was the first influence you had through your parents and other adults. Your parents taught you how to eat, dress, behave, etc., even before you started going to school, when education started its own influence. Although you might have been going to church with your parents when you were little, you probably paid little attention to religion at that time. You were probably doing religious things to please your parents. So culture was the first exposure to life you had and that is why it has more influence on your life than religion or education.

Culture and tradition in themselves are not bad. After all, culture is simply a way of life acceptable to a group of people. However, some aspects of a culture may have damaging effects on your marriage, especially in areas where it conflicts with God's will. A graphic example is that of Joseph in Genesis 48. According to tradition, by which Joseph was abiding, Jacob was to put his right hand on the first-born in pronouncing blessing on Joseph's sons. But it was God's design that the younger brother should be greater than the older one, the first-born. In trying to follow tradition, we become rigid and subjective and miss out on what God is about to do. This is why you should constantly reprogram your mind and replace the old stuff of culture in your memories with God's Word.

Do not be conformed to this world, but be transformed by the renewal of your mind, that you may prove what is the will of God, what is good and acceptable and perfect (Romans 12:2).

You want to know the will of God? You need a transformation, a reprogramming, a renewal of your mind. Computer programmers are fond of using the slogan "Garbage in, garbage out." What you feed into your mind is what you are going to become. To know God's will, feed His Word into your mind.

Make it a goal to learn and know more about God's Word. Through this, you get to know God better and His will for your life. There is no limit to how much you can learn of God. God's will for your life is that you grow to maturity

(Ephesians 4:11-14). Let me suggest some practical steps you can take to grow with God, get to know Him better, and know His will for your life and marriage.

Step 1: *Endeavor to read daily four chapters of the Bible.*

By doing this, you can cover the whole Bible in nine to twelve months. The Appendix provides you with a systematic way to go about it. This systematic approach of going through the Bible is adopted by many people. However, it can become boring to someone like myself. So let me suggest the randomized approach I use. (My wife follows the systematic approach.) Start with your favorite book in the Bible, e.g., John, Romans, Psalms. Read four chapters of the book a day until you come to the end of the book. Select another book, not necessarily the one following the first one. Say the first one is Romans, the next one could be John. Read four chapters a day until you finish it. Choose another one—maybe Proverbs, this time—and follow the same procedure. You keep selecting books in the Bible until you cover them all. This may seem unsystematic; it is surely not boring. I have found this approach very helpful and I have used it to go through the Bible more than seven times. You may want to try it if you don't like the systematic approach in the Appendix.

Step 2: *Take a correspondence course on the Bible.*

This will help you feed your spiritual person continually and you will accumulate college credits toward a diploma or degree. Although you could buy the same book, recommended for the correspondence course and read it on your own, there is a limit to how much you can learn by yourself. Most of us are not self-disciplined enough to learn much on our own. Also, without a credit or diploma as a motivating goal, we are easily discouraged and distracted by other "urgent" things. Paying for the course may be an additional motivation to spend time and study God's Word.

You may ask, "Which correspondence course do you recommend?" It depends on what you are looking for and your level of maturity in the faith. In my opinion, the best one would cover as much of the Bible as possible and by the end of it you would have earned some credit or diploma. With this in mind, I strongly recommend:

Liberty Home Bible Institute
2220 Langhorne Road
Lynchburg, VA 24514
(804) 528-4119 or 1-800-446-LHBI

This course is offered by Liberty University and covers a chronological study of the entire Bible, every major Bible doctrine, practical seminars, and six electives with study notes, textbooks, and audiocassettes or videocassettes. At the completion of the course, you will receive a general Bible diploma. If you are interested in taking short courses on some topics of interest (e.g., Old Testament Hebrew, New Testament Greek), write:

Moody Bible Institute
Correspondence School
820 North La Salle Drive
Chicago, IL 60610-9975
(312) 918-2620 or 1-800-955-1123

For correspondence courses leading to advanced degrees, up to Ph.D., write:

Christian International
Route 2, Box 351
Point Washington, FL 32454
(905) 231-5308

or

Trinity Theological Seminary
4233 Medwel Drive
P. O. Box 717
Newburgh, IN 47629-0717
(812) 853-0611

These courses are essentially in-depth, planned Bible studies. They allow you to study in the privacy and convenience of your own home and help you derive the maximum amount of truth in the minimum amount of time. Knowing God's will comes from knowing His principles, His mind, His Word.

Step 3: *Study on your own.*

Depending on your area of interest or ministry, buy well-written books on that area and study them for growth. I personally like commentaries; so I buy commentaries on Romans, John, Genesis, etc., one at a time and study them. Maybe your interest is in witnessing, counselling, or even marriage; buy books in that area and study. You can get good books from your local bookstore or at a lower price through mail order from:

Christian Book Distributors

P. O. Box 3687
Peabody, MA 01961-3687
(508) 532-5300

Whether you start at step 1, 2 or 3 depends on your level of maturity.

Studying the Word of God helps you develop some doctrinal beliefs, which are essentially your convictions of faith and life. Failure to follow sound doctrinal beliefs leads to erroneous living, which is not God's will. Sound doctrinal beliefs provide a solid base on which everything else depends. They are the navigational stars for your life's journey. They undergird you through life.

2. *Believe His Word*

It is one thing to learn and know God's Word; it is another thing to believe it. You can give mental assent to it, but you can't obey what you don't believe. Believing is merely taking God at His Word, and that is the only absolute this world has (Matthew 24:35).

> *The message which they heard did not benefit them, because it did not meet with faith in the hearers* (Hebrews 4:2).

You don't benefit from God's Word until you combine it with faith, obey it, and live it. The reason many Christians don't live victoriously is that they don't combine faith with what they hear or know. A Christian who is seriously sick knows that God can heal, but he may not have faith that God is willing to heal him.

Faith is what the secular world calls risk taking. The more risks one can take, the more likely one is to succeed in the secular world. The same is true in the spiritual world. The heroes of faith listed in Hebrews 11 and noted elsewhere are men and women of faith—Abraham, Moses, Rahab, Samuel, etc. Without faith, it is impossible to please God or move with Him (Hebrews 11:6).

3. *Learn His Will*

It is important that we know God's will for our lives, our marriages, our children, etc. Otherwise we lose focus, we go through life feeling miserable, we experience frustration and confusion, and we suffer from identity crises. Life is without meaning apart from doing God's will. We can see the difference between people who live according to God's will and those who are ignorant of God's will for their lives. It is the difference we observe in the lives of Moses and the Israelites he was leading. Moses knew God's mind and principles, but the people knew only God's acts. Psalm 103:7 puts it this way:

He made known his ways to Moses, his acts to the people of Israel.

The people murmured and complained because they did not understand God's will, plan or purpose for their lives. The greatest tragedy of life is to pass through life without knowing God's will.

Knowing God's will for one's life is not an easy task, but it can be learned. There are no formulas or short cuts. But you can know it if you are willing to pay the price. It takes effort and diligence to know God's will.

God's will for your life is your life's calling. Why were you born? What are your special gifts and talents? What would God want you to accomplish in your lifetime? You may not have answers to these and similar questions right away, but with time you should be able to find answers as you move with God and let His Word illuminate your mind. You will discover that you have talents, things you love to do, things you are good at doing. You will also discover that your community has needs you can recognize. Using your talents in meeting the needs of the community is doing God's will. The will of God is your goal for life. It is your life's vision.

Needless to say, prayer is essential in confirming God's will for your life. Knowing God's will could be a subject of prayer or an answer to prayer. Also, we must be sensitive to the guidance of the Holy Spirit and be flexible. We must look for open doors of opportunity when other doors are closed (1 Corinthians 16:9; 2 Corinthians 2:12; Revelation 3:8). So leave a door open for providence so that God may enter your life as He chooses.

Consultation with serious Christians is essential in learning the will of God. The Bible, the Holy Spirit, and the church (the body of believers) constantly complement each other in providing guidance. You don't want to reinvent the wheel and make the same mistakes others have made. You can benefit from the experience of others who are doing the will of God and are more mature in the Christian faith. They clarify your own views. They also give you encouragement and strength. They probably have passed along the same path and see you more clearly than you see yourself sometimes. However, the final decision should be made by you. Take their advice as guides, not as commands. You must be in the driver's seat when it comes to making your life decision.

Finally, the way you discover God's will for your home is similar to how you discover His will for your personal life.

Making Christ the Focus

If Christ is the focus of your life and marriage, you should show it by your:

- surrender to His lordship,
- family devotion,
- obedience to His will,
- commitment to His body, and
- pursuit of holiness.

1. *Surrender to His Lordship*

A life that is focused on Christ must fully yield and surrender to His lordship. Jesus said,

> *Why do you call me 'Lord, Lord,' and not do what I tell you?* (Luke 6:46).

We must commit ourselves to the lordship of Jesus Christ as a continuing act of the mind, will, and heart. As we surrender to Him, we allow His Spirit to take charge of every area of our lives and we become vessels of honor that God can use to accomplish His purposes.

A typical example of what God can accomplish with a man who is fully surrendered to Him is found in the life of the apostle Paul. Many Bible scholars consider the conversion of Paul as the climax and consummation of Christianity. When

Paul surrendered himself to the lordship of Jesus Christ, he entered a new ministry and a new life. He got a new Captain and a new Boss. Humility became his foundation and love his goal. God has demonstrated that he can shake the world with a yielded man: a Moses, an Elijah, a Daniel, a Peter, a Paul, a Luther, a Wesley, a Moody, a Spurgeon, etc. He is now waiting for you and me. Make Christ your Master, and he will make you a master.

2. *Family Devotion*

A family that is Christ-centered must set aside some time to read God's Word and pray. A family devotional time is vital to your marriage. Although you alone are responsible for your personal relationship with God, family devotions give you a better perspective on life and on each other. They provide you with time to grow closer to God and to each other because you communicate with each other and pray together. The individual and corporate devotional life of a family can provide a stability that is refreshing, enjoyable, and helpful to the health of the family. The importance of prayer in the fabric of family life will be discussed fully in the next chapter.

3. *Obedience to His Will*

If Christ is the center of your life and marriage, you show it by obeying His Word and acting on it. Hearing God's Word alone will not change your life. You must hear and obey by living the Word:

> *Be doers of the Word, and not hearers only, deceiving your-*
> *selves. For if anyone is a hearer of the word and not a doer,*
> *he is like a man who observes his natural face in a mirror;*

for he observes himself and goes away and at once forgets what he was like. But he who looks into the perfect law, the law of liberty, and perseveres, being no hearer that forgets but a doer that acts, he shall be blessed in his doing (James 1:22-25, emphasis mine).

Not every one who says to me, 'Lord, Lord', shall enter the kingdom of heaven, but he who does the will of my Father who is in heaven (Matthew 7:21).

As Christians, God has called us for a single purpose—that we may be conformed to the image of His Son, Jesus Christ (Romans 12:2). He wants us to live through Christ (1 John 4:9; 2 Corinthians 5:15; Galatians 2:20). We must let Christ live through us. His love must be the controlling factor of our life. We must live for Him, not for ourselves, and let His light shine through us. The blessing of God is guaranteed on our marriage as we obey God's Word (Deuteronomy 5:29,33; 6:24; 30:20).

4. *Commitment to His Body*

A life that is surrendered to Christ is evident through involvement and commitment to a local church, the body of Christ. You cannot claim to belong to the head while you dissociate from the body. Church involvement is important for your family's spiritual development. It is important that you look for a church where you can grow and be committed for such a long time that your children will be able to identify it as their church. Your involvement could be active or supportive. Active involvements include singing in the choir, teaching Sunday school, helping in the nursery, being an usher, being the director of youth ministry, etc. Supportive involvements include not-so-obvious tasks such as making a call, writing to missionaries, participating in the prayer chain, etc. As one writer said:

> *What I can do to share my faith and support my church:*
> *Have phone ... will call.*
> *Have pen ... will write.*
> *Have interest ... will come.*
> *Have car ... will bring.*
> *Have money ... will tithe.*
> *Have voice ... will witness.*
> *Have concern ... will pray.*
> *Have love ... will share.*

Whatever you choose to do, do it as unto the Lord.

5. *Pursuit of Holiness*

To be Godlike in character means to be holy, for God is holy. We have been called and set apart to live a holy life (1 Peter 1:16). In 1 Thessalonians 4:3,7, Paul wrote:

> *For this is the will of God, your sanctification: that you abstain from unchastity ... For God has not called us for uncleanness, but in holiness.*

It is God's will for our lives not to conform any longer to the pattern of this world, but to be renewed in our minds (Romans 12:1,2). This process of renewing or reprogramming our minds involves constant exposure to the Word of God and establishing convictions. As we expose ourselves to the Scriptures, our values begin to change so that God's standard becomes our desire and delight. Through the ministry of the Holy Spirit, we are transformed more and more into the likeness of our Lord.

The Rewards of a Christ-Centered Home

Human beings are reward-oriented by nature. This is why God made a lot of promises for those who obey Him. God is not asking us to obey His Word for nothing in return. There are blessings and rewards for obeying God.

What are the benefits or rewards for living according to God's will and making Christ the focus of your marriage? They are so many that it is impossible to enumerate them all. I will mention only four of them. Apart from having a lasting, satisfying marriage, you have:

- meaning to life,
- guidance,
- fulfillment, and
- harmony.

1. *Meaning to Life*

We all search for meaning in life. The search for meaning is a primary force that drives us in one direction or another in life. Life without meaning is boring and not worthwhile. Living according to God's will helps you discover meaning and purpose for living. It helps you to answer the basic questions of life: Who am I? Why am I here? And for what reason? You get a special word from the Lord, which could be your vision or mission in life. Your mission is your life because it gives breath to your system. It is your purpose because it is the reason for your existence. It is your future because it keeps you focused. When you live according to God's will, He directs and orders all your steps. Life becomes meaningful and purposeful. It doesn't mean that your life and marriage are without problems. But it does mean that you don't see problems as obstacles on your way. Rather, you see problems as opportunities, as stepping stones.

2. Guidance

Life is so complex that sometimes it is very difficult to decide which way to go. Sometimes you are troubled, uncertain or confused. You don't really know what to do. You need divine guidance. God guides those who follow Him. He is your shepherd; you will not lack guidance. He leads you in paths of righteousness for His name's sake (Psalm 23:1-4). But God doesn't always interfere in human lives when He is not asked to do so. He has designed man with a free will. Man may exercise the right to choose against God. However, when man voluntarily chooses to obey God and seek His guidance, God interferes and directs.

> *The steps of a man are [ordered] from the LORD, and he establishes him in whose way he delights* (Psalm 37:23).

> *A man's mind plans his way, but the Lord directs his steps* (Proverbs 16:9).

Your influence on your spouse and children is tremendous. If you aren't seeking God for wisdom and guidance, you may influence them in the wrong direction.

3. *Fulfillment*

The Lord fulfills the desire of those who love, fear, and obey Him (Psalm 145:19). Your will becomes His will because you have been transformed by His Word. As you allow Christ to control your life and marriage, all areas of your life will begin to fall in line with God's plan. Under His plan, you can expect maximum benefits and optimal returns. There will be no regrets.

4. *Harmony*

Harmony in marriage is not total agreement on every point, but a concord that comes by each one making his/her unique contribution to the whole. For that harmony to exist, there must be a common faith based on solid Christian principles. A husband and wife who are in touch with God and seek to do His will in all areas of their lives will eventually be blended in perfect harmony.

Marriages break down largely because of character failure. If a man or a woman is faithless to God, it is no surprise if he/she is faithless to the marriage covenant. Religion at home is vital to keeping a home together. Religion based on love is the only foolproof guarantee in a marriage relationship and in home life.

Religion in the home is the best preventive measure against juvenile delinquency. The best guarantee for good, well-behaved children is religious instruction in the home. A Christ-centered home puts into action Christian principles such as obedience to divine commandments, submission to constituted authority, faithfulness, trust, love, and giving.

These principles and values naturally lead to stability to the marriage and produce harmony among family members.

Without a doubt, making Christ the center or focus of your marriage is the greatest secret of a happy, successful marriage. As Secret Number 1,

> *Unless the LORD builds the house, those who build it labor in vain* (Psalm 127:1).

Secret Number 1 is the most important of all. Although the secret or principle by itself is not enough, without it other principles will not work. It is the foundation on top of which everything must be laid. Christ should be the foundation of your home. He is the sure foundation that will not fail. Build your marriage on Him.

Notes

[1] Josh McDowell, *The Secret of Loving* (Wheaton, IL: Living Books, 1989), p. 33.

CHAPTER TWO

THE SECRET OF PRAYER

You do not have, because you do not ask
James 4:2

... Ask and you will receive, that your joy may be full
John 16:24

They say the family that prays together stays together. This belief has passed the test of time. Several marriages have been completely transformed by initiating a practice of regular prayer. If a husband and wife read the Bible and pray together, not only will they stay together, they will communicate more effectively with each other and enrich their marital relationship. This is due to the fact that prayer time provides you an opportunity to share things you have forgotten to share because of the busy activities of life. The prayer time also provides a forum for sharing your beliefs with each other. This sharing, providing either information or items of prayer or thanksgiving, further broadens the common bond that exists between a couple.

Prayer is not only vital in a husband-and-wife relationship, it is the divine rule for living. It is prayer that gives significance to life. Prayer is the first sign of spiritual life, and also the means of maintaining it. Prayer is the key to the problems of our day, especially family problems.

"Whether we like it or not," said C. H. Spurgeon, "asking is the rule of the kingdom." Whatever concerns your highest welfare, and whatever has to do with God's plans and purposes concerning men on earth, must be a subject of prayer. Our temporal matters have much to do with our health, happiness, and home. Not to pray about such matters is to leave God out of the largest sphere of our existence. One who cannot pray in everything has never learned the nature and worth of prayer. In John 15:1-11, our Lord teaches that prayer and fruit-bearing are not matters of our choices; He has chosen us for the very purpose of praying. Why? Because without prayer the Lord's promises are dim, shadowy and impersonal. As E. M. Bounds excellently put it:

Promises are God's golden fruit to be plucked by the hand of prayer . . . . Promises, like rain, are general. Prayer embodies, precipitates, and locates them for personal use. Prayer goes by faith into the great fruit orchard of God's exceeding great and precious promises, and with hand and heart picks the ripest and richest fruit.[1]

We do not naturally know how to pray, although our hearts long for God. John the Baptist had to teach his disciples how to pray, and Jesus, too, taught His disciples how to pray. Just as with every other thing in life, we must be taught how to pray and how to receive from God. If prayer were taught in every church as it should be, there would be no need of including a chapter on it in this book on marriage.

Since prayer is vital to a happy, successful marriage, it is important to briefly cover the fundamentals of effectual prayer. We will cover:

- results of prayerlessness,
- the necessity of prayer,
- hindrances to prayer,
- how to pray, and
- rewards of prayer.

Results of Prayerlessness

A prayerless Christian is a weak believer because prayerlessness is the absence of the work of the Holy Spirit in one. It is easy to let things, legitimate and right in themselves, so engross our attention and preoccupy our minds that prayer is given little or no attention. Even the apostles had to guard themselves at this point (Acts 6:2). Prayerlessness may manifest itself in our routine life or even in our spiritual service. This fact was well noted by E. M. Bounds:

Sacred work—church activities—may so engage and absorb us as to hinder praying, and when this is the case, evil results always follow. It is better to let the work go by default than to let the praying go by neglect .... "Too busy to pray" is not only the keynote to backsliding, but it mars even the work done. Nothing is well done without prayer for the simple reason that it leaves God out of the account. It is so easy to be seduced by the good to the neglect of the best, until both the good and best perish. How easily are many men, even leaders in Zion, led by the insidious wiles of Satan to cut short our praying in the interests of the work! How easy to neglect prayer or abbreviate our praying simply by the plea that we have church work on our hands. Satan has effectively disarmed us when he can keep us too busy doing things to stop and pray.[2]

Prayerlessness is disobedience to God. To fail to pray is to disobey the Lord's command that we watch and pray (Matthew 26:41). It is to leave God out of our existence and depend on our flesh. In First Samuel, the people of Israel begged Samuel to pray for them. Samuel responded by saying:

Far be it from me that I should sin against the LORD by ceasing to pray for you (1 Samuel 12:23).

In spite of the pressures and challenges we face today, a husband and wife should guard against "sinning against the Lord" by not praying for each other.

Because prayerlessness is a sin, it leads to many awful consequences. It results in

- want,
- trouble,
- defeat,
- destruction, and
- lack of revelation from God.

1. *Want*

Prayer is receiving from God. It is a means by which we let God bless us. God has pledged Himself to supply all our needs—physical, spiritual and intellectual.

If you ask anything in my name, I will do it (John 14:14).

Truly, truly, I say to you, if you ask anything of the Father, he will give it to you in my name. Hitherto you have asked nothing in my name; ask, and you will receive, that your joy may be full (John 16:23,24).

If our God has promised to supply our needs and nothing is impossible with Him, how come most of us do not have our needs met? One reason is our lack of prayer: *We have not because we ask not.* God's promise is conditioned on our praying. We are weak and impoverished because we fail to pray. God is restrained in doing because we abstain from praying.

2. *Trouble*

Prayerlessness leads to trouble on the inside. We worry, panic, and fret when we do not pray.

What causes wars, and what causes fightings among you? Is it not your passions that are at war in your members? You desire and do not have; so you kill. And you covet and cannot obtain; so you fight and wage war. You do not have, because you do not ask (James 4:1,2).

Praying calms disturbing forces, allays tormenting fears, brings conflict to an end. Prayer brings joy and peace into one's soul. Prayer casts all our anxieties on Christ (1 Peter 5:7; Philippians 4:6,7).

God intends that we enjoy peace not only on the inside, but on the outside as well. But that will not be realized until we pray for all men, especially for rulers in church and state, *that we may lead a quiet and peaceable life* (1 Timothy 2:1,2).

Prayerlessness brings trouble, war, and economic disaster to a nation, and believers consequently suffer along with others.

3. *Defeat*

A believer is in a constant spiritual battle. The nature of this warfare will be fully discussed in the next chapter on vigilance. Here it will suffice to say that prayerlessness leads to defeat in the spiritual warfare against Satan and his ministers. The life of a believer is no primrose path. It is a battle against invisible foes. We wrestle not against flesh and blood, but against spiritual wickedness in high places (2 Corinthians 10:3,4). This is why Paul, who understood the nature of the battle, urged us to *put on the whole armor of God* and to pray with all prayer and supplication in the spirit (Ephesians 6:10-18). Prayer is one weapon to combat our adversaries. A prayerless believer is not utilizing all the aids God has supplied for his combat with the enemy and is consequently subject to defeat by the enemy. Without prayer and vigilance, we cannot win the battle, overcome our adversary, and ultimately prevail.

4. *Destruction*

Although Satan is the ruler of this world (John 14:30; 16:11), God intervenes to salvage or destroy depending on our response. After the apostasy with the golden calf, Israel as a nation would have met their just destruction had Moses not prayed (Exodus 32:1-14). It was Moses' prayer that restrained God's wrath on Israel (Psalm 106:23). It was the fasting and prayer of Esther with all Israel that made God intervene and thwart the plan of Haman against the Jews (Esther 3 to 6).

Prayerlessness brings shame, defeat, and destruction to God's people.

> *I sought for a man among them who should build up the wall and stand in the breach before me for the land, that I should not destroy it; but I found none. Therefore I have poured out my indignation upon them; I have consumed them with fire of my wrath; their way have I requited upon their heads, says the Lord God* (Ezekiel 22:30,31).

We lose and miss the golden opportunity to change God's plan for destruction when we fail to intercede in prayer.

5. *Lack of Revelation from God*

God does not talk to those who have no time to listen. God does not reveal His secrets, His mind, His plans and purposes to a prayerless believer or family. A prayerless man in the church of God is like a paralyzed organ in the physical body. He is out of place among the saints, out of harmony with God, and out of tune with His purposes for mankind. The man of prayer, whether layman or preacher, is God's right-hand man. To such a person, God commits Himself and His work. Praying men are the only men who represent God in this world. It is to them that God reveals His secrets.

> *Surely the Lord GOD does nothing, without revealing his secret to his servants the prophets* (Amos 3:7).

> *The secret of the LORD is with them that fear him; and he will show them his covenant* (Psalm 25:14, KJV).

A typical example of this is Abraham's intercession for Sodom and Gomorrah. The Lord said, *Shall I hide from Abraham what I am about to do* (Genesis 18:17). Men have never risen to eminence in spiritual experience unless prayer has been the controlling factor of their lives. Every great man of God is a man who is committed to prayer. There seems to be no exception to this rule. There are no short cuts. Think of Abraham, Moses, Samuel, David, Nehemiah, Daniel, and the apostles. Martin Luther, John Wesley, Andrew Murray, John Knox, Samuel Morris, Charles Finney, and Edward Bounds were all men of great accomplishments who received revelations from God because they were mighty in prayer.

The Necessity of Prayer

Prayer is part and parcel of Christian living. The Christian way of life is of necessity the way of prayer. Prayer is a channel through which we talk to God and let Him talk to us. Just as man needs air to survive, a family needs prayer to exist spiritually.

Prayer is essential to both God and man. There are at least five reasons why we ought to pray. Prayer is:

- God's command,
- our spiritual service,
- the weapon of our warfare,
- the way out of trouble, and
- the way to advance God's work.

1. *God's Command*

Since prayer is receiving from the Lord, we are commanded several times in the Bible to pray.

Call upon me in the day of trouble; I will deliver you, and you shall glorify me (Psalm 50:15).

If my people who are called by my name humble themselves, and pray and seek my face, and turn from their wicked ways, then I will hear from heaven, and will forgive their sin and heal their land (2 Chronicles 7:14).

Ask, and it will be given you; seek, and you will find; knock, and it will be opened to you. For everyone who asks receives, and he who seeks finds, and to him who knocks it will be opened (Matthew 7:7,8).

Watch and pray that you may not enter into temptation (Matthew 26:41).

Have no anxiety about anything, but in everything by prayer and supplication with thanksgiving let your requests be made known to God (Philippians 4:6).

Pray constantly, give thanks in all circumstances; for this is the will of God in Christ Jesus for you (1 Thessalonians 5:17,18).

First of all, then, I urge that supplications, prayers, intercessions, and thanksgivings be made for all men, for kings and all who are in high positions, that we may lead a quiet and peaceable life, godly and respectful in every way (1 Timothy 2:1,2).

Cast all your anxieties on him, for he cares about you (1 Peter 5:7).

The list of commands on prayer is endless. We see from these Scriptures that we are commanded by God, Christ, and the apostles to pray. God's promises are dependent and conditioned on our praying. Our prayer is the only means by which God's promises become a reality in our lives. Not to pray is to sin or disobey God. It is to exclude God from our lives and show our independence of Him.

2. *Our Spiritual Service*

There are three major offices in the Old Testament: king, priest, and prophet. A king represents God's rule over men. A priest is a representative of the people before God. A prophet is a voice of God to His people. Our Lord Jesus Christ was a prophet, he is now a priest, and He will be a king. As believers, we share in the priesthood of Christ, His present ministry. Our priesthood is described by Peter as *a royal priesthood* (1 Peter 2:9). The priesthood becomes the birthright of every believer. Like our Old Testament counterparts, we as believer-priests have the privilege of direct access to God. However, with this privilege comes a twofold responsibility: sacrifice and intercessory prayer. We are to offer to God as sacrifices our bodies (Romans 12:1,2), our substance (Romans 12:13), our service (Hebrews 13:16), and our praise (Hebrews 13:15). We are to intercede on behalf of others (Colossians 4:12).

As priests, we are to intercede, stand in the gap, on behalf of our loved ones, our fellow brethren, our pastors, our civic leaders, and all men (1 Timothy 2:1,2). People who are not close to God need us to stand between them and God and plead their case.

Since we married, Chris and I put ourselves under the obligation of setting one day apart each week to pray for our immediate and extended family members. Besides praying for ourselves and our daughter, we pray for our parents, sisters, brothers, uncles, nephews, etc. We pray for their needs, their salvation, their protection, their deliverance from the bondage and blindfolding of the enemy, and so forth. Though we cannot move mountains, we can pray and touch God to move the mountains in their lives. Although we often don't see the immediate effects of the weekly prayers, it is amazing to see how God moves in the lives of those we pray for.

As parents, we are ordained by God as priests unto our children. Pray for your kids. Pray for their salvation, their wholeness in Christ, their sound, divine health, their safety, their dreams, their education, their success, and so forth. If you want your children to know God, and not rebel against Him, you must cultivate your personal relationship with God. First and foremost you must be prayerful. Dr. James Dobson related the story of his grandfather who for eleven years prayed half an hour a day for the salvation of his children and grandchildren. As an answer to his constant, persistent prayer, all his children and grandchildren became Christians, and many are in full-time Christian ministry. Our prayers for our children have a lasting impact on them. Blessed is a child who sees his parents on their knees from time to time. That child has learned that God matters to mom and dad, a lesson no lecture can impart.

3. *The Weapon of Our Warfare*

As mentioned earlier, a believer is in constant warfare against the devil and his demons. Prayer is one of the spiritual aids God has provided for His children to combat the enemy and be victorious. Paul wrote:

> *For though we live in the world we are not carrying on a worldly war, for the weapons of our warfare are not worldly but have divine power to destroy strongholds* (2 Corinthians 10:3,4).

Of these weapons, prayer is most formidable and potent in our conflict with the spiritual forces in heavenly places (Ephesians 6:12). Oswald Sanders said, "The fulcrum on which defeat or victory turns is our ability to pray aright and make intelligent use of our weapons." Satan fears nothing from prayerless studies, preaching, and teaching, but he trembles when he sees the weakest saint on his knees.

4. *The Way out of Trouble*

Job said:

> *Man that is born of a woman is of few days, and full of trouble* (Job 14:1).

Trouble belongs to the present state of man on earth. It is the disciplinary agent of God's moral government. There are at least five sources of trouble. First, some troubles are human in their origin: they happen to everyone in the world. Second, there are self-originated troubles: troubles caused by our ignorance, carelessness, lack of vigilance, and prayerlessness. Third, some troubles arise from others and we have no control over them. Fourth, some troubles are Satanic in origin, as we see in the case of Job. Lastly, some troubles are of the Lord; they are meant to punish or straighten certain things in us or test our level of faith in Him. No matter what the source of our trouble is, prayer is a way out of it.

When it comes to trouble, prayer plays a double role. Prayer prevents you from getting into trouble and can deliver you out of trouble.

The self-originated troubles due to prayerlessness and lack of vigilance can be prevented by praying. It is better to stay out of trouble than to have to pray having got into trouble. As the hymnist rightly said:

Oh what peace we often forfeit,
Oh what needless pain we bear,
All because we do not carry
Everything to God in prayer.

We bear unnecessary burdens, suffer needless pain, pass through avoidable troubles just because we do not pray.

Prayer can also deliver us out of trouble. Since prayer is a way of getting things from God, it is also a way of rejecting what you do not want and getting out of trouble. Trouble has a way of driving us to God. Nothing shows our helplessness more than trouble knocking at our door. But prayer gives us joy and strength to bear trouble. Prayer instills patience in the midst of trouble. Prayer opens us to see God's hand in trouble. How foolish and vain are the complaints and rebellion of men under trouble. Blessed is the man who, like the Psalmist, sees wise ends in trouble and understands that his troubles are blessings in disguise:

It is good for me that I was afflicted, that I might learn thy statutes (Psalm 119:71).

You want to be delivered out of all your troubles? Do what David said:

This poor man cried, and the Lord heard him, and saved him out of all his troubles (Psalm 32:6).

5. *The Way to Advance God's Work*

God's work must be done in God's way, using God's tools. God's work is threefold: reaching *up* through prayer, reaching *out* by way of evangelism, and reaching *in* by ministering to the needs of the saints. Prayer is God's work, and human nature does not like taxing, spiritual work. Also, prayer plays an important role in evangelism, revival, and ministering to the saints through intercessory prayer.

John Wesley said, "It seems God is limited by our prayer life—that He can do nothing for humanity unless someone asks Him." God's work makes progress in the hands of praying men and women. Praying believers and families are God's agents for carrying on His work on earth. They are always the forerunners of spiritual prosperity. It was Hannah's prayer that provided Israel with Samuel, the kind of a man God knew Israel needed as a prophet and a ruler of His people. It was Zacharias' prayer that brought about John the Baptist, the kind of man God saw fit to be the forerunner of His beloved Son. It was in answer to prayer and fasting that the apostles Paul and Barnabas were filled with the Holy Spirit and set apart for missionary work.

As Dwight Moody well said, it is foolish to try to do God's work without God's power. The real test of a genuine work of God is the prevalence of the spirit of prayer. Prayer is the secret of powerful preaching, effective soul-winning, and revival. Prayer is a secret of a successful, happy marriage. The family that prays knows God's will and works with God in carrying out His will.

Hindrances to Prayer

In his book *The Art of Intercession*, Kenneth Hagin gave a testimony that ought to be the experience of every Christian. He said:

> *In the 45 years since I learned to really pray, I've never prayed a single prayer concerning myself or my own needs without almost instantly getting the answer. Why? Because I know how to pray. I know what belongs to me. I know how to take authority over the devil.*[3]

Every believer ought to have day-by-day intercourse with God, asking and receiving from Him. That is the way Jesus Himself lived. But we often pray and obtain no answer. Why? Because we don't know how to pray. The whole secret of prayer is in the matter of approach. We must approach God the right way. We must learn what hinders prayer and what helps it, the false way of praying and the true way of praying. Our Lord deals with both of them.

Since prayer is asking and receiving from God, it must be done in His way. Certain conditions must be met in order for our prayer to be answered. In this section, we learn what keeps prayer from being answered, while the next section will cover what gets prayer answered. Hindrances to prayer include:

- sin,
- pride,
- unforgiveness,
- doubt,
- asking wrongly,
- disunity, and
- Satan's opposition.

Of course, there are other minor hindrances, such as time-consciousness, tiredness of the body, mental and emotional problems, and the place of prayer, but we will limit our discussion to only the seven major hindrances.

1. *Sin*

God is holy and hates sin. Sin hinders prayer because it separates you from God.

> *If I regard iniquity in my heart, the LORD will not hear me* (Psalm 66:18, KJV).

> *Your iniquities have made a separation between you and your God, and your sins have hid his face from you so that he does not hear* (Isaiah 59:2).

Sin is essentially a disposition, a state of heart. It follows us even to the very presence of God. Sin could take any form of disobedience to God's will. It could be rebellion against constituted authority (Romans 13:1,5). It could be wrongs against others that you have not straightened out (Matthew

5:23,24), debts that you have decided not to pay (Romans 13:8), unkindness to widows or the fatherless (Exodus 22:22,23). Wives could have their prayer hindered if they are not submissive to their husband (Ephesians 5:22). If husbands do not love or deal scripturally with their wives, their prayers will be hindered (1 Peter 3:7).

The sin could also be disobedience to God's Word. If you refuse to listen to God's Word or you are indifferent to it, your prayers will not be acceptable to God. To see the full import of this, read Proverbs 28:9 in three modern translations:

If one turns away his ear from hearing the law, even his prayer is an abomination (RSV).

If anyone turns a deaf ear to the law, even his prayers are detestable (NIV).

God doesn't listen to the prayers of men who flout the law (LB).

Receiving from God, spiritual and physical prosperity, blessing, and fruit-bearing all depend on our meditating on the law of the Lord on a daily basis (Psalm 1:1-3; Joshua 1:8). God has not promised to bless us if we live out of His will. Here is what our Lord promised:

If you abide in me, and my words abide in you, ask whatever you will, and it shall be done for you (John 15:7).

A disinclination to read God's Word, mediate on it, and obey it, shows sin in the heart.

If you want to get along with God and have your prayer answered, you must honestly confess your sins, ask for God's forgiveness, and repent of them. As you do so, God is faithful and just to forgive you your sins and cleanse you from all unrighteousness (1 John 1:9).

2. *Pride*

To be proud is to think of oneself more highly than one ought. It is to boast of one's ability as if it were not a gift from God (1 Corinthians 4:7). As we shall see in the next chapter, pride is the sin of Lucifer. Pride is a hindrance to prayer. What brings the praying soul near to God is humility of heart.

If my people who are called by my name humble themselves
... then I will hear from heaven, and will forgive their sin
and heal their land (2 Chronicles 7:14).

The parable of the Pharisee and publican is a picture of humility against pride in praying. The Pharisee's prayer is impregnated with self-conceit, self-praise, and self-exaltation. This praying religious leader, though schooled to prayer by training and habit, prayed not. God heard his words only to condemn him. On the other hand, the publican was overwhelmed with self-depression and inward sinfulness. Realizing how poor in spirit he was, he cried for mercy for his sins. The Pharisee's proud estimate of himself and his contempt for his neighbor closed the gates of prayer to him, while humility opened wide those gates to the publican. I must avoid the danger to show off, to be interested in myself as the one who prays, to be known among others as one who prays, or to be seen as praying by others.

In order to receive from God, we must be clothed with humility. God puts a great price on a humble heart (Isaiah 66:2). Our prayers must be set low before they can ever rise high. Humility is an indispensable access to God when other qualities fail.

3. Unforgiveness

As husband and wife, it is hardly possible to avoid offending each other, but you must learn to forgive each other. Unforgiveness or resentment is a barrier to prayer. If you don't forgive others, God can't forgive you. That is just the way the law of forgiveness works. George Herbert well said, "He who cannot forgive others breaks the bridge over which he must pass himself." Unforgiveness, holding grudges against others, resentment is a sin. When boiled down to its essence, unforgiveness is hatred and *whoever hates his brother is a murderer* (1 John 3:15).

In the Lord's prayer, it is clearly taught that the basis of our receiving forgiveness from God is our willingness to forgive others. In Matthew 6:12-15, we read:

Forgive us our debts, as we also have forgiven our debtors. For if you forgive men their trespasses, your heavenly Father also will forgive you; but if you do not forgive men their trespasses, neither will your Father forgive your trespasses.

In Mark 11:25, Jesus said:

Whenever you stand praying, forgive, if you have anything against any one; so that your Father also who is in heaven may forgive you your trespasses

Our praying is in vain and useless unless we forgive others who may have wronged us. It is therefore imperative that you make sure that all grudges, bitterness, wrongs are forgiven. Follow Paul's instruction in Ephesians 4:26. Before sunset each day, search your heart, confess any grudge or wrong to God, forgive, and ask God for forgiveness.

Let all bitterness and wrath and anger and clamor and slander be put away from you, with all malice, and be kind to one another, tenderhearted, forgiving one another, as God in Christ forgave you (Ephesians 4:31,32).

4. *Doubt*

The whole basis of prayer is believing and trusting God.

For whoever would draw near to God must believe that he exists and that he rewards those who seek him (Hebrew 11:6).

Doubt blocks prayer and prevents it from being answered because doubt short-circuits faith. Doubt and fear are the twin foes of faith. Doubt limits and therefore cannot receive from God.

Let him ask in faith, with no doubting, for he who doubts is like a wave of the sea that is driven and tossed by the wind. For that person must not suppose that a double-minded man, unstable in his ways, will receive anything from the Lord (James 1:6-8).

In order to receive from God, we must get rid of doubt. We must guard against doubt or unbelief as we would against an enemy. We must reprogram our mind with God's Word. We must exercise faith in little things and let our faith grow to a level of maturity whereby we ask God for big things. Faith needs to be cultivated. It is increased by exercise, by being put into use. It grows by reading and meditating on God's Word.

5. *Asking Wrongly*

Our prayer must be according to God's will, plan, priority, and purpose. James said:

> *You ask and do not receive, because you ask wrongly, to spend it on your passions* (James 4:3).

And John said:

> *This is the confidence which we have in him, that if we ask anything according to his will He hears us* (1 John 5:14).

Asking wrongly, for selfish reasons, for reasons that will not glorify God, can block our prayers. To ask rightly, you must seek to know God's will for your life and your family. This takes feeding your soul with God's Word. Millions of people—are you one of them?—are starving their souls by refusing to feed them. One of life's tragedies is the possession of a starved soul in a well-fed body. Remember,

> *Man shall not live by bread alone, but by every word that proceeds from the mouth of God* (Matthew 4:4).

Study God's Word on daily basis so as to discover God's mind and pray appropriately.

6. *Disunity*

Unity or praying with one accord is essential to group praying. This is particularly significant in prayers involving a husband and wife. Jesus said:

> *Truly, I say to you, whatever you bind on earth shall be bound in heaven, and whatever you loose on earth shall be loosed in heaven. Again, I say to you, if two of you agree on earth about anything they ask, it will be done for them by my Father in heaven* (Matthew 18:18,19, emphasis mine).

The apostles understood this teaching of Jesus and put it into practice in their praying (Acts 1:14). The enemy too understands the spiritual import of unity in prayer, especially family prayer. So he attacks the husband and wife with bitterness, resentment, or anger so that they either find it hard to come together in prayer or there is no agreement in their praying.

If there is anything that will hinder unity between you and your spouse, be humble enough to approach your spouse about it. Follow Jesus' instruction in Matthew 18:15-35.

7. *Satan's Opposition*

Satan opposes anything God does. He opposes prayer in many ways. He prevents believers from prayer through laziness, self-indulgence, wrong teaching, and wrong attitude toward prayer. If he fails in preventing believers from praying, he tries seducing them to pray wrongly, seeking things from God for self-gratification. If he does not succeed at this level, he opposes the receiving of whatever is being asked. It is this last aspect of his opposition that we are interested in here.

Satan is *the prince of the power of the air* (Ephesians 2:2). He is not without power. Daniel, one of God's great prophets, could not interpret a prophetic vision. He sought the Lord in prayer and fasting for twenty-one days (Daniel 10:2-14). Daniel was heard and answered the first day of his praying. God sent an angel to deliver the meaning of the vision, but Satan withstood the angel for twenty-one days, until Michael came to the angel's rescue and then the answer to prayer got through. There are countless prayers of the saints hanging up there, half-way between earth and heaven, waiting for faith to bring them down.

This is why a believer must have faith to persist in prayer. To this end, Jesus gave two parables on the relevance of persistence in prayer when our prayers are not answered right away (Luke 11:5-13, 18:1-8). Delays in receiving answer to prayer are not denials. The fact that we do not receive an immediate answer to prayer is no evidence that God does not hear prayer. We must not only be courageous, determined, and persistent in our praying, we must also be patient. We must learn to wait and see the salvation of the Lord. God will surely answer our prayer if we persist long enough.

How to Pray

Having examined how not to pray or hindrances to prayer, we shall now discuss what makes prayer effectual. Just as with anything else, we must learn how to pray and receive from

God. John the Baptist taught his disciples how to pray, and Jesus did the same thing, too (Luke 11:1-4).

In learning how to pray, we will examine five major aspects of prayer:

- different kinds of prayer,
- constituent elements of prayer,
- elements of successful prayer,
- what to pray for, and
- when to pray.

1. *Different Kinds of Prayer*

Just as there are all kinds of sports and they are not all played by the same rules, there are several kinds of prayer in the Bible and rules governing them. Each kind of prayer has its own approach and objective. Many prayers are not being answered because we apply the wrong rules and have our rules all mixed up. We tend to take rules that govern one kind of prayer and apply them to other kinds of prayer. Obviously, this kind of praying will not work; it will fail to achieve its intent.

The Bible teaches the following kinds of prayer:[4,5]

(a) The prayer of faith is the prayer of petition. It is the prayer to change things (Matthew 21:22; Mark 11:24). It must be based on God's revealed will. The prayer is primarily for yourself. However, baby believers could be carried temporarily on your faith. Since this kind of prayer is based on God's revealed will, which we know for sure, it must not contain "if." Using "if" in such prayer only shows doubt, fear or unbelief. It is this kind of prayer that needs fasting (Matthew 17:14-21).

(b) The prayer of guidance involves dedicating our lives for God's use (Luke 22:42; James 4:13-15). It is the prayer that involves decision, going somewhere to do something. The phrase "if it is your will" is appropriate in this kind of prayer since we do not know for sure what God wants us to do. It takes waiting patiently on God. The condition for receiving an answer to such prayer is openness to God's way. God may come to you in various ways and you must be open to receive from Him. Perhaps the best illustration of this kind of prayer is found in the life of David (1 Samuel 23:2,3; 2 Samuel 2:1,2; 5:19,23).

(c) The prayer of worship is the prayer that focuses on God, to praise and adore Him (Daniel 2:17-23; John 11:41,42). This is where songs, hymns, and words of praise and adoration are appropriate. Some of the prayers recorded in the Psalms fall into this category.

(d) The prayer of intercession is praying on behalf of someone else (Job 42:8; 1 Timothy 2:1-4; Philippians 1:3-5). An intercessor is one who pleads on behalf of another. Intercessory prayer involves identifying with the object of our prayer. Some of our loved ones are dead in trespasses without knowing it, and somebody has to stand in the gap for them. Some believers are babies spiritually; they need somebody to care for them (Galatians 4:19).

(e) The prayer of agreement is group prayer (Matthew 18:18-20; Acts 12:5). Of course, the prayer of worship could also be group prayer if more than one person is involved, but the prayer of worship is focused on God while the prayer of agreement has to do with those praying. It is in this kind of prayer that unity is vital.

(f) Prayer in the Spirit is essentially speaking in tongues (1 Corinthians 14:14,15; Ephesians 6:18). Prayer can be offered either in your own language or in other tongues. As spirit beings, we need to pray in the Spirit especially when we do not know how to pray (Romans 8:26,27). Praying in the Spirit is edifying yourself (Jude 20; 1 Corinthians 14:4).

Understanding these different kinds of prayer should help us apply the right rule to our praying.

2. *Constituent Elements of Prayer*

Many people often regard prayer as asking for things from God. But prayer is multi-dimensional in nature. Prayer can be resolved into six constituent elements: adoration, thanksgiving, confession, consecration, petition, and intercession. Each element must be part of a balanced devotional prayer.

Adoration is meeting God with worship. It is paying humbling obeisance before God, our Creator and Maker. Only God deserves such honor as evident in the Ten Commandments (Exodus 20:4-6). In our prayer we must worship Him in spirit and in truth (John 4:24).

Thanksgiving is expressing our appreciation of God's manifold blessings and mercies on us. We must be thankful for what God has done for us in the past, what He is doing now, and what He is yet to accomplish in our lives. This three-fold pattern of thanksgiving is evident in Psalm 103:2-5 where David said:

> *Bless the LORD, O my soul, and forget not his benefits, who forgives all your iniquity, who heals all your diseases, who redeems your life from the Pit, who crowns you with steadfast love and mercy, who satisfies you with good as long as you live so that your youth is renewed like the eagle's.*

Confession of sin is the next. As mentioned earlier, we cannot approach the throne of the holy God with sin in our life and expect Him to hear. Sin must be put out of the way. Confession is the process by which we express our transgression and failure, by omission or commission, to attain the divine standard. By confession, we dig out the evil things inside us in the presence of the Holy One of Israel and ask for His forgiveness.

Consecration is an act of surrender to God. It is willingness to accept God's will for our life. It is a process where we remind ourselves before Him of our vows to forsake all and follow Him. It is putting our whole life as a sacrifice on His altar.

Petition is casting our anxieties and personal needs before our loving heavenly Father. It is asking God to give us "this day our daily bread."

Intercession is remembering to pray on behalf of others who do not enjoy the same access to the presence of God. As William Sangster said, "The burdens of mankind are so numerous and heavy that those who do not intercede lack either faith in prayer or feeling for their fellows."

Is it hard for you to pray ten minutes? Try spending two minutes on each of these elements in your daily prayer. Your prayer life will never remain the same.

3. *Elements of Successful Prayer*

In the previous section, we discussed the hindrances or don'ts of prayer. Here we now consider the do's of prayer, those things that will make our prayer receive answers from the Lord. There are basically four elements that make our prayer effective. These are praying according to God's will, being definite or specific, having faith in God, and being persistent in prayer.

(a) Praying according to God's will involves seeking to pray for issues which are pleasing to Him as we know from the Bible. This is why the importance of daily study of God's Word cannot be overemphasized. Martin Luther's motto helps along this line: "To have prayed well is to have studied well."

Praying in God's will is praying for things that will please God and honor Him, things that will give God the maximum glory and do us the maximum good. When we pray in God's will, we will be confident that He hears us (1 John 5:14).

(b) Praying on definite, explicit issues is vital to receiving from God. Jesus said:

> *In praying do not heap up empty phrases as the Gentiles do; for they think that they will be heard for their many words. Do not be like them . . . .* (Matthew 6:7,8).

God is not interested in our use of vain repetition. There is no merit to saying prayers over and over again. This is the way the Gentiles do, thinking that they may impress God, but Jesus said we should not be like them. He wants our prayers to be expressed in a clear and intelligent manner.

Instead of praying in lump sums and indefinite terms, God desires that we be specific. *Give us this day our daily bread* is specific, definite praying. Examine your Bible and see how specific men and women were in prayer. Abraham's servant prayed that God would send him a bride for Isaac and got exactly what He prayed for (Genesis 24:12-14). Gideon specifically asked for a sign and got it the next morning (Judges 6:36-39). Hannah prayed for a child, and Samuel was given to her. Elijah prayed specifically for drought and got drought, prayed for rain and got rain, prayed for fire from heaven and got just that; he went about as though he had the key of heaven in his possession because he knew how to be specific in prayer. Peter prayed for Dorcas to come back to life and she did. So pray for specific items and expect specific answers.

(c) Having faith in God is the very first requisite of pleasing God and receiving from Him (Hebrews 11:6). James urged that we ask for anything we lack, including wisdom from God. But the asking must be in faith; otherwise we receive nothing from God.

But let him ask in faith, with no doubting, for he who doubts is like a wave of the sea that is driven and tossed by the wind. For that person must not suppose that a double-minded man, unstable in all his ways, will receive anything from the Lord (James 1:6-8).

And Jesus said:

Have faith in God. Truly, I say to you, whoever says to this mountain, "Be taken up and cast into the sea," and does not doubt in his heart, but believes that what he says will come to pass, it will be done for him. Therefore I tell you, whatever you ask in prayer, believe that you have received it, and it will be yours (Mark 11:22-24).

Only God is capable of moving mountains, but faith moves God to act on our behalf. Faith and prayer can get you anything in the world. With faith, *nothing will be impossible to you* (Matthew 17:20,21; Mark 9:23,29). Faith can do anything because it brings God to undertake for us, and nothing is impossible with God.

Bound by His irrevocable promises, God is willingly ready to supply exactly and fully all we ask in prayer with faith. Faith and prayer select the thing, and God commits Himself to do the supplying. It is those who diligently seek God in prayer and faith who are richly rewarded.

The right spirit in which to approach the throne of grace is with confidence (Hebrews 4:16). As the hymn puts it: "Thou art coming to a king, large petitions with thee bring." Who shall doubt the King? Shame on us if we are unbelieving before the throne of the King of heaven and earth. May our faith grow to the level at which we can act on confident faith in God in every detail of life and receive all the fullness there is in the Name that guarantees to do so much.

(d) Being persistent in prayer means praying through with long, continued supplication and waiting on God until He answers. Tepid praying does not move God's arm. We see again and again in the Bible men and women who persisted in prayer. Jacob persisted in prayer about his problems and burdens until he prevailed with God and got a new name and a new blessing (Genesis 32:24-29). Daniel's prayer was answered the first day of his fasting and prayer, but he did not receive the answer until after twenty-one more days of prayer. Queen Esther with other Jews in Persia prayed through and got their prayer answered. John Knox persistently prayed, "Give me Scotland or I die." His prayers terrified tyrants.

Our Lord said to His disciples that men *ought always to pray and not lose heart* (Luke 18:1). We should not give up because God delays in answering. When God delays, it is either because He has some better things for us, or because there is something He wants to accomplish in us that cannot be effected otherwise.

Sometimes it is necessary to persist in prayer with fasting. As Dr. John Rice well put it:

Real persistence in prayer, letting other things go and giving God the right way often involves fasting. In fact, I think there is little point to fasting or depriving ourselves of other things simply as a matter of self-punishment if we do not pray. If a man is to be just as absorbed in business as ever, with no more thought for God, then what good would it do him spiritually to do without food or drink or sleep? Fasting is the accomplishment of persistent, fervent prayer that will not be denied.[6]

So learn to pray effectual prayer, which must be specific, aligned with the will of God, offered in faith, and persistent until the answer is received. Such prayer prevails with God.

The effectual fervent prayer of a righteous man availeth much (James 5:16, KJV) for God and man.

4. *What to Pray For*

Sometimes believers just don't know whether to pray on a particular issue or not. Since each person has some unique needs and problems, it will be difficult to be very specific about what you should pray for. We will talk about what you can pray for in principle and you can apply these principles to your specific needs and problems. As mentioned earlier, a well-balanced devotional prayer will include all the constituent elements of prayer. Here we will concentrate on the items for petition and intercession.

First, you can pray about temporal matters. Our temporal matters have much to do with our health and happiness. They are the main source of our cares and worries. Prayer can be applied to every matter that concerns us, whether it affects our body, mind or soul. The wants of the body, food, business, finances, or anything that affects us in life can be a subject of prayer. Paul says,

Have no anxiety about anything, but in everything by prayer and supplication with thanksgiving let your requests be made known to God (Philippians 4:6).

The King James Version reads: *Be careful for nothing* .... This includes all kinds of cares—job cares, business cares, body cares, domestic cares, financial cares, and soul cares. All are to be brought to God in prayer. How much needless pain, care, and worry we save ourselves if we use prayer as a means of relieving those temporal cares and learn to cast all our cares in prayer on God "who cares for us" (1 Peter 5:7).

Second, you can pray about spiritual matters. Whatever concerns man's highest welfare, and whatever has to do with God's plans and purposes concerning men on earth, is a subject for prayer. God's work languishes because of our prayerlessness. Missionaries are called home, fields are closed, church congregations dwindle, revival efforts fail—all because we fail to intercede and ask God for mighty things. God's people live in poverty, in sickness, in disappointment, and in defeat because we do not intercede. We do not experience miracles today as in the apostolic days because we do not do exploits with God in prayer. God invites, commands us to ask for big things. He is looking for those through whom He can perform wonders.

Open your mouth wide, and I will fill it (Psalm 81:10).

Call to me and I will answer you, and will tell you great and hidden things which you have not known (Jeremiah 33:3).

God is eager to give more than we can ask and is pleased with big prayers.

Third, pray for divine guidance. When you are making a decision and not sure which way to go, pray for the Lord's direction, in big and little things, sometimes for yourself, sometimes for others. Wait on the Lord and be receptive to His leading.

Be still, and know that I am God (Psalm 46:10).

Fourth, pray for your family members. Help your spouse spiritually by praying for his/her needs and problems. Lift up one another in prayer. As husband and wife, commit your children to God through prayers of blessing, guidance, and protection. Bless them and lay your hands on them as believer-priests. God has vested you with spiritual authority over your children. Pray for their souls to be saved at an early age. Pray for their spiritual growth as they live the Christian life.

Finally, pray and intercede on behalf of others. Pray for your extended family members—your parents, brothers, sisters, uncles, in-laws, etc. Pray for your fellow believers. Pray for your spiritual leaders—pastors, elders, deacons, deaconesses, Sunday school teachers, music directors, etc. Pray for your boss at your workplace and for your co-workers. Pray for your job and company. Pray for your political leaders—representatives, mayors, governors, presidents, etc.

5. *When to Pray*

If prayer is so important in our day-to-day life, we must set aside some definite time to devote ourselves to prayer. If we only pray at convenient times, we will never pray as much as we ought to and our spiritual life will never be what it could be. We see throughout the Bible that men of prayer always set aside some specific times and we must follow their examples. Daniel prayed three times a day (Daniel 6:10). David praised the Lord seven times a day (Psalm 119:164). Our Lord was used to withdrawing to the mountain to pray all night after His busy ministry during the day (Luke 5:16; 6:12; Matthew

14:23; Mark 1:35). The apostles prayed day and night (Acts 3:1; 12:1-17; 16:25; 1 Thessalonians 3:10).

To be definite in your prayer, plan a schedule just as you have a menu for each day. You can concentrate on different prayer items for different days in the week. A typical example of a weekly prayer schedule is shown in Table 2.1.

Table 2.1
A Typical Family Prayer Schedule

Day	Prayer Item
Monday	Prayer for your jobs as husband and wife.
Tuesday	Prayer for immediate family members.
Wednesday	Intercessory prayers for extended family members.
Thursday	Intercessory prayers for missionaries, your city, your nation, and other nations.
Friday	Prayer and fasting for your specific ministry, other ministries, and other brethren, particularly those who asked you specifically to pray for them.
Saturday	Prayer of worship. Sing hymns and psalms. Thanksgiving for the blessings of the week.
Sunday	Prayers for your church. Pray for the pastor, Sunday school teachers, etc.

This schedule is a slight modification of my weekly family prayer schedule. Since we married, Chris and I have designat-

ed two days a week for fasting and prayer because we realize
the spiritual warfare we are involved in. In addition to this,
we hold vigils every Friday night. Friday night has always
been looked forward to because it is the best part of our week.
The time is not only for praying, it is the time to talk and
share our experiences during the week. We share what each of
us has learned independently through reading and studying
during the week. This act of fasting and having vigil each
week is a continual reminder of our goals and priorities in life.
It has drawn us closer to one another and to God more than
anything else can. We have watched each other grow spiritually. We have seen prayers answered in specific ways.

The prayer of agreement works best between a husband and
wife. As mentioned earlier, for such prayer to be effective,
there must be unity and agreement among the people praying.
Where can one find a stronger agreement than in a couple
who are committed to God and to each other? Take advantage of that conducive atmosphere for prayer and pray often
with your spouse. Agree to pray together on issues even when
you disagree. Whatever you bind, God binds (Matthew 18:18-
20).

The Rewards of Prayer

The Bible is replete with the blessings and rewards of believing prayers. When God's people go on their knees, God is
moved to action. Israel in the land of bondage cried to God,
and was miraculously delivered. Samson prayed and his
strength was restored so that he slew more enemies at his
death than during his life. Elijah prayed and the heavens were

closed for three and a half years; he prayed again and the heavens gave rain. A dead child was brought back to life as a result of Elisha's prayer. The secrets of heaven were revealed to Daniel when he prayed. The great discourse we call the Sermon of the Mount was preceded by a night of prayer by our Lord. Paul and Silas in the prison at Philippi prayed, the place was shaken, and an entire family was converted. These examples are enough to show that prayer has its own rewards. These rewards include:

- promoting personal holiness,
- preparing us for God's use,
- providing power in your work, and
- blessing to humanity.

1. *Promoting Personal Holiness*

The ultimate goal of the Christian life is conformity to the image of Christ. God saved and set us apart to be His own people. To be His people is to have His characteristics, one of which is holiness. Prayer will promote your attainment of that goal. It will promote your personal holiness as can nothing else but study of the Word of God. Our growth into the likeness of Christ is in direct proportion to the time, heart, and effort we put into prayer.

2. *Preparing Us for God's Use*

God works through men and women to carry out His agenda for this world. If men and women will not work for God, His work will not be done. Prayer makes us more conscious of God's work, His intents, and His purposes for our lives. It brings us into sympathy with the mind of God. It prepares us as ready vessels for God's use. It leads us to the point of surrender, where we open up our whole being to God and are ready to be filled with His fullness. Men God has used greatly were men of prayer. Think of Martin Luther, John Knox, George Whitefield, John Wesley, Charles Finney, and Dwight Moody.

3. *Providing Power in Your Work*

Christianity is a supernatural religion from start to finish. If you are trying to serve God and man in your poor, weak way, quit. Your duty as a Christian is to serve in God's supernatural power. It is the privilege of every Christian to have at his/her disposal the power of God. We must perform our service with supernatural power, the power of God ministered through Jesus Christ by the Holy Spirit. Prayer will bring the power of God into our work. As Isaiah 40:31 said:

> *They who wait for the LORD shall renew their strength, they shall mount up with wings like eagles, they shall run and not be weary, they shall walk and not faint.*

To have prayed well is to have worked well, to have lived well, and to have died well. We bring all our troubles, overcome all our obstacles, and conquer all our circumstances in life in the field of prayer. It is in prayer that life's critical battles are lost or won. As a parent, you need the power and wisdom of God to raise up your children in the "nurture and admonition of the Lord," to train them in the way they should go, and to lead them to accept Christ into their lives as Lord and Savior.

4. *Blessing to Humanity*

This world is bad enough, but if it were not for us Christians it would be worse. If we take our place in prayer, we can change things. Our access to God opens every possibility because prayer is the sovereign remedy to every human problem. John Jowett said:

> *When, therefore, I commune with God in prayer I become a point of contact, an inlet through which the divine life flows into the veins and arteries of humanity. That is no idle figure of speech. Every man is an inlet through which clean or unclean energies pour into the general life-pool of the human race. We cannot help it .... The hands that make contact with the battery direct the electrical dynamic to every fiber and tissue of the body. And hands that are lifted up in prayer are conductors of the divine dynamic to the general brotherhood of humanity. And therefore our Master counsels us to retire into the secret place.*[7]

The wonders and blessings of prayer have not ceased. Prayer is the key to success in both your spiritual and secular life. It is the key to a happy, successful marriage. Only time and eternity can tell the impact and rewards of a family that prays together.

As Secret Number 2,

> Pray with and for your family.

Notes

[1] E. M. Bounds, *The Possibilities of Prayer* (Grand Rapids, MI: Baker Book House, 1979), pp. 17, 23.

[2] E. M. Bounds, *The Weapon of Prayer* (Grand Rapids, MI: Baker Book House, 1931), pp. 13, 14.

[3] Kenneth E. Hagin, *The Art of Intercession* (Tulsa, OK: Kenneth Hagin Ministries, 1980), p. 118.

[4] Ibid., pp. 5-7.

[5] Larry Christenson, *The Christian Family* (Minneapolis, MN: Bethany House Publishers, 1970), pp. 184-187.

[6] John R. Rice, *Prayer: Asking and Receiving* (Murfreesboro, TN: Sword of the Lord Publishers, 1942), p. 218.

[7] John H. Jowett, "Where Our Greatest Battles Are Fought" in *Classic Sermons in Prayer*, compiled by Warren W. Wiersbe (Grand Rapids, MI: Kregel Publications, 1987), p. 59.

CHAPTER THREE

THE SECRET OF VIGILANCE

Be sober, be watchful. Your adversary the devil prowls around like a roaring lion, seeking some one to devour. Resist him, firm in your faith.... And after you have suffered a little while, the God of all grace, who has called you to his eternal glory in Christ, will himself restore, establish, and strengthen you
1 Peter 5:8-10

F ew Christians today are aware that they are engaged in a spiritual war. Families are confronted with conflicts under many different circumstances. The conflict may be between husband and wife, between children and parents, between family standards and social demands. You often hear couples say, "I feel like there's something wrong, but I can't put my finger on it," or, "We start out in a good discussion, and the next thing you know, we're yelling at each other, and nobody knows who started it," or still, "We've made it to the top—many would call us successful. But we don't really know where we're going. We feel like we're groping in the dark." There are conflict and confusion of roles in the family—the husband doesn't know his duties, nor do the wife and children. Insufficient attention is paid to the activities of the enemy and we allow him to outwit us in strategy.

Whether you know it or not, every believer is involved in a global war, for our commission is to take the gospel to the whole creation. We are fighting spiritual warfare with unseen forces. We are engaged in a war against a ruthless enemy. Behind international conflict, social conflict, personal conflict, and family conflict lurks the master agitator—Satan.

In 2 Corinthians 2:11, Paul warned that we should not be ignorant of the devices of Satan lest he gain advantage over us. The god of this world uses ignorance and blindfolding to capture people (2 Corinthians 4:4). He keeps believers in ignorance of many things. They fear when they don't have to; they run from the enemy when they are supposed to oppose and stand firm; they suffer defeat when they are to be victorious; they live like slaves when they are sons of the King of kings and Lord of lords; they lack many things they are supposed to possess by right. Too much goes by default because we are not aware of the insidious activity of the enemy.

Just as a military commander cannot be victorious in battle unless he understands his enemy, you will suffer defeat unless you understand the adversary of your soul and the way he operates. Your life will either count for God or it will be sidetracked through the opposition of a little-known enemy. We can't afford to be ignorant of the enemy's devices. God desires that we be fully informed and understand His will and provision (Ephesians 5:17). We must seek to know what the Scripture teaches about:

- the enemy's person,

- the enemy's methods of operation,
- how to overcome the enemy, and
- how to watch your mind (the battleground).

Perhaps the best book ever written on Satan is *Your Adversary, the Devil* by J. Dwight Pentecost.[1] Unfortunately, the book is out of print. Since I quote or paraphrase Dr. Pentecost in the next two sections, I have placed a dagger sign (†) at the end of each paragraph taken, paraphrased or adapted from his excellent work.

The Enemy's Person

Time and space would not permit us to have a thorough discussion on Satan. We will briefly consider:

- Satan's origin,
- Satan's fall and judgment,
- Satan's hierarchy, and
- Satan's conquest of the earth.

1. *Satan's Origin*

The one we call Satan was originally known by the name Lucifer, which means "the light bearer," "the brilliant one," "the shinning one." In Ezekiel 28:11-13 we discover why that name was so appropriate. Lucifer was a created being, as verse 15 reveals:

You were blameless in your ways from the day you were created, till iniquity was found in you.

Not only was Satan perfect or blameless in his ways, he was the epitome of wisdom and beauty. He was the wisest of all of God's created beings. God had established him as administrator of the affairs of the angelic realm. Lucifer was perfect in beauty, for no creature so fully reflected the glory of God.†

2. Satan's Fall and Judgment

Lucifer was placed in a position of authority over all the cherubim (angelic beings of high rank, associated with God's presence) who surrounded the throne of God. It was the responsibility of the creature to be in subjection to the Creator, for privilege brings responsibility. As in Ezekiel 28, Lucifer's heart was lifted up because of pride in his beauty, wisdom, privileges, and responsibilities. In Isaiah 14:12-14, God has seen fit to reveal to us what went on in Lucifer's heart. Sin or trouble originates in the *heart.* Five times Satan said in his heart, "I will."

> *I will ascend to heaven;*
> *above the stars of God*
> *I will set my throne on high;*
> *I will sit on the mount of assembly in the far north;*
> *I will ascend above the heights of the clouds;*
> *I will make myself like the Most High* (Isaiah 14:13,14).

Thus, we see Lucifer's heart being filled with selfishness, pride, and rebellion. He wanted to act independently of God. A fire burned within Lucifer because of his glory, beauty, and authority. That which was given him became a consuming passion and snare. This burning passion to sit on God's throne, rule over angels and the earth, bring the earth into subjection to himself, cover himself with God's glory and then exert his independence, led to his rebellion and eventual destruction. Apparently, Lucifer pitted his will against God's will and led a revolution among the angels. According to Revelation 12, one third of the angelic realm followed Lucifer.†

God judged Lucifer and changed his name to Satan, meaning "adversary." Satan was banished from God's presence. All this happened before man was created, before God restored the earth from the chaotic mess caused by Satan's rebellion. God had an agenda to resolve this pre-history rebellion led by Satan.

The pride of Lucifer is being reproduced in unsaved men and women today. An unsaved person says, "If I acknowledge Jesus Christ as my Savior, I'll have to admit that my righteousness is nothing. I'll have to admit that my intellect is not enough to discover divine truth." It is the pride of their father the devil that keeps them from Jesus Christ. Also, Satan's sin may be reproduced by the child of God. That is why Paul warned Timothy against selecting a novice as an elder.

He may be puffed up with conceit and fall into the condemnation of the devil (1 Timothy 3:6).

God cannot use a proud person. Like Moses (Numbers 12:3) and John the Baptist (John 3:30) we must decrease that Christ might increase for God to use us. As husband and wife, you must learn to respect and honor one another out of reference for Christ (Ephesians 5:21). Therefore, let no man *think of himself more highly than he ought to think* (Romans 12:3) lest we think like our adversary, the devil.†

3. *Satan's Hierarchy*

In order for Satan to realize his ambition to be like the Most High, he had to take over God's control over all created things and exercise that control in every realm. Let us consider first Satan's plan to take the angelic realm. We will later examine his intention to rule over the earthly realm.

Angels are created beings, created by the authority of God through His Son:

> *All things were made through him [Christ], and without him was not anything made that was made* (John 1:3).

> *Christ himself is the Creator who made everything in heaven and earth, the things we can see and the things we can't; the spirit world with its kings and kingdoms, its rulers and authorities; all were made by Christ for his own use and glory* (Colossians 1:16, LB).

Angels have personalities, having bodies not limited in time or space (Daniel 9:21). They voluntarily worship God (Psalm 148:2) and possess the capacity of knowledge (Matthew 24:36). They were created to live and exist in the sphere of the heavenlies (Mark 13:32). When man was created to live on earth, angels were to execute and administer God's will on the earth. Thus they are referred to as ministering spirits, supervising the life of all men (Hebrews 1:14).†

Angelic beings are divided into many different ranks, and each rank has its own responsibility. In Colossians 1:16, for example, the angelic creation in heaven is divided into categories called *thrones, dominions, principalities,* and *powers.* These four words evidently represent different ranks or graduations of angels with their own responsibilities. *Thrones* would refer to angels who were created to sit on thrones and to rule. *Dominions* refers to those who exercise rule under God. *Principalities* refers to those who govern, and *powers* refers to those who exercise some particular assigned authority. Thus we see that God has a system of governing the universe. He is sovereign and rules over all things, but God as an administrator delegates authority. For example, in Daniel 12:1, Michael is referred to as the angel who stands for Israel. In Daniel 10:13, reference is made to the Prince of the kingdom of Persia, while Daniel 10:20 refers to the Prince of Greece. God has assigned a throne, a "prime minister," who exercises authority over each nation. Thus a hierarchical, administrative authority is vested in angels.†

When Lucifer rebelled against God, he was successful in leading away after him a third of the angelic creation (Revelation 12:4). Satan brought that group of fallen angels, called demons, into a kingdom like God's system. A child of God is surrounded every moment by these hosts of fallen angels as well as by that of ministering angels. Having once chosen to obey Satan, these demons obey him perfectly and completely. They persist in executing Satan's will for you and your marriage. And Satan's will for you is to defeat the will of God for you at every moment of your life. His plan for your family is to destroy it so that God's purpose for marriage is not achieved. Every moment you disobey God and succumb to the temptation of Satan, you are casting a vote for Satan instead for God.

4. *Satan's Conquest of the Earth*

Before God created man, He restored the earth from the chaotic mess caused by Satan's rebellion. In Job 38:4-7, we find that God created the universe before Satan's rebellion and consequently before man's existence on the earth. We may consider Genesis 1 and 2 as a record of God's reconstruction of the earth. Once man was created, he was watched by both the holy and the fallen angels. Man was created in the image of God and made to rule on earth as God's representative. Thus man was given the legal right, the scepter of authority, to rule and dominate the whole earth.

However, Satan's desire to gain control over the earth prompted him to devise a strategy to steal the title deed of the earth. He craftily lied to Adam and Eve. Adam committed high treason and sold out to Satan. As with the fallen angels, Satan was successful in leading man to go against the will of God. Since then Satan has been the god of this world (2 Corinthians 4:4). He will have that dominion until Adam's lease runs out. Though God is sovereign and all-powerful, He cannot legally and justly move in and take away the legal right of dominion from the devil.

Satan, after his conquest of the earth, became man's absolute master, the ruler of this world (John 12:31). Man not only lost the title deed—of himself, all his dominion, and all his descendants—over to Satan, he lost his spiritual life. He could no longer communicate with God. He became dead in trespasses and sins (Ephesians 2:1; 4:18). He became self-centered, lawless, and rebellious against God.

The Enemy's Methods of Operation

You can hardly win a battle when you don't understand your adversary, his philosophy, his plans, his programs, his devices, his strategies, his methods of operation. In order to gain advantage over Satan, we must be aware of his devices (2 Corinthians 2:11). Satan's war against you and your marriage can be summed up in the phrase *wiles of the devil* (Ephesians 6:11). The word *wiles* means "methods" of doing things. Satan's methods of operation include:

- deception,
- temptation,
- perversion,
- imitation,
- opposition to God's will, and
- fear.

We will see how Satan uses these deadly weapons in his insidious activity toward his ultimate goal in the life of a believer. We will later consider the mightier weapons God has placed in the minds of His own to overcome the enemy, to take advantage of our own position and the weaknesses of our foe.

1. *Deception*

The greatest weapon the prince of darkness relies upon to keep the world under his influence is deception. This was the weapon he used at the beginning of his deal with the fallen angels, and he still deceives and leads men and women away from God.

To reign as a god, Satan had to lead astray those whom God created. He had to lie and deceive. That is why Jesus in his conflict with the Pharisees said:

> *You are of your father the devil, and your will is to do your father's desires. He was a murderer from the beginning, and has nothing to do with the truth, because there is no truth in him. When he lies, he speaks according to his own nature, for he is a liar and the father of lies* (John 8:44).

Satan is a deceiver. He operates in the realm of denial of truth or in the realm of lies. In order to persuade the angelic hosts to follow him, he had to lie. He deceived Eve into following his idea. The apostle Paul traced the sin of Eve to its ultimate source—she responded to a deception by the deceiver:

> *Adam was not deceived, but the woman was deceived and became a transgressor* (1 Timothy 2:14).

This deceit is the characterization of Satan the Scripture presents to us, and it gives us the first principle by which Satan operates. Until we understand that Satan cannot, under any circumstances, operate in the realm of truth, we will be unprepared for his manifestation or temptation.†

The Bible is very specific about how Satan lies. First, Satan lies in the area of the Word of God. In 2 Corinthians 4:2, Paul said:

> *We do not use deception, nor do we distort the word of God* (NIV).

Deception suggests hypocrisy so that things do not appear as they actually are. The apostle was comparing himself with false teachers, who are Satan's ministers. If Satan is to hold the minds and hearts of men captive to his lie, it is necessary to blind men to the truth. We see men today openly repudiating the Word of God. That is a part of Satan's plan and purpose—to propagate his lie that the Bible is not the Word or that it only contains some words of God, is not authoritative, is only to be studied as a historical record, has no relevance in our life today.†

The second area in which Satan propagates a lie is the person and work of Jesus Christ. Men, instigated by Satan, have denied the virgin birth of Jesus, His deity, His resurrection, the fact that only through Him can man be saved, His second coming, and so forth. In anticipation of the categorical denial of Christ, the apostle John warned severely:

> *Who is the liar but he who denies that Jesus is the Christ?*
> *This is the antichrist, he who denies the Father and the Son*
> *. . . . Beloved, do not believe every spirit, but test the spirits*
> *to see whether they are of God; for many false prophets have*
> *gone out into the world. By this you know the spirit of God:*
> *every spirit which confesses that Jesus Christ has come in the*
> *flesh is of God, and every spirit which does not confess Jesus*
> *is not of God. This is the spirit of the antichrist* (1 John
> 2:22; 4:1-3).

The apostle said that a man's teaching concerning the person and work of Christ must conform with the Word of God, otherwise he is of the devil and he is propagating lies.†

The third area in which Satan uses deception is the doctrinal sphere. Satan uses the doctrines of demons to entice believers and by deception draw them away from the path of simple faith in Christ. In 1 Timothy 4:1-3, Paul mentioned some of these doctrines of demons: forbidding of marriage and abstaining from meats. In Galatians 5:4,18, Paul identified another doctrine of demons: legalism, seeking to live for God by the principle of the law rather than being led by the Spirit. Christ Himself warned about this onslaught of deceiving spirits upon the saints in the close of the age.

Take heed that no one leads you astray. For many will come in my name, saying, "I am the Christ," and they will lead many astray ... For false Christs and false prophets will arise and show great signs and wonders, so as to lead astray, if possible, even the elect (Matthew 24:4,5,24).

There are myriads of men and women who propagate the doctrines of demons. They weaken the authority of the Scriptures and provide other ways of salvation. Some offer no Savior, no cross, but a moral religion with man as his own savior. In the Christianized world, some doctrines of demons are found in Christian Science, Theosophy, Spiritism, and New Theology. In the heathen world, they are found in Islam, Confucianism, and Buddhism. Even in the professing Christian church, countless thoughts and beliefs are injected into the minds of believers by deceiving spirits or the father of lies, rendering them ineffective in the warfare with sin and Satan.

There are many other minor areas in which Satan deceives people. For example, in the area of drugs, such as cocaine and marijuana, Satan deceives people to believe that they will get out of their problems by using these stimulants. In spite of the danger, Satan convinces people that the drugs will enhance their creativity and productivity, reduce their feelings of loneliness and isolation, help fill the emptiness in their lives.

Can an honest believer be deceived? Christ would not have warned His disciples to *take heed ... be not deceived* if there had been no danger of deception. However, if one keeps his mind open to truth and light from God, one cannot be deceived for long. A mind closed to light and truth is a sure guarantee of deception by Satan. As one's mind is open to receive from God, God's Spirit will illuminate and expose any area in which a believer has been deceived.

When Satan lies to you about your spouse, do not believe him. Think of something good about your spouse and repudiate his lie. Remember, Satan is the acusser of the brethren (Revelation 12:10). Just as he accuses you falsely before God, he will lie about your spouse. His intention is to cause trouble between you and your spouse.

2. *Temptation*

According to the Word of God, there are three channels through which Satan can gain access to the citadel of a man's life. Satan can enter through the lust of the flesh, the lust of the eyes, or the pride of life (1 John 2:16). It is a comfort to know that Satan cannot tempt through a multitude of channels but can enter one's life through only three gates. All sin falls into one of these three classifications: the lust of the flesh, the lust of the eyes, and the pride of life. Jesus was tested in these three areas, yet without sin (Matthew 4:1-11;

Hebrews 4:15). In the first division, the realm of the flesh, Satan recognizes that man, because of Adam's sin, is possessed by a nature characterized by selfishness and inordinate passions. Satan may tempt and appeal to these sins of the flesh as he did with Jesus. In the second category, the lust of the eyes, Satan capitalizes on another characteristic of human nature. Satan realizes that what man sees he desires and covets and what he covets he will attempt to attain for himself. Satan may lead man astray in temptation through covetousness. In the third category, the pride of life, Satan appeals to pride because the human nature is basically proud; it loves and strives for that which promotes and elevates the individual.†

When Satan comes to tempt an individual he must appeal to one of these three basic characteristics of human nature—its carnal capacity, its selfish interests, or pride. He may use the mind or heart or a combination of these two. He may plant a seed in the mind and leave it over a long period until a person eventually comes to love Satan's proposal and then finally gives in Satan's bidding. We see this illustrated in David's sin with Bathsheba (2 Samuel 11). The steps of temptation that carried David to disgrace are the steps Satan uses in the experience of every person to bring that individual out of God's will and to obedience to himself. Satan begins with the mind. He plants a desire in that mind whether through the flesh, selfishness or pride. He moves from the mind to the area of the heart. What he has planted in your mind that appeals to the lust of the flesh, the lust of the eyes or the pride of life becomes the object of your affections.†

Solomon, who had great experience in wrestling with Satan, wrote:

Keep your heart with all vigilance; for from it flow the springs of life (Proverbs 4:23).

The Living Bible puts it this way:

Above all else, guard your affections. For they influence everything else in your life.

You need to examine your affections. Whatever you hunger for, Satan will appear to offer it in exchange for a spiritual compromise. Because we are prone to put ourselves in situations where we subject ourselves to Satan's attack, Paul advised us to:

Put on the Lord Jesus Christ, and make no provisions for the flesh, to gratify its desires (Romans 13:14).

And Peter advised us to:

*Abstain from the passions that **wage war** against your soul* (1 Peter 2:11, emphasis mine).

We need to safeguard our minds and hearts so that we are not providing that which Satan can use to produce sin in us.

3. *Perversion*

Satan is not only a deceiver and a tempter, he is also a perverter. To pervert is to change something from its intended use. Satan perverts or distorts what God has given man for his blessing and benefit. There is no blessing, no benefit, no good gift that Satan does not distort.

One area where Satan perverts is in the realm of food, either by deceiving people to abstain from it or to take it in excess. God at the time of creation gave food as a blessing to man so that his physical body might be sustained. Whereas God intends food as good and that it should be received with thanksgiving (Genesis 1:29; 2:16; 1 Timothy 4:3,4), Satan deceived the Colossian church by introducing a philosophical thought that would restrict the diet of the Colossians (Colossians 2:21): that spirituality is judged by what a person eats and doesn't eat.

On the other hand, Satan causes men to resort to excess of food and wine. He has made them gluttons, and by their gluttony they pervert the intended use of food (1 Peter 4:3; Proverbs 23:1,2,20,21). Men and women now wrestle with the problems of obesity and, consequently, heart trouble, high blood pressure, and all that goes with being overweight. The man who leans on alcohol to get himself through some trying situation will never learn to walk by faith and depend on the Holy Spirit. Satan doesn't want you to walk by faith, but to substitute alcohol. That is his perversion.†

The second area in which Satan perverts is the realm of sex. This area of perversion, of immorality, and promiscuity, is open evidence that Satan is a perverter of those God-given appetites and desires. By perverting and diverting them from their intended use, Satan produces all manner of uncleanness, immorality, and impurity. The apostle Paul dealt with premarital sex in epistle after epistle lest young men and women follow Satan's path into premarital relationships, which the Scripture forbids as fornication. Satan deceives young people by calling premarital sex fun and normal. Paul also dealt with divorce in First Corinthians, as our Lord did in Matthew 19, for divorce is a perversion of Satan.†

The third area in which Satan perverts and distorts is in the realm of material wealth, either by asking people never to desire riches or asking those who are already rich not to use their wealth for its intended purpose. On one hand, Satan makes people believe that they can't be rich and be good Christians, citing Scriptures such as Luke 18:24,25 and 1 Timothy 6:9,10. It is interesting to note that in the same passage where Paul seemed to forbid the desire to accumulate riches, he gave a specific instruction on the use of wealth for those who are rich (1 Timothy 6:9,10,17-19). It is not money or wealth that is the problem, but the love of it. Poverty is not God's desire for His people, although He permits it (Deuteronomy 15:4,7). People choose to be poor due to ignorance of God's will (Ephesians 5:17; Proverbs 10:22; Deuteronomy 15:4,5), disobedience to God (Deuteronomy 8:17-19; 28:1-68), laziness (Proverbs 10:4; 26:13-15), and lack of goals, plans, and priority (Proverbs 16:1,3).

On the other hand, Satan says to a businessman that if he runs his business on Christian principles his competitors will win out; if he is honest in running his business, he will lose; if he pays his tithes, he will never make it. That is Satan's perversion to make the will of God appear too expensive, whereas God's will is not burdensome (1 John 5:3). It is God's will that His people be rich so that you can enjoy His provision (Genesis 1, Psalm 24:1), glorify Him (Job 1:8-10; Ephesians 1:12; John 17:4), carry out His mission (Matthew 28:18-20; Romans 10:14-17), and be a blessing to others and to His work (Matthew 25:14-30; 1 Timothy 6:17-19).

A final area of Satan's perversion is the standard of God's holiness. Satan perverts God's standard of morals, ethics, and conducts. People have adopted the philosophy that the end justifies the means, that good is relative, "if it feels good do it." Satan has distorted love through television screen and music. Men call good evil and evil good (Isaiah 5:20) because Satan is a perverter.†

4. *Imitation*

One of Satan's strategies is to imitate God, to deceive people concerning his plans so that when they follow his imitation they will be convinced they are following God. Satan and his evil spirits work under cover of light:

> *For such men are false apostles, deceitful workmen, disguising themselves as apostles of Christ. And no wonder, for even Satan disguises himself as an angel of light. So it is not strange if his servants also disguise themselves as servants of righteousness. Their end will correspond to their deeds* (2 Corinthians 11:13-15, emphasis mine).

Truth and light are the very nature of God. If Satan operates directly in the realm of truth and light, his deeds will be exposed. In order for believers not to recognize his lies, Satan presents himself under the guise of light. This is a part of Satanic deception, the Satanic system that imitates God's program.

One area in which Satan imitates is the realm of miracles. God sends men with authority to proclaim a message and authenticates that authority by miracles. But Satan as an imitator sends his representatives to perform the same miracles to deceive men and turn them away from the truth (2 Thessalonians 2:9). Satan has one whom he transforms into a minister of righteousness to imitate the miracles of God. He imitated the miracles of Moses to deceive Pharaoh and the Egyptians (Exodus 7:11,12,22). He sought to imitate the miracles of Elijah to deceive the Israelites (1 Kings 18:26-39). He will imitate the miracles of Moses and Elijah during the tribulation period (Revelation 13:13-15).†

The second area Satan imitates is evangelism. God has an agenda of reaching sinners and edifying saints (Matthew 28:18-20; Acts 1:8). As Satan saw the purpose and program of God to send men out to witness to Jesus Christ, he sent out his emissaries to deny the central truth: Jesus Christ and Him crucified. Satan preaches another Jesus by the power of another spirit that results in another gospel. While Satan is reaching unbelievers with another gospel (2 Corinthians 11:4; Galatians 1:8), he is reaching the saints with the doctrines of demons (1 Timothy 4:1; 2 John 10). It is significant to observe that God's method of reaching men is to preach the truth concerning the person and work of Jesus Christ. Satan has not devised another method. He imitates the program of God and sends his ministers, whom he claims to be ministers of righteousness, into the world to do what the saints of God are commanded to do: preach the gospel. His ministers preach a counter-gospel, propagate a lie, and substitute the false for the true. Satan seeks to produce a perfect man apart from Christ. He appeals to men and women: "By following me you can become like God."†

There is danger in indiscriminate listening to your radio and TV, hearing of preachers and reading of books. We are commanded to test everyone who professes to be a minister of the gospel of Christ (1 John 4:1-3). Satan is at work to deceive, to propagate a lie, and he does it by the subtle imitation of the truth or counterfeiting of the divine.†

5. *Opposition to God's Will*

Satan opposes everything God does. No matter from which direction you look at Satan, he has no good side. He is a liar, he is a cheat, he is an imitator, he is an opposer. He opposes and hinders God's will in the world, in the church, in your home, and in your life. To see how Satan opposes God's will entails scanning through the Scriptures, from Genesis to Revelation, or looking at human history from the divine viewpoint. Time and space would not allow us to do that here. But we see Satan's opposition in the garden of Eden, the birth of Isaac, the birth of Moses, the history of the nation of Israel, after the birth of Jesus Christ, and in the garden of Gethsemane.

One area where Satan opposes God's will is the realm of human life and existence. Jesus made mention of this fact when He said:

> *The thief comes only to steal and kill and destroy; I came that they may have life, and have it abundantly* (John 10:10).

Here Jesus revealed three ways by which Satan attacks human existence: stealing, killing, and destruction. Satan kills human lives through war, suicide, abortion, poison, and the like. He steals and robs us of that which legitimately belongs to us, which God has designed for us to enjoy and glorify Him. He destroys lives through sickness, diseases, and infirmities so that those lives are unable to glorify God. Through stealing, killing, and destruction, Satan opposes God's will for our lives—that we enjoy life to its fullness, life in abundance.

The second area in which Satan opposes God's will is in the sphere of spiritual growth. It is God's will that we be not conformed to this world but be conformed to the image of His Son (Romans 12:2). It is His will that we be not babes but grow to maturity in Christ (Ephesians 4:11-14). Satan opposes God's will and tries hard to make believers carnal and immature in faith. This opposition of the devil is graphically illustrated in the parable of the sower (Matthew 13:1-9). In the parable, we see three strategies the enemy uses to hinder growth. As soon as the Word of God is preached or sown, Satan with his emissaries leaps into action. First, Satan makes the heart and mind unprepared so that the truth is not received—*some seeds fell along the path.* Second, if Satan cannot prevent one from hearing the Word of God, he tries to make sure that the Word is not deeply rooted in the person. He uses persecution, doubt, ridicule, and skepticism to ensure that God's Word has no lasting impact on our lives—*other seeds fell on rocky ground.* Third, if Satan fails in uprooting the Word before it germinates, if he fails in preventing the Word from growing to the point where it is ready to bear fruit, he will get us occupied with unnecessary things—*thorns grew up and choked them.* What the Word of God produces in your life is directly related to the preparation you have permitted the Holy Spirit to do in your life and heart.†

The third area in which Satan opposes God's will is the progress of God's work, the expansion of His kingdom here on earth. The work of God progresses in three ways—through our reaching *up* in prayer, through our reaching *out* in evangelism, and through our reaching *in* by ministering to fellow believers. Satan opposes each of these three avenues. He hinders the propagation of the gospel (1 Thessalonians 2:18). He tries his best to make us prayerless, to make us do God's work with human resources rather than spiritual weapons. And he restrains us from reaching out in love and meeting the needs of our fellow brethren.

The final area in which Satan opposes God's will is the realm of law and order or authority and submission. Human government is a divine institution necessitated by the rebellion of Satan and by Satan's program to produce utter lawlessness and rebellion upon the face of the earth. God has placed authority and human government in three spheres: state, church, and home. Any form of government that fulfills the divine purpose for government, that is, any government that maintains law and order, that curbs selfishness, lawlessness, and rebellion, is a government that has divine approval. The believer is responsible to submit to it (Romans 13:1-7; 1 Peter 2:17; 1 Timothy 2:2; Titus 3:1). When we fail to submit to authority either at home, at church or in the state, we are casting our vote for Satan whose plan is to lead men in lawlessness and rebellion. Be on guard against lawlessness and rebellion.†

"God opposes the proud, but gives grace to the humble." Submit yourselves therefore to God. Resist the devil and he will flee from you (James 4:6,7).

*For who sees anything different in you? What have you that
you did not receive? If then you received it, why do you
boast as if it were not a gift?* (1 Corinthians 4:7).

6. Fear

Like a roaring lion, Satan uses fear to intimidate a believer.
He uses fear in three major ways to instil doubt and unbelief
in you. The first area is anxiety about needs. We look ahead
and think of tomorrow with fear. What shall we eat and wear?
Where shall we live? What will happen tomorrow? How I am
going to pay that bill? Is there a possibility of the company
closing and firing every employee? Does the economy seem to
be going against your business? Is the news so terrifying that
you think you will not see tomorrow? Do the children have
problems that seem impossible to handle? Satan uses fear,
worry, doubt, anxiety, and tension to torment us and keep us
off balance. We see the effect of fear in the life of the people
of Israel as they were led by Moses out of Egypt, the land of
bondage. Would God be able to take them across the Red
Sea? Would God be able to feed them? Would God be able
to provide water for them in the wilderness? They soon forgot
the numerous miracles God had performed to take them out
of Egypt. The fear of having your needs met is destructive
because it threatens your very existence. It paralyzes the faculty
of reason, destroys faith in God, undermines enthusiasm in
godly things, discourages your initiative, encourages procrasti-
nation, makes self-control impossible, and leads to worry and
dissipation. This is why Jesus severely warned:

*Do not be anxious about your life, what you shall eat or
what you shall drink, nor about your body, what you shall*

*put on. Is not life more than food, and the body more than
clothing? Look at the birds of the air: they neither sow nor
reap nor gather into barns, and yet your heavenly Father
feeds them. Are you not of more value than they? ... For
the Gentiles seek all these things; and your heavenly Father
knows that you need them all. But seek first his kingdom
and his righteousness, and all these things shall be yours as
well. Therefore do not be anxious about tomorrow, for
tomorrow will be anxious for itself. Let the day's own
trouble be sufficient for the day* (Matthew 6:25-34).

Rather than yielding to fear and worry about life, you should
be concerned about God's kingdom, His business, His agenda,
His righteousness, and how to please Him; let Him take care
of your needs. We should cast our cares and burdens on Him
who cares so much about us (1 Peter 5:7). As you learn to
walk with God by faith, not in fear and doubt, and cast your
cares on Christ, He supplies every need of yours according to
His riches in glory (Philippians 4:19).

The second area in which Satan uses fear is the realm of
criticism. We don't want to be criticized. So we conform and
compromise. The fear of criticism robs you of initiative when
God wants you to do something different and you fear what
others would say about you. It limits your individuality and
uniqueness and makes you conform to the status quo. But as
Peter and the apostles said:

We must obey God rather than men (Acts 5:29).

And as David said:

In God I trust without a fear, what can man do to me?
(Psalm 56:11).

Lastly, Satan uses fear in the area of death—loss of your own life or a loved one. The fear of death is more common among the aged, but sometimes it grips the hearts of the young as well. We fear death when our kids don't come back from school on time or when our spouse's plane doesn't arrive at the scheduled time. Maybe the kids had an accident. Perhaps the plane crashed. The enemy brings fear of death. When Satan sends fear of the loss of a loved one, you should, instead of accepting the fear and meditating on it, rebuke Satan and start praying for that loved one. If the fear is concerning the loss of your own very life, tell the devil what Dr. Jerry Falwell is fond of saying: "The man of God cannot die until it is the time appointed by the Lord." Remember:

Your life is hid with Christ in God (Colossians 3:3).

He who touches you touches the apple of His eye (Zechariah 2:8).

No weapon that is fashioned against you shall prosper (Isaiah 54:17).

Surely he will save you from the fowler's snare and from the deadly pestilence. He will cover you with his feathers, and under his wings you find refuge; his faithfulness will be your shield and rampart. You will not fear the terror of night, nor the arrow that flies by day ... For he will command his angels concerning you to guard you in all your ways (Psalm 91:3-5,11, NIV).

A believer must have a proper attitude toward death. Death is an appointment for every man or woman (Hebrews 9:27). We need not fear death, since Christ has swallowed death in victory (1 Corinthians 15:54) and death is mere transition from here to glory. Fear is of the devil.

For God hath not given the spirit of fear; but of power, and of love, and of a sound mind (2 Timothy 1:7, KJV).

Your best bet against fear is to fear God. God is the only person to be fearful about. God told Isaiah:

Do not call conspiracy all that this people call conspiracy, and do not fear what they fear, nor be in dread. But the LORD of hosts, him you shall regard as holy; let him be your fear, and let him be your dread (Isaiah 8:12,13).

Fear God and you will have nothing else to fear.

7. *Satan's Ultimate Goal*

The ultimate goal of Satan is to weaken your faith and destroy your marriage. Faith is a way of life; it is the sum total of your profession as a believer in Christ. Without faith, it is impossible to please God (Hebrews 11:6), and the just shall live by faith (Romans 1:17). Satan will make you doubt the Word of God. If Satan succeeds in stealing or weakening your faith and destroy your family through deception, temptation, perversion, imitation, and opposition to God's will in your life, he has defeated you. In order to overcome the enemy and have a victorious family, you must avail yourself of the tools God has for you.

How to Overcome the Enemy

God has not saved us, made us His children, and brought us into His royal family only to be victims of Satan's defeat. It is not God's will that we live a defeated life. He has provided us with spiritual weapons to overcome the enemy of our body, soul, and spirit. In our human strength, we don't stand a chance against the attacks of the devil, his incredible power, and insidious schemes. By ourselves, we are no match for Satan who has thousands of years of experience fouling up God's children. The apostle Paul said:

> *For though we live in the world we are not carrying on a worldly war, for the weapons of our warfare are not worldly, but have divine power to destroy strongholds* (2 Corinthians 10:3,4).

We must constantly be aware of the fact that our warfare is spiritual and that it takes spiritual weapons to fight a spiritual battle. We should not be afraid of the warfare, because we are going to win. God has not sent us to do battle with inadequate weapons. He has provided us with weapons, strong and adequate to overcome the devil. Such weapons include:

- the power of the Holy Spirit,
- the weapon of Scripture,
- the weapon of prayer,
- your authority in Christ,
- spiritual armor, and
- willful resistance of the devil.

God has placed in your hand these six mighty weapons to combat the enemy of your soul. As shown in the Table 3.1, there is one or more corresponding weapons a believer can use for each of the six weapons of the enemy. If we are to overcome the enemy, we must be aware of these weapons and learn to use them.

Table 3.1
Weapons for Overcoming the Enemy

Satan's Weapons	Believer's Weapons
Deception	Scripture
Temptation	Scripture, Holy Spirit
Perversion	Willful resistance
Imitation	Scripture, Discernment by the Holy Spirit
Fear	Faith, Scripture
Opposition to God's Will	Authority in Christ

1. *The Power of the Holy Spirit*

We are to overcome the enemy in just the same way Jesus did. We are told that Jesus was *full of the Holy Spirit* (Luke 4:1) and so was able to overcome the temptations of Satan. He lived His life as He expects us to live, in a moment-by-moment, absolute reliance on the Father, who worked through Him by the Holy Spirit (John 5:19; 1 Peter 2:21). Since it takes spiritual power to overcome spiritual power, Jesus promised:

You shall receive power when the Holy Spirit has come upon you (Acts 1:8).

The Holy Spirit energizes the believer with power to carry out God's work: witnessing to unbelievers, praying, healing, casting out demons, binding, and resisting the power of the enemy.

We should not be satisfied with a one-shot exposure to the power of the Holy Spirit. God wants to give us a pattern of living in which He fills us moment by moment with new and spiritual energy. This pattern of living was called "being filled with the Spirit" in Ephesians 5:18:

Do not get drunk with wine, for that is debauchery; but be filled with the Spirit.

The filling of the Spirit is the means God has given us for living the Christian life with power. It is not optional; it is a command.

2. *The Weapon of Scripture*

The believer must learn to wield Scripture as the divinely provided weapon for victory over Satan and the evil spirits. Jesus overcame Satan during His temptation by appealing to the Word of God (Matthew 4:1-11). There are three ways by which the Scripture serves as a weapon in warfare against the devil. First, knowledge of the truth is the surest safeguard against deception of the devil. Knowledge of the truth enables the believer to recognize the lies of Satan. A knowledgeable believer will be able to judge or examine all things (1 Corinthians 2:14,15). We are to abound in knowledge and all discernment so as to approve what is excellent and of the Lord

(Philippians 1:9,10; Ephesians 5:17). To overcome the devil as a liar, the believer must walk in truth. There is no way to victory over falsehood but by truth.

Second, knowledge of the truth helps you to know your rights, your authority as a believer in Christ. Satan's desire is to keep you in fear and bondage of culture, sickness, disease, poverty, and so forth. Jesus' desire is for you to be free from all that (John 8:31,32). When you meditate on the Scripture on a continual basis, the Holy Spirit will illuminate your heart with truth. You will know your rights in Christ and Satan will no longer be able to dupe you.

Third, the Scripture is the sword of the Spirit, an offensive weapon to combat the enemy.

For the word of God is living and active, sharper than any two-edged sword, piercing to the division of soul and spirit, of joints and marrow, and discerning the thoughts and intentions of the heart (Hebrews 4:12).

The Word of God has power to destroy strongholds of the enemy and every obstacle to the knowledge of God (2 Corinthians 10:4,5).

3. *The Weapon of Prayer*

The sword of the Spirit and prayer are the Christian's offensive weapons against Satan. Much has been said about prayer as a spiritual weapon in the last chapter already. It will suffice to add a few lines. The importance of prayer in spiritual warfare is best described in the words of Samuel Chadwick:

Satan dreads nothing but prayer .... The church that lost its Christ was full of good works. Activities are multiplied that meditation may be ousted, and organizations are increased that prayer may have no chance. Souls may be lost in good works, as surely as in evil ways. The one concern of the devil is to keep the saints from praying. He fears nothing from prayerless religion. He laughs at our toil, mocks at our wisdom, but trembles when we pray.[2]

4. Your Authority in Christ

Christ by His resurrection was placed in authority over every realm: in heaven, on earth, and under the earth (Matthew 28:20; Philippians 2:9-11). Christ is far above all power and principality (Ephesians 1:20-22). Through baptism, we have been identified with Christ in His death, burial, and resurrection. When He ascended and was seated at the right hand of the Father, we ascended and were seated with Him. We participated in all that Jesus Christ has done. When God gave the Son authority over every realm, He gave us that authority because we are in Christ Jesus. Now the believer has authority over Satan that he did not have naturally. The believer was placed under the angels by the fact of his creation, but by virtue of his new creation in Jesus Christ he is elevated to a position above angels (Psalm 8:5; Hebrews 1:5-14). It is important to realize that we have no authority of our own (Acts 19:13-17). Only in His name is our victory guaranteed.

In Revelation 12:7-11, we are told that:

Now war arose in heaven ... the great dragon was thrown down, that ancient serpent, who is called the Devil and Satan, the deceiver of the whole world—he was thrown down to the earth, and his angels were thrown down with him. And I heard a loud voice in heaven, saying, "Now the salvation and the power and the kingdom of our God and the authority of his Christ have come, for the accuser of our brethren has been thrown down, who accuses them day and night before our God. And they have conquered him by the blood of the Lamb and by the word of their testimony, for they loved not their lives even unto death . . . . "

Here we are given five vivid words that describe our enemy's character and methods of operation. He is called the dragon, meaning that he is a dreadful, cruel, ferocious monster. He is the old serpent in that he is cunning and crafty, working under cover. He is designated the devil, the slanderer. He is Satan, the adversary of God, the church, and the brethren. Finally, he is the accuser of the brethren, the father of all lies. But the same passage provides three invincible weapons of offense:[3]

• the judicial weapon—*they overcome him by the blood of the Lamb,*
• the evidential weapon—*they overcome him . . . , by the word of their testimony,* and
• the sacrificial weapon—*they loved not their lives even unto death.*

The secret of victory is not our prowess, but our union and identification with Christ in His victorious death. The blood of the Lamb is the ground of victory. We are to regard Satan as already defeated and to claim Christ's victory over him as ours, for Satan has no counter-weapon to the blood of the Lamb. So when we plead the blood of the Lamb in prayer, we are resting on Christ's mediatorial work and claiming victory purchased by His blood.

The sacrificial weapon is to defeat the enemy when he uses the fear of death against you. Remember, your life is not in Satan's hand to control, but it is hid with Christ in God (Colossians 3:3). So when the enemy threatens you with fear, tell him that he has no control over you; you have been purchased by Christ (1 Corinthians 6:19,20). Christ is the only one who can take away your life, and when He does, it will be for your maximum good and His maximum glory.

5. *Spiritual Armor*

As noted earlier, Satan uses natural needs such as food, sex, and the need for a mate, when these needs are not under the control of the Holy Spirit. He can use a normal sex drive to break up a marriage. He is on constant guard, watching every believer, and waiting for the believer's armor to slip so that he can fling in his fiery darts.

Therefore take the whole armor of God, that you may be able to withstand in the evil day, and having done all, to stand. Stand therefore, having girded your loins with truth, and having put on the breastplate of righteousness, and having shod your feet with the equipment of the gospel of peace; besides all these, taking the shield of faith, with which you can quench all the flaming darts of the evil one. And take the helmet of salvation, and the sword of the Spirit, which is the word of God. Pray at all times in the Spirit, with all prayer and supplication (Ephesians 6:13-18).

The armored and non-armored believer may be briefly contrasted as shown in the Table 3.2. The armor is provided that a believer may stand against the wiles of the adversary, the devil. Satan is prowling around like a roaring lion, seeking someone to devour, and watching every believer. We must be vigilant and watchful. A soldier puts on his armor in preparation for battle, not at the battle front. So arm yourself with the belt of truth—a growing knowledge and understanding of the Word of God and how to apply it to daily living. Arm yourself with the breastplate of righteousness, a protection over your heart—against the enemy's slander and accusation, against the enemy's temptation to sin. This involves claiming your righteousness in Christ (2 Corinthians 5:21) and living a holy life before God (1 Thessalonians 4:3,7). Arm yourself with your feet shod with the gospel of peace. Don't let Satan knock you off balance with fear. Rest assured in God's promise to give you rest and peace of mind. Claim God's Word for provision and protection. His Word is a covenant you can trust. Arm yourself with faith, as a shield against doubt and fear. The apostle John said:

> *Whatever is born of God overcomes the world; and this is the victory that overcomes the world, our faith* (1 John 5:4).

Arm yourself with the helmet of salvation—against any doubt as regards your salvation—knowing that your salvation is complete and secure. Arm yourself with the weapon of Scripture, the sword of the Spirit (Hebrews 4:12). Let the Word of God dwell richly in your heart (Colossians 3:16).

Table 3.2

Comparison Between Armored and Non-armored
Christians.[4]

The Armored Christian	The Non-Armored Christian
Armored with truth	Open to lies through ignorance
Righteous living	Unrighteous living through ignorance
Making and keeping peace	Divisions and quarrels
Self-preservation and control	Reckless unwatchfulness and lack of discipline
Faith as a shield	Doubt, fear, and unbelief
Scripture as a weapon	Relying on human reason
Praying without ceasing	Prayerless toil

Putting on the whole armor is not enough. You must be
bold and courageous. As Paul said:

... *having done all to stand. Stand therefore ...* (Ephesians 6:13,14).

*Be watchful, stand firm in your faith, be courageous, be
strong* (1 Corinthians 16:13).

6. *Willful Resistance of the Devil*

God's method of meeting the devil is to launch a counter-
offensive, to resist him, or to stand actively against him. That
is exactly what Jesus did at His temptation. Christ confronted

the enemy by actively resisting or repudiating him. Peter learned from Christ and so he advised:

> *Be sober, be watchful. Your adversary the devil prowls around like a roaring lion, seeking some one to devour. Resist him, firm in your faith* (1 Peter 5:8,9, emphasis mine).

Notice that Satan is not called a lion; he is *like* a lion. Jesus is the Lion of Judah (Revelation 5:5). James gave an advice similar to Peter's:

> *Submit yourselves therefore to God. Resist the devil and he will flee from you* (James 4:7, emphasis mine).

Although Satan is described as prowling around "like a roaring lion," he is an abject coward who will run at the strong opposition from the believer. This is where the believer's will and right to make decisions come in. Satan cannot force you to do anything; he can only lure and deceive you. Your refusal and resistance of the enemy's proposal is an aggressive weapon in the spiritual conflict.

We must utilize all these weapons of warfare. Depending on the situation, we may need just one of the weapons or all of them to fight the enemy. Power must be used against power, and force against force. Through the energizing power of the Holy Spirit, prayer, Scripture, standing on our position of authority in Christ, putting on our spiritual armor, and willful resistance, victory over Satan, your adversary, is certain.

How to Watch Your Mind

Satan is a manipulator; he plays with your mind. So you need to watch and guard your mind. To do this will involve watching what comes to your mind and arming yourself with the right mind.

Watch what you say and hear. Words dominate us. What you confess, what you say with your mouth, whether positive or negative, will control your life. Don't allow Satan to feed your mind with garbage. What you eat becomes part of your flesh. If you eat junk, junk becomes part of you. The same is true spiritually. Feed your mind with positive thoughts and let your confession also be positive.

Whatever is pure, whatever is honorable ... whatever is gracious, if there is any excellence, if there is anything worthy of praise, think about these things (Philippians 4:8).

Stop confessing failure, doubt, weakness, inability. That is Satan's suggestion. Start confessing positive things, what God says about you. As Dr. Frederick Price is fond of saying, "Your faith will never register above the words of your lips."

Arm yourself with the right mind. This has to do with how you hear or receive information. If doubt, unbelief, fear, defeat, and failure dominate your daily thoughts, you have a mind dominated by the devil. Everything of God is positive, while everything about the devil is negative. Since Satan plays with your mind, it is important that you have the right mind, the mind of Christ. It is a mind of humility, accepting that you have nothing that you did not receive from God (1 Corinthians 4:7; Philippians 2:5-11). It is a mind of total dependence on God, evident in your prayer life, realizing that without Him you can do nothing (Luke 5:16; 6:12; 9:28; John 15:5). It is a mind of faith, believing that what God says in His Word will come to pass and that what you confess will become reality. It is a mind of gratitude and appreciation toward God, your spouse, and others.

Most of the conflicts between you and your spouse are instigated by the enemy, and your mind is the battleground. Therefore, as Secret Number 3,

> *Keep your heart with all vigilance, for from it flow the springs of life* (Proverbs 4:23).

Notes

[1] J. Dwight Pentecost, *Your Adversary, the Devil* (Grand Rapids, MI: Zondervan, 1969).

[2] E. M. Bounds, *The Possibilities of Prayer* (Grand Rapids, MI: Baker Book House, 1979), p. 52.

[3] J. Oswald Sanders, *A Spiritual Clinic* (Chicago, IL: Moody Press, 1958), pp. 128-130.

[4] Jessie Penn-Lewis, *War on the Saints* (Fort Washington, PA: The Christian Literature Crusade, 1977), p. 138.

PART II

SOCIAL SECRETS

CHAPTER FOUR

THE SECRET OF COMMUNICATION

Can two walk together, except they be agreed?
Amos 3:3, KJV

Communication has always been a major problem in most homes. It is often the missing link in unhappy marriages. Through extensive studies, it has been found that the happiest couples are the ones who talk most with each other. Communication is therefore not a dispensable luxury in a successful marriage; it is an indispensable necessity. It is the lifeblood of strong relationships. Ability to communicate is fundamental to a successful marriage because it is the means by which a husband-wife relationship or parent-child relationship is established and maintained. It is your ability to communicate personal thoughts, feelings, experiences, and preferences that will allow your marriage to pass through the changing seasons. There can be no unity and happiness in a home where there is lack of communication.

The word *communication* is derived from the word *communus,* meaning "having something in common." Communication in a marriage is a process whereby a man and woman come to an agreement. Having grown up in different back-grounds, it is hard for the two to see or reason the same way. But how can they walk or live together happily unless there is a mutual agreement? (Amos 3:3). In order for them to agree, there must be effective communication, which does not come naturally.

According to Dr. Norman Wright, a marriage counselor and the author of numerous books on family communication:

Communication is a process (either verbal or nonverbal) of sharing information with another person in such a way that he understands what you are saying. "Talking" and "listening" and "understanding" are all involved in the process of communication.[1]

The understanding aspect of communication is very broad and will be covered in the next chapter. If we limit communication to talking and listening, it basically involves at least eight steps:

1. What you intend to say.
2. What you actually say.
3. What the other person hears.
4. What the other person thinks he hears.
5. What the other person intends to say back.
6. What the other person actually says back.
7. What you hear.
8. What you think you hear.

It is evident that to say what you mean and mean what you say is not an easy task. But we can all learn to improve the way we communicate. Communication is a developmental skill; it gets better as we work on it and cultivate it.

As shown in Figure 4.1, communication involves transmitting and receiving signals. The signals may be a word, tone of voice, look, touch or gesture. For effective communication, signals must be properly transmitted, well received, understood, and acted upon. In this chapter, we shall zero in on the following aspects of communication:

- talking: the art of transmitting,
- listening: the art of receiving,
- communication killers,
- improving your communication skills, and
- the rewards of effective communication.

Talking: The Art of Transmitting

A couple cannot really know each other unless they talk and confide in each other. Communication is an act of the will. Just as we would never know God if He chose not to reveal Himself and communicate to us through His Spirit, we cannot know each other unless we choose to communicate (1 Corinthians 2:11). Talking brings out what is inside of us. If we are to be loved, we must be willing to talk and be known. If others cannot fully know us, they cannot fully love us. For example, just talking about the kind of home you prefer to live in, the kind of car you want to drive, and the number of kids you plan to raise helps you learn a lot about each other. As another example, talking about money in your marriage teaches you more about each other, creates oneness, and frees your minds.

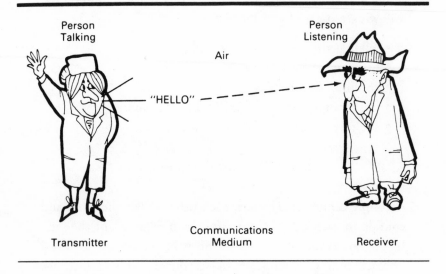

Fig. 4.1 Communication involves transmitting and receiving.
Source: Malcolm G. Lane, *Data Communications Software Design* (Boston: PWS-KENT Publishing Co., 1985), p. 5.

We must understand the mechanism of talking before we can be effective communicators. When you talk to another person, a filtering process takes place as illustrated in Figure 4.2. What you say is not necessarily what is being received.

Five major ingredients must accompany an effective talk:

- honesty,
- speaking the truth in love,
- speaking your spouse's language,
- speaking with understanding, and
- thinking before you speak.

1. *Honesty*

Honesty is one of the most important qualities in a person and particularly in a successful marriage. It is unfortunate that there are too many dishonest husbands and wives who lie to one another on a continuing basis. The reason for this is rather obvious. We live in a world that does not honor honesty. The world's philosophy is: "Tell everything that will keep you out of hot water. Never tell your wife or husband everything." But this is contradictory to God's will. Total honesty must be practiced at home. A child of God should have nothing to hide.

This reminds me of my arrival from Amsterdam at John F. Kennedy Airport in New York one day. As soon as I got out of the plane, I was approached by two men who identified themselves as airport police. I couldn't figure out what was the problem, but I wasn't afraid because I had nothing to hide. After they searched my hand luggage, I asked them what the problem was. They said that I had a stolen ticket. Knowing fully well that I hadn't stolen the ticket, I was very calm and

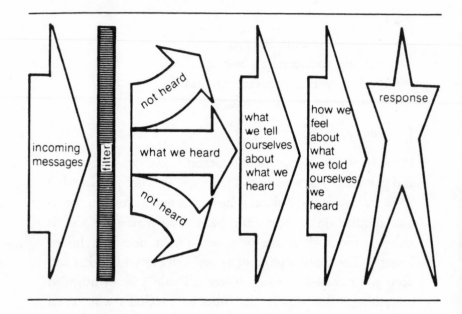

Fig. 4.2 Filtering process in talking. Taken from *How Do You Say "I Love You"?* by Judson J. Swihart © 1977 by InterVarsity Christian Fellowship of the USA. Used by permission of the InterVarsity Press, PO Box 1400, Downers Grove, IL 60515.

ready for investigation. To cut the long story short, they found that the problem was with the travel agency and not with me. A child of God should be willing to write his testimony in the skies, having nothing to hide.

Honest or open talk is perhaps the best medicine for a shaky marriage, because it helps husband and wife understand what each other is feeling. Deception only compounds misunderstanding. Manipulation, deceit, and lying do not belong in a happy marriage. If you have committed a sin that is affecting your marriage, you need to confess it to God, let your spouse know about it and ask for his/her forgiveness. Although your honesty may cause your spouse to be heartbroken at the moment, he/she will surely appreciate your honesty and forgive you. Most couples find relief from their marital tensions in honest talk about things that seem to threaten their marriage.

A couple who lie to each other are undermining their relationship. Suppose, for example, Bob lies to Sarah that he enjoys pork and beans. This will encourage Sarah to serve pork and beans on a regular basis and Bob will end up being upset. Suppose, on the other hand, that Sarah lies to Bob that she spent forty-five dollars for a dress instead of thirty-five dollars because she spent ten dollars on something Bob doesn't like. If Bob finds out about the lie, it may be difficult for Bob to trust Sarah again.

Therefore, putting away falsehood, let every one speak truth with his neighbor, for we are members one of another (Ephesians 4:25).

> *Do not lie to one another, seeing that you have put off the old nature with its practices and have put on the new nature, which is being renewed in knowledge after the image of its creator* (Colossians 3:9,10).

> *O LORD, who shall sojourn in thy tent? Who shall dwell on thy holy hill? He who walks blamelessly, and does what is right, and speaks truth from his heart* (Psalm 15:1,2).

Unity and love are based on being thoroughly and completely honest with one another. Absolute honesty should be practiced in a Christian home.

2. *Speaking the Truth in Love*

As Christians, we must say the truth, but the truth must be said in love if it is to accomplish its intent (Ephesians 4:15). Honesty must be balanced with love. To speak the truth in love means to take into consideration the other person's feelings. It means to use kind words in expressing what is on your heart because love is kind (1 Corinthians 13:4). When love is evident in your communication, it makes your words sweet to the ear and encouraging to the heart. Love makes up for bad grammar and twisted sentences.

When dealing with our spouses, we must bear in mind that we are not dealing with creatures of logic but creatures of emotion and prejudice. Anybody can criticize, condemn, and complain. But it takes character and discipline to be understanding and forgiving. So couple your criticism with compliments. Follow the biblical pattern for criticism in Revelation 2:1-4: three compliments, one criticism. For example, the wife may say, "Honey, what a wonderful painting you gave me yesterday! You're a great artist. No one ever gave me his own original painting before. You have so much talent, and I'm proud of you." (She waits for his response.) "Next time, can you make the painting larger so that we place it in the living room?"

The compliments makes me feel I am doing a good job, so I am motivated to improve. If, however, you give me the criticism without the compliments, I am likely to give up because it makes me feel I am a failure.

3. Speaking Your Spouse's Language

Your spouse is a foreigner! Your spouse may be of your race and nationality, but you speak different languages because of your different backgrounds. You may both use the same English words but with different meanings. You have a set of values, beliefs, terms, and style of talking that are different from your spouse's. We all understand things best when they are said in our own language. The languages couples commonly use include the following:

1. Meeting material needs.
2. Meeting emotional needs.
3. Helping.
4. Spending time together.
5. Saying it with words.
6. Saying it with a touch.
7. Making it brief.
8. Giving a lot of details.

Suppose, for example, that Karen's primary language is helping. George may tell Karen that he loves her and demonstrate it by spending time with her and meeting her material needs. Karen may not really feel that she is being loved, and George gets frustrated. George is talking in a language other than Karen's primary language. She does not hear his total message of love until she is being helped. It is as if she is saying, "I can't accept language 1 or 4 unless you also speak 3. But if you speak language 3, I can also accept languages 1 and 4." For your relationship to blossom, learn your spouse's dominant language and communicate in that language.

4. *Speaking With Understanding*

It is a fundamental error to assume that others view life as we do. This wrong assumption leads to misunderstanding, false judgment, misconception, resentment, breakdown in communication, and weakening of the relationship. Although we will discuss extensively the differences in people in the next chapter, it is appropriate here that we see the differences in people as far as communication is concerned. When people communicate, they are processing information to be transmitted or received in different ways. In terms of information processing, people can be classified as visual, auditory, and feeling-oriented.

A visual person experiences things with his eyes. He demonstrates this trait through reading, watching, taking pictures, and so on. He would prefer seeing something to being told. In a speech, he uses terms such as *look, see, pattern, picture, point of view, clear,* and *show.* Communicate with a visual person by providing him something he can see.

An auditory person is interested in what he hears. He relates more to sounds than sights. He thinks best when he speaks to himself. He prefers listening to a message on audiocassette to reading the same message in a book. He prefers receiving your call or hearing your voice to receiving a letter from you. He tends to remember what he hears better than others. A hearing-oriented person often uses terms such as *hear, call, sound, loud, clear, ear, music,* and *talk.*

A feeling-oriented person responds on the basis of his feelings. He has a heightened sense of emotion or intuition. He loves closeness and affection. He is more spontaneous than a visual or auditory person. He is known for his sensitivity. He uses terms such as *happy, love, near, sense, close, feeling, warm, touch, soft, smooth,* and *tense.*

Though we all use the three modes, one mode tends to be more developed and dominant in us than the others. Men tend to be more visual than women, while women are more feeling-oriented than men. We need to understand these different perceptions so that we respond to an idea with an idea and a feeling with a feeling. Understand your spouse's dominant mode of information processing and learn to communicate with him/her in that mode.

5. *Thinking Before You Speak*

It is not enough to be truthful and honest about what you say; you must think before you say it. Before you open your mouth, consider your partner's best interests and the long-range health of your marriage. As James said:

Let every man be quick to hear, slow to speak, slow to anger (James 1:19).

And as the wise man said:

Do you see a man who is hasty in his words? There is more hope for a fool than for him (Proverbs 29:20).

To help evaluate what you are about to say, ask yourself the following questions before you open your mouth:

Is it true?
Is it necessary?
Is it edifying?
Is it kind?

Thinking before you speak can save you a lot of troubles in your marriage.

Listening: The Art of Receiving

Listening is more than hearing. Few people really take the time to listen to others. True listening requires discipline and full concentration. Listening is not our natural preference. We like to speak and assert our position, feelings, opinions, and ideas rather than listen to others. Because of this we tend to concentrate more on getting our word into the conversation, rather than giving full attention to what the other person is saying. Josh McDowell noted:

From the fact that God gave us two ears and one mouth, the Irish have drawn the thoughtful conclusion that we should listen twice as much as we talk.[2]

Most of the time, our communication is in the form of a monologue: a one-way talk. We talk just to get our ideas across to others and not to hear others' views. Communication must be a dialogue, a two-way talk, in order to be effective. You must be willing to give and take, transmit and receive, talk and listen.

Your spouse, like any other person, has a deep need to be heard and listened to. Listening to a person makes him/her feel loved, respected, and esteemed. It is well said that the best way to get someone to listen to you is to listen to the person.

Listening is a learned behavior; we can all learn to listen and improve how we listen. First, we consider why people want us to listen to them. Later we consider how to listen. There are four reasons why people want you to listen or why you want to listen to them:

- to pour out,
- to inform or learn something,
- to reflect, and
- to get advice, help, or comfort.

Sometimes people need to pour out their hurts, frustrations, and pains. They need you to listen, not for you to fix things or give advice. They simply want someone to listen with patience, mercy, and integrity. Maybe your husband comes back from work and needs to ventilate his feelings to someone who will listen, understand, and sympathize. If you try to comfort him, he may get more frustrated. Just listening may be all he needs.

Often people are eager to share with you what they have just learned. Sometimes we feel bored if what is being shared is of no interest to us. But with love you can listen patiently to your spouse when he/she has something to share with you.

At other times, people need you as a sounding board to reflect and clarify thoughts. This happens a lot with public speakers, such as pastors and politicians. They are not really asking for your advice, but your view. They need you as a mirror to reflect their thoughts and see their opinions from another frame of reference. All you need is to listen and try to say back what you hear, only in a different way. If your wife is the speaker, maybe all she wants is a male perspective on her thinking process.

The need for ventilating and reflection was demonstrated by president Lincoln during the Civil War. Lincoln invited an old friend in Springfield, Illinois, asking him to come to Washington. Lincoln said he wanted to discuss some problems with him. When the friend arrived at the White House, Lincoln talked to him about the advisability of issuing a proclamation freeing the slaves and went over all the arguments for and against such a move. After talking for hours, Lincoln shook hands with his friend and sent him back to Illinois without even asking for his opinion. Lincoln had done all the talking himself. Lincoln was not seeking advice. He just needed his friend as a sounding board to help clarify his thinking. He wanted merely a friendly, sympathetic listener to whom he could unburden himself. That is what we all want when we are in trouble. As the *Reader's Digest* once said: "Many persons call a doctor when all they want is an audience."

Lastly, sometimes people are not sure about what to do and may need your advice, help, and comfort. This is where counseling comes in. Of course, the kind of comfort or guidance you provide will depend on your experience, maturity, and knowledge of the Scriptures.

We need to be aware of these different reasons for listening so that we can respond in a proper manner. If we assume the wrong reason, we will not listen creatively and the speaker may feel that he/she has not been heard.

To improve your listening skill:

• listen in an active manner,
• listen with understanding, and
• listen with openness.

Being an active listener means you get involved in what the other person is saying by paraphrasing, clarifying, and providing feedback. It means that you observe facial expression, body posture, and voice tone as well as words. Active listening lets the sender know that he/she is being understood and encourages the sender to continue communicating. It is a valuable tool for facilitating thinking on the part of the sender. To be an active listener, you need to concentrate on the person and the message. Listen with your ears, eyes, and body. You may need to say, "OK," or, "I see," or something similar in order to show your involvement.

To listen with understanding means that you get inside the other person's world and see things from that person's perspective. People see things differently due to different backgrounds, beliefs, values, experiences, and personality traits. You may not like or agree with what is being said, but you understand because you can see the situation from the other person's point of view.

Like filtered talking, filtered listening is receiving partial information. It is the opposite of open listening. Two common problems inhibit open listening. One problem is the preconceived idea that the speaker is trying to promote or "sell" his/her interests. The other problem is failure to listen to the other person with either the mind or the heart. Sometimes we are so busy figuring out what we are going to say next that we close our minds and fail to hear much of what is being said. Open listening means you listen without bias or judgment to all that is being said. It means you care enough to let the other person be free to talk. It involves taking the time to know what the situation is before jumping to conclusions.

If one gives answer before he hears, it is his folly and shame (Proverbs 18:13).

Learn to listen with action, understanding, and openness.

Communication Killers

We now examine the common problem areas in communication. In order to communicate effectively, we must overcome certain communication barriers or killers. These include:

- anger,
- selfishness,
- silence,
- wrong words, and
- wrong timing.

1. *Anger*

Anger is a sure communication killer. It is hard, if not impossible, to communicate effectively when one is angry. Anger is an emotion with has its positive and negative aspects.

Most of our anger does not arise from a concern for righteousness as we see in the case of Jesus (Mark 3:5) but from a self-centered heart. When a person is told his shortcomings, rather than accept and face them honestly, his natural reaction is to explode. We must not allow anger to control us and lead us to taking wrong actions. Let us heed Paul's advice:

Be angry but do not sin; do not let the sun go down on your anger (Ephesians 4:26).

Couples often complain that they are having trouble with sex, but the real trouble often has nothing to do with sex. The real difficulties in bed at night may come from the fact that all kinds of problems have been carried into bed from the day, problems that ought to have been resolved before going to bed. Husbands and wives must learn not to let the sun go down on their anger.

How do we control our anger in a marital setting? If you are the one upset, the best thing is to withdraw and stop discussion until you can get your feelings under control. If your spouse is the one upset, the best thing is not to argue or counterpunch, but just to let your spouse talk himself or herself out. As the old adage says, "Silence is golden."

He who is slow to anger has great understanding, but he who has a hasty temper exalts folly. He who is slow to anger is better than the mighty, and he who rules his spirit than he who takes a city (Proverbs 14:29; 16:32).

2. Selfishness

Remember, the goal of communication is to bring you to a point of agreement on an issue. But selfishness is a great barrier to achieving agreement or oneness. We always seem to be right in our own eyes. But as Christians, we should follow the example of John the Baptist:

He must increase, but I must decrease (John 3:30).

Only as we let Christ increase in us can we experience effective communication, which leads to oneness in our marriage.

The list of areas in our life where we manifest selfishness is endless and some of these areas hinder communication. A typical example is overcommitment due to pursuit of uncommon goals. A couple pursuing different goals and working in opposite directions will have little or no time to communicate; they will have little to talk about. A way of solving the problem is to become more involved in things that are of mutual interest. This is graphically illustrated in Figure 4.3. When the spheres of interest of a husband and wife do not overlap as portrayed in Figure 4.3(a), there is little or not room for communication. As in Figure 4.3(b), mutual interests provide more things to talk about. As Paul said:

Let us then pursue what makes for peace and for mutual upbuilding. Let each of us please his neighbor for his good, to edify him. For Christ did not please Himself (Romans 14:19; 15:2,3).

3. *Silence*

It is common among older couples to use silence as a weapon in resolving their conflicts. One partner simply refuses to talk to the other. Perhaps the silent partner feels less vulnerable to the other partner's attack by remaining silent. Or maybe

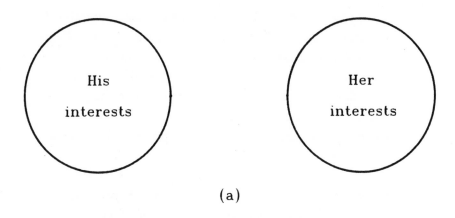

(a)

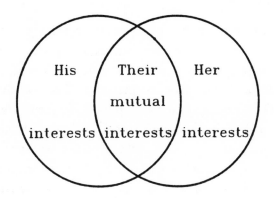

(b)

Fig. 4.3

(a) Totally different interests leave no room for communication.

(b) Overlapping interests provide things to talk about.

silence is used as the last resort to get what is being demanded of the other partner. Whatever the reason for being silent, silence is a childish trait in this regard. It is a sign of immaturity. It is a dangerous tool in resolving conflict. Prolonged silence often leads to anger, which may have some adverse consequences for the silent partner.

If you have something against your spouse, it is better to discuss it, rather than being silent about it. You must be willing to open up so that your partner can have a chance to know what is wrong. If you are silent about it, your partner may have no idea of what is bothering you. Cultivate the habit of not leaving your spouse in suspense through your silence.

4. *Wrong Words*

The words we use in communicating ideas can build or destroy. Unwholesome communication includes sarcasm, destructive criticism, put-down jokes, obscene words, rejection, and ridicule. They attack the person, pull or tear the person apart. They are likely to foster poor self-esteem, fear, and a climate of fighting and resentment. This equally applies to communication with your child. A child who suffers from name calling or ridicule will quickly learn to withdraw into defeat or failure. Since it is easier to destroy than to build, you must learn the art of using the right words to build up your spouse and children. As Paul said,

> *Do not let any unwholesome talk come out of your mouth, but only what is helpful for building others up according to their needs, that it may benefit those who listen* (Ephesians 4:29, NIV).

Resist the temptation to put your spouse down. Fight the urge to be negative, critical or judgmental. Avoid using phrases such as:

"That is stupid. Don't you know any better?"
"I feel sorry for you."
"You never learn to do things right."
"You don't know what you're talking about. Any fool knows that is not true."
"You never listen to me when I'm trying to explain something."
"You always act like a two-year-old when I express a different view."
"You never do the things around the house that you promise to do."

Not only are such phrases exaggerating and untrue, they are negative and destructive. Avoid the words *never* and *always* because they tend to create never and always. "You never" and "you always" tend to program your spouse toward fulfilling the expectations that are laid out for him/her. Remember:

Death and life are in the power of the tongue (Proverbs 18:21).

5. *Wrong Timing*

In the introductory chapter, it was said that an important key to success in anything is doing the right thing in the right way, at the right time, and for the right reason. This secret or principle applies to communication. Timing is crucial to communication, especially when the issue under discussion is important. *When* something is said is equally as important as *what* is said. Trivial matters could be discussed at any time, but important issues should be delayed till an appropriate time. As the wise man said:

> *For everything there is a season, and a time for every matter under heaven: a time to be born, and a time to die ... a time to keep silence, and a time to speak ...* (Ecclesiastes 3:1-8).

> *For there is a proper time and procedure for every matter* (Eccelesiastes 8:6, NIV).

> *A word in season, how good it is!* (Proverbs 15:23).

There is a time to say things, and a time to keep quiet.

It takes time to communicate and reach agreement on important issues. A couple should seek a convenient time to communicate, should choose carefully what they say or how they say it, and when it is said. A wise wife will share with her husband something difficult after she has fed him; she knows that he could handle things better when he has eaten. A wise husband may have to wait till morning to share unpleasant news with his wife if he knows that she may not sleep after hearing such disturbing news.

To discuss serious matters with your spouse, plan a convenient time. When you have a question, an idea, or even a criticism and you don't have the right words to use or your spouse is not in the right mood, wait for a better time. For example, if your partner is not an early riser, the morning may be a bad time to discuss it. Many couples find that after supper is a good time for serious communication. However, after supper may be a bad time for a home with little children. Each couple should find a convenient time when they are in the best possible mood to discuss things objectively.

Improving Your Communication Skills

Fortunately, communication is a learned behavior. We can all learn and improve our communication skills if we are willing. To improve your communication, certain actions must be taken, but don't expect a miracle overnight. It takes time for actions to bear fruits. Here are some of actions you can take to enhance your ability to communicate and enjoy a happy marriage:

- tame your tongue,
- spend more time together,
- learn to accommodate, and
- learn to COMMUNICATE.

1. *Tame Your Tongue*

Each of us has power in our words:

Death and life are in the power of the tongue.... A gentle tongue is a tree of life, but perverseness in it breaks the spirit (Proverbs 18:21, 15:4).

The tongue is a fire.... With it we bless the Lord and Father, and with it we curse men, who are made in the likeness of God. From the same mouth come blessing and cursing. My brethren, this ought not to be so (James 3:6-10).

We must learn to use our tongue positively. There is power in our words that can change things for the better. There is power in the word of encouragement, the word of hope, the word of praise, the word of confidence, the word of love to transform a hopeless, despairing partner into a confident, radiant, positive person. Our communication must be such as to enrich, build, and edify.

Let no evil talk come out of your mouths, but only such as is good for edifying, as fits the occasion, that it may impart grace to those who hear (Ephesians 4:29).

Let your speech always be gracious, seasoned with salt, so that you may know how you ought to answer every one (Colossians 4:6).

Watch what comes out of your mouth. Weigh it before you speak it. An African proverb says, "Words are like eggs; once broken they cannot be gathered." Wouldn't it be better not to make a statement than to make five statements to explain what you mean? Say what you mean and mean what you say.

To say what you mean is not an easy task. To make what you say agree with what you mean, you need to do two things: think before you say it and increase your vocabulary. The last part is usually where more work is needed. As mentioned before, we were all born as ignoramuses, having to learn everything, especially words. There is no end to the learning process. Most of the time, we run out of the right words to convey our ideas. We must read more and learn more words. The more words you have at your disposal to say something, the more choices you have in selecting the words, and the more effective is your communication. Pray for wisdom to know how to say the right thing, at the right time, in the right way, and for the right reason.

2. *Spend More Time Together*

The element of time is vital to effective communication between a husband and wife. There are two aspects of timing of which a couple must be aware. One aspect is that communication takes time. The other is that there is a right time to communicate, especially at a deep level. The second aspect has already been discussed. For a happy, successful marriage, a couple must realize that quantity and quality go hand in hand. The time they spend with each other needs to be good time; no one enjoys hours of arguing, bullying, or bickering. Time also needs to be sufficient; a quality relationship is not likely to develop in a few minutes together.

Dr. Willard F. Harley, in his best-selling book *His Needs, Her Needs*, recommended to his male clients that they learn to set aside as much as fifteen hours per week to give their wives undivided attention. How did Harley come up with this "huge" amount of time? Let Harley himself answer that question:

> *A given activity qualifies to be part of the fifteen-hour goal if you can affirmatively answer the question: "Does this activity allow us to focus primarily on each other?" Going to see a movie for three hours does not meet our criterion. You may exchange some affection during the running of the film, but in most cases you cannot truly say that you focused on each other.*
>
> *Activities like taking a walk, going to a restaurant, boating on a quiet pond, golfing, sunbathing at the beach—*

things of that nature—better qualify. Any recreation that requires intense concentration or so much exercise that conversation becomes difficult does not qualify.

If you engaged in conversation while riding together in the car, however, count it toward the fifteen hours . . .

I had to ask myself, "What would Joyce like more: money to spend or the time with me?" . . . I decided to spend the time with Joyce, despite the tighter money situation, because I had learned the importance of being with my wife. In subsequent years, during my counseling experiences I would learn the truth: Money or a career serves a marriage; a marriage should never serve money or a career. In many of the failed marriages I have observed, the couple abandoned their relationship to build a fortune. In the end they had a fortune at the expense of their marriage.[3]

Chris and I spend fifteen or more hours a week in conversation. Each morning, we wake up early and spend at least half an hour in morning devotion. Our devotion usually involves reading a short passage in the Bible and then meditation. It is in the meditation that we communicate, learn from each other, and edify each other. It is amazing how much we learn and grow together each day. On Friday nights, we have a vigil for four to six hours. Most of that time is spent sharing what we have learned individually from personal devotions during the week and the rest of the time is spent in prayer. This has made Friday night the best part of each week in our home and we both look forward to it each week. Also, as we come back from church on Sunday morning, the first thing we do is share what each of us gained in the sermon. This usually takes thirty to sixty minutes of communication. (The fact that you have to share what you gain in the service forces you to be very attentive to the pastor's sermon.)

Without doubt, happy families communicate well, but time, the price of effective communication, must be sacrificed.

3. Learn to Accommodate

As mentioned earlier, selfishness is a communication killer. If you want your marriage to be successful and happy, you must learn to give and take, to accept and accommodate your spouse as he/she is. The two of you are different in many respects. Therefore it is no surprise that you do things differently, see things differently, and communicate differently. Each person needs the freedom to be himself or herself while still adapting to the other's needs.

The concept of accommodation is a key to resolving communication conflicts in a marriage. Your idea is not necessarily better than or superior to that of your spouse. So learn to respect your spouse's opinion even when you disagree.

Do nothing from selfishness or conceit, but in humility count others better than yourselves. Let each of you look not only to his own interests, but also to the interests of others. Have this mind among yourselves, which is yours in Christ Jesus (Philippians 2:3-5).

4. Learn to COMMUNICATE

Byron Emmert suggested the following tips to help you and your spouse communicate[4]:

C   Commit yourself to listening to your spouse every day.
O   Observe each other's unspoken needs.

M   Make regular appointments to spend time together
     and talk.

M   Mend your arguments before you go to bed.

U   Utilize the opportunities to let your actions speak
     louder than words.

N   Notice the positive things your spouse does, and say
     thanks.

I   Initiate conversation by asking feeling-oriented ques-
     tions.

C   Care about your spouse's opinions, even if they differ
     from yours.

A   Admit to your spouse when you're wrong.

T   Touch each other when you listen or talk.

E   Expect the best of your spouse.

The Rewards of Effective Communication

The effort and time spent in communication will pay dividends. Through effective communication, a husband and wife
can better love, accept, and understand each other. By talking
and listening intently, we can discover the treasures in our
mates' minds—their likes and dislikes, their strong points and
weak points, what they can and can't become. The benefits
and rewards of effective communication are numerous; they
include:

- intimacy,
- sexual compatibility,
- understanding, and
- happiness.

1. *Intimacy*

Partners get drawn closer together through the process of communicating their experiences, thoughts, desires, aspirations, plans, and weaknesses. They get to learn and know more about each other. For example, communication about money in your marriage brings you closer together, teaches you individual values, creates oneness of purpose, and frees your minds from uncertainty.

2. *Sexual Compatibility*

A couple must communicate freely about their sexual needs. Apart from taking time to learn about human sexuality, they need to talk to each other about their sexuality. The more they know and talk to each other of their likes and dislikes about their lovemaking, the more they will enjoy each other.

Tim and Beverly LaHaye in their excellent book *The Act of Marriage* noted:

> *Most Christian women go into marriage relatively uninformed about sex and often retain the naive idea that their husbands know it all and will teach them.... Most young brides expect their husbands to inform them of male needs. Unfortunately this does not usually happen. We have found that open communication between a husband and wife remains the best possible sex education. After all, a young bride does not need to know how man functions; she must simply learn to recognize the sexual responses of one. Who best can teach her about his needs but the object of her love—her husband?*[5]

3. *Understanding*

Married partners increase their understanding of each other through effective communication. Communication helps them to be in each other's world. As a result of this, you understand your partner so well that you can predict his/her behavior.

Without communication, resentments smolder. When communication is done in love, it rules out misunderstanding, a tool of strife.

4. *Happiness*

Effective communication is a marriage booster. It strongly influences other areas in marriage. As a husband and wife engage in caring communication, with each other's needs at heart, they experience deeper feelings of affection and appreciation. As each need is discussed, understood, and fulfilled, their marriage is enriched as never before. They become satisfied and happy.

As Secret No. 4,

> The happiest couples are those who talk the most with each other.

Notes

[1] H. Norman Wright, *Communication: Key to Your Marriage* (Ventura, CA: Regal Books, 1974), p. 52.

[2] Josh McDowell, *The Secret of Loving* (Wheaton, IL: Living Books, 1989), p. 60.

[3] Willard F. Harley, *His Needs, Her Needs* (Old Tappan, NJ: Fleming H. Revell Co., 1986), pp. 59, 60.

[4] Byron Emmert, "Communication Counsel" in *Husbands and Wives* (Wheaton, IL: Victor Books, 1988), Howard and Jeanne Hendricks (eds.), p. 286.

[5] Tim and Beverly LaHaye, *The Art of Marriage* (Grand Rapids, MI: Zondervan, 1976), pp. 92, 93.

CHAPTER FIVE

THE SECRET OF
UNDERSTANDING

By wisdom a house is built, and by understanding it is established
Proverbs 24:3

Understanding is an important aspect of communication, as mentioned in the previous chapter. As far as communication goes, understanding is being able to see from someone else's viewpoint, to view life through another person's eyes. However, communication is not the only reason why understanding is an essential ingredient in a successful, happy marriage. In a husband-wife relationship, it is important that we understand how and why men and women reason and behave the way they do, what they like or dislike.

When a man and woman get married, you have a coming together of different sexes, different families, and possibly different educational trainings, different cultural backgrounds, different religious affiliations, different views of life, etc. The man has inherited the way his wife was treated by her father, her mother, her brothers and sisters, and even her former male friends. She is the sum total of her background as a single person. The same is true for the man. This is why the first five years of marriage are a period of adjustments. It is also the reason why God instructed ancient Israel through Moses that a man was to be exempt from military service and all business responsibilities for one year after his marriage so that he could "know" his wife (Deuteronomy 24:5). If a couple has been married for more than five years, any prolonged disharmony in their marriage is usually attributable to lack of communication or lack of understanding.

Like any other worthwhile endeavor, a successful, happy marriage takes time and study. It is pathetic that our educational system emphasizes how to make a living, not how to live. A plumber's license, for example, requires four years of training; a marriage license requires no training but only two willing bodies. Since our educational system does not require a training program for husbands-to-be or wives-to-be, their only education may be the example they observed in their homes. For many of us, that example is inadequate.

The fact that the training we received at home is grossly inadequate is evident in a breakdown of understanding between husbands and wives. Our society has developed a strong strain of individualism. To put it in Dr. George McKinney's terms:

"You know, I can make it; I can do my own thing; I'm independent; I don't need you. If I don't really need you, there is no reason for me to suffer with you or try to understand you. I can make it without you."

That attitude is shattering marriages all over the world. You see, it is rather ridiculous to get married if you don't need one another.[1]

To have a happy, successful marriage, you need understanding. You need to:

- understand the differences in people,
- understand your roles as a husband or
- understand your roles as a wife,
- understand your husband's needs or
- understand your wife's needs,
- understand your roles as a father or
- understand your roles as a mother, and
- understand your children's needs.

Only the first five issues will be discussed in this chapter; the last three will be covered in Chapter 10 on parenting. To get understanding takes some effort and time. There must be a willingness to learn and change our views about life, ourselves, and others.

Wisdom is the principal thing; therefore get wisdom: and with all thy getting get understanding (Proverbs 4:7, KJV).

Happy is the man who finds wisdom, and the man who gets understanding, for the gain from it is better than gain from silver and its profit better than gold. She is more precious than jewels, and nothing you desire can compare with her (Proverbs 3:13-15).

Understand the Differences in People

It is a commonplace experience that people are different. What makes people different is simple: background and natural makeup. One's background is the sum total of his family upbringing, educational training, culture, nationality, etc. One's natural makeup has to do with one's sex. Most spontaneous reactions or prejudices are largely the result of our background. Fortunately, we can effect change in the impact that background has had on us, but it is hardly possible (unless God intervenes, of course) to change the natural makeup. Men will be men and women will be women; there is little we can do about that. We need to understand from the outset what can be changed and what can't be changed; otherwise we will be asking for the moon. In fact, our objective in this section is to examine those differences that cannot be changed. Understanding them will help us accept our mates the way they are. The differences between men and women include but are not limited to:

- personality,
- physical makeup,
- sex,
- emotion, and
- intuition.

A husband and wife need to understand these basic differences in the sexes. They also need to understand that the differences don't make women inferior to men; men and women are simply unique beings.

1. *Personality*

Psychologists have found that there are basically four personality types with many minor variations. The four basic traits are Dominant, Influencing, Steady, and Compliant[2,3]—or DISC, for short. Most of us are a combination of these traits. Often one personality trait predominates in an individual while strains of one or two other traits may be found. It is worthwhile to briefly examine these traits.

• *Dominant* is the hot, quick, active, and strong-willed person. He is a self-sufficient, independent, and decisive person. He easily make decisions for himself and for others. Life is activity to Mr. D. He has endless ideas, plans, and ambitions. He is self-willed and often succeeds where others fail. His emotional nature is the least developed part of his temperament. He hardly sympathizes with others. He is quick to find opportunities and is often regarded as an opportunist. It is not hard to recognize this personality because they seldom follow instructions manual. They always feel they know what to do and they don't need somebody's help. Many of the world's leaders and generals fall into this personality group. They make good executives, dictators or criminals, depending on their moral standards. Their weaknesses usually make them difficult to live with. They are most often more appreciated by colleagues than by family members.

• *Influencing* is the outgoing person who makes friends easily. He is warm, lively, and receptive. He likes recognition, group activities, social clubs, and parties. Mr. I is very social and hates solitude. He is never at a loss for words or jokes, often speaks before thinking. His noisy, buoyant, friendly ways make him appear more confident than he really is. It is easy to recognize Mr. I because everything he has ever done can be found on his walls. People in this category make good salesmen, public speakers, politicians, pastors, teachers, hospital workers, leaders, entertainers, and actors. Their weakness of will usually makes them ineffective and undependable; they tend to be undisciplined, restless, and emotionally explosive.

• *Steady* is a calm, easy-going and well-behaved person. He gets along with others easily. He tends to be a spectator in life; he tries not to get too involved with the activities of others. He is usually sympathetic, kind, and permissive. He is a natural peacemaker. He enjoys a meticulous type of work. To recognize Mr. S, involve him in decision making. He changes his mind several times and, after he has finally decided, he regrets having made the decision. Many teachers, leaders, and scientists fall into this group. Their weakness is lack of decisiveness. They are usually easy to live with, but their careless, easy-going way of life can be irritating to a dominant type of partner.

• *Compliant* is the gifted perfectionist with a very sensitive emotional nature. He likes clear-cut guidelines and conformance to detail. He is a self-sacrificing, faithful friend, but he does not make friends easily because he is usually dominated by his emotions and doesn't want to hurt or be hurt. His analytical prowess causes him to diagnose accurately the obstacles and dangers of any project he has a part in planning. You recognize Mr. C when he buys equipment because he must ask for the instructions manual and correct the spelling and grammar before using the manual. People in this category include the world's great artists, inventors, philosophers, musicians, and researchers. Their weaknesses are many; they are sensitive, self-centered, critical and vengeful. They often have more problems making emotional adjustments to life than others.

I hope this rather brief presentation of the four personality traits will help you to better understand your spouse. The personality difference may result in differences in lifestyle, which are often a major source of conflict in marriage relationships. If you are not very careful, the qualities that attracted you will make you resent your mate. For example, Cynthia greatly admires Tim's hard work and success in business, but resents the fact that Tim is busy and frugal. The most irritating characteristic in Tim is a by-product of the quality Cynthia most appreciates. As another example, Jimmy respects Laura's selectivity. She has a good taste in selecting clothes, housewares, etc., but Laura is very selective in what she eats and that causes problem when Jimmy and Laura visit friends. The point is that people are attracted to each other on the basis of strengths, but each natural strength has a corresponding weakness.

You must learn that God gave your spouse the temperament he or she wears and you must accept those characteristics that cannot be changed. Like Paul, we must learn to be content and accept others just as they are (Philippians 4:11-13). Also we must understand that God has designed a man and woman to complement each other; to be more than mates, but to be *helpmates*, supplying the needs of each other. The extremes of one person are balanced by the partner's extremes. You may call it "balanced opposites" like night and day, summer and winter, light and darkness. Learn to understand that the differences are for your good, to make you a balanced person.

2. *Physical Makeup*

It is unscientific to claim that men and women are physically, biologically identical except for the ability to bear children. Research has shown that maleness and femaleness are rooted in the human brain. The differences in brain function between the sexes are innate, biologically determined, and relatively resistant to change through cultural influences. We differ anatomically, biochemically, and emotionally. Men and women differ in skeletal structure, women having shorter heads, broader faces, less protruding chins, shorter legs, and longer trunks. Women have several unique functions: unique chromosome makeup, menstruation, pregnancy, and lactation. On the average, men possess fifty percent more brute strength than women. Women endure heat better than men because their metabolism slows down less.

It is true that men and women are about equal in intelligence—inherited mental capacity—but they are not alike. Some of the strongest interests of men are physical activities, scientific effort, adventure, business, and activities that call for courage and exertion of strength. Women's prime interests tend to lie in pursuits that are sedentary, domestic, esthetic, humanitarian, artistic, and emotionally expressive, and in the milder forms of action. Men excel in curiosity, reasoning power, ingenuity, comprehension, abstract thinking, mathematical formulation, and athletics. Women rise to their best in verbal aptitude, memory, association, vividness of mental imagery, cooperativeness, self-control, sympathy, kindness, and personal warmth. Of course, there are variations from the general patterns among both men and women.

3. *Sex*

Men and women differ in their sexual drive and experience. A man's sexual drive is fairly constant, while a woman's sexual drive is sporadic and related to her menstrual cycle. In spite of modern sex education and "liberation," young men and women often come together in marriage from opposite ends. He is more sexually experienced and motivated by strong desires; she is less experienced, less motivated and sometimes naive.

An average woman is sexually aroused more by touch and romantic words. She is far more attracted by a man's personality and appearance. Her arousal is more of a matter of mindset. She can choose to experience arousal depending on her emotional attachment to a particular man. A man characterized by affection, attentiveness, kindness, and tender sensitivity will have little difficulty arousing his wife. While a man requires little or no time to prepare for sex, a woman may need hours of emotional and mental preparation.

A man is stimulated by sight and other means: a scent of perfume, watching a woman's walk, looking at a photo of a naked woman, even daydreaming. A man can easily experience arousal, which may happen several times a day. It may occur relatively effortlessly, and it sometimes happens whether he wants it or not.

4. *Emotion*

Men and women display unique emotional characteristics. A man derives his emotional satisfaction from achieving in academics, being successful in business, becoming financially independent, supervising others, conquering dominions, or by being appreciated by his patients or colleagues at work. A woman, by contrast, derives her emotional satisfaction by being loved, respected, warmly treated, and accepted. Female emotions are also influenced by exclusively female functions such as the menstrual cycle, lactation, and pregnancy.

The business world capitalizes on the twelve basic emotional hungers of men and women, which are as follows: security, progress, health and beauty, superiority, companionship, acquisition, activity, competition, group urge (as in family and race), curiosity, sex, and religion. Other human emotions include desire, fear, anger, jealousy, hatred, and revenge. The way these emotions are satisfied or controlled is another major difference between men and women.

5. *Intuition*

Women tend to be more intuitive than men. It has been observed that women do catch subliminal messages faster and more accurately than men. Because their intuition is based on a subconscious mental process, many women can't give specific explanations for their feelings. They simply feel something about a deal, person or situation without a logical reason. Men tend to logically analyze a deal, person or situation. For most women, intuition is the ultimate weapon for solving mysteries. A woman tends to have built-in radar. She intuitively knows that little Rob is making a mess when he should be taking a nap. She knows it wasn't the neighbor's kid who broke dad's favorite chair. She knows when Jane is lying about what she was doing out until 1:10 a.m. She is aware of imminent danger. Men and kids need women who acknowledge and use their intuition.

Perhaps the best way to close this section is to list Norman Wright's summary of male/female differences:[4]

1. Men and women are very different by nature in the way they think, act, respond, etc. These differences can be complementary, but very often lead to conflict in marriage.

2. A woman is an emotional-feeler; a man is a logical-thinker.

3. For a woman language spoken is an expression of what she feels; for a man language spoken is an expression of what he's thinking.

4. Language that is heard by a woman is an emotional expression; language that is heard by a man is the receiving of information.

5. Women tend to take everything personally; men tend to take everything impersonally.

6. Women are interested in the details, the nitty-gritty; men are interested in the principle, the abstract, the philosophy.

7. In material things, women tend to look at goals only; men want to know the details of how to get there.

8. In spiritual or intangible things, the opposite is true. Men look at the goals; women want to know how to get there.

9. Men are like filing cabinets. They take problems, put them in the file and close the drawer. Women are like computers; their minds keep going and going and going until the problem is solved!

10. A woman's home is an extension of her personality; a man's job is the extension of his personality.

11. Women have a great need for security and roots; men can be nomadic.

12. Women tend to be guilt-prone; men tend to be resentful.

13. Men are stable and level off; women are always changing.

14. Women tend to become involved more easily and more quickly; men tend to stand back and evaluate.

15. Men have to be told again and again; women never forget!

16. Men tend to remember the gist; women tend to remember details and distort the gist.

You are welcome to add your own observations to Wright's list.

As Wright said, instead of the differences between men and women being complementary, they often lead to conflict in a marriage. We must see God's design in these differences. The rib God used in making woman was symbolic of certain characteristics God took from Adam to make Eve. The qualities that God took from Adam and placed in Eve are what we today consider the woman's nature. We can see that the Divine Architect has made it such that a husband and wife complement each other. Each fulfills what is lacking in the other. For this reason, a man is not complete without a wife; a woman is incomplete without a husband. Men and women need each other, not just for sexual or biological reasons, but for completeness's sake.

Understanding these personality, physical, sexual, emotional, and intuitive differences in people, in males and females, helps in building mutual tolerance and acceptance between a man and woman. A husband who understands his wife's physiological makeup and its impact on her emotions can enter her world to discover what and why she feels. A wife who understands will take her husband the way he is, knowing that the way he behaves is characteristic of all men.

Understand Your Roles as a Husband

When we talk about roles in a home, we don't mean a rigid role structure. A husband and wife must be willing to share thoughts, jobs, and projects based upon ability, giftedness, and cooperation rather than upon a rigid role structure. However, due to some basic differences between males and females, certain things are better done by men than women and vice versa. For example, a mom is better qualified for detective work at home than a dad because of her intuitive capacity.

At least for the sake of the kids, the husband's and wife's roles should not be confused. The blurring of mother-father roles can have harmful effects on kids. If everybody does whatever he or she likes, children will get confused and will never learn what it means to be a man or a woman. The roles of a man in a husband-wife relationship include:

- headship,
- loving his wife,
- handling her with understanding, and
- learning to meet her needs.

1. *Headship*

The husband's role as the head of his wife was partly explained in Chapter 1. Here we simply add a few more thoughts. Being the head does not make a husband the boss over his wife. Just as with the human head, being the head means that you play a very important role. It is a position of awesome responsibility. A husband should set the pace by being a leader.

Christ's authority in the home is centered in the husband. The husband has been endowed with delegated authority. It is his duty to make sure that the authority is exercised properly in ways that honor Christ. As a Christian husband, he is responsible to God to head up his family. His headship does not mean merely privilege and right. It means leadership; it means assuming the responsibilities that go with such authority.

Headship or leadership of the family means seeing that all the members of the family are cared for. Physical welfare, food, clothing, shelter, and protection must be provided. Leadership must be exercised also in spiritual matters: family worship, prayer and fasting, witnessing, Bible study, church attendance, and witness to the community.

A husband must exercise his headship and authority with humility. Jesus said:

Whoever would be great among you must be your servant, and whoever would be first among you must be slave of all. For the Son of man also came not to be served but to serve, and to give his life as a ransom for many (Mark 10:43-45).

Jesus exemplified this principle in the foot-washing and crucifixion. We must follow in His steps (1 Peter 2:21).

2. *Loving His Wife*

Apart from your responsibility to God, your first responsibility as a husband is to your wife. You are to love her as part of yourself (Ephesians 5:33). Your headship as well as your love should be patterned after that of Christ. Christ took the initiative to love and serve the church. A husband must follow this pattern in caring for his wife. Your love must be sacrificial, meaning that you are willing to give all it takes to fulfill your wife.

Love your wife as a person, not as a sex object. There are many things a man can do to express his love for his wife as a person. For example, when a man returns from work, he should indicate a personal interest in his wife and what she has been doing during the day, either at home or at work. His spending time with the kids rather than being obsessed with the sports page or TV sends a message to his wife that he cares and is committed to his marriage.

A loving husband doesn't need to demand that his wife obey or submit but gives her the freedom to do so. Since love is irresistible, the love you sow in your wife returns to you, perhaps multiplied. As you play your role effectively, your wife submits freely and returns your love joyfully, because she knows she is loved.

3. *Handling Her With Understanding*

The husband-wife relationship is so close that a man can hurt himself by hurting his wife. Yet few men understand how to nourish and cherish their wives. Peter was aware of this when he wrote:

> *You husbands, live considerately with your wives, bestowing honor on the woman as the weaker sex, since you are joint heirs of the grace of life, in order that your prayers may not be hindered* (1 Peter 3:7).

In the New American Standard Bible, this verse says that husbands should *live with your wives in an understanding way.*

Husbands should not expect their wives to behave like men. A husband should treat his wife tenderly because she is feminine. To be understanding, he must try to enter her world to see how she sees and feel how she feels. That is not an easy task, but that is what it means to be understanding. It means attempting to get into her shoes; they will naturally not fit exactly. Yet Peter said that husbands must try to understand what it is to be a woman. Now and then it does a husband good to stay with the kids eight hours on Saturday while his wife is out, if for no other reason than to become more understanding. Now and then it does him good to change a dozen diapers in order to acquire a little more understanding. A husband needs to put on his wife's shoes so that he can understand her problems. According to Peter, lack of understanding on the part of a husband can hinder his prayer. God closes His heart against him because he has closed his own heart against his wife.

4. *Learning to Meet Her Needs*

A wise and loving husband will learn as much as possible about life in general and marriage in particular. If you do what comes naturally, you will be wrong most of the time. In order for you to be an understanding husband, you need to learn as much as you can about your wife. This means you are willing to discover your wife's needs so that you can meet them. It means you try to listen to your wife and reason with her. It means you are sensitive to her emotions, moods, and ideas. Here we see the need for a selfless attitude in discharging your role as the husband.

Your learning as a husband is not limited to discovering your wife's emotional, sexual, and material needs; it extends to learning to meet her spiritual needs. The fact that Paul instructed inquisitive women to ask their husbands at home questions of concern to them (1 Corinthians 14:34,35) should make every husband desire to learn more about spiritual things.

Chris and I are age mates. In spite of this, I try to know more than she about things in general and spiritual matters in particular. I realized this aspect of my role as a husband several years before we married and made every effort to learn. Not knowing that I was going to marry a very inquisitive person like Chris, I was preparing myself through personal reading, formal training, and correspondence courses. When we married, I didn't have any difficulty answering most of my wife's questions about life and the Bible.

Understand Your Roles as a Wife

Your role as a wife is basically developing a relationship with your husband that will bring happiness to both of you. This basic role leads to some roles including

- submission to your husband's leadership,
- teaching him,
- studying him, and
- helping him.

1. *Submission to Your Husband's Leadership*

The husband-wife relationship functions properly when we follow biblical guidelines. Following biblical guidelines not only helps your relationship grow, it helps you reach the destination of a happy, successful marriage. One of the guidelines is for the wife to submit to her husband's leadership (Ephesians 5:22-24). The reason for the submission is related to the order and purpose of her creation. Submission does not remove freedom; it allows it.

Wives have been given the opportunity to choose freely the submissive role even as Jesus chose to be submissive to the Father, and He was highly exalted (Philippians 2:5-9). The submissive role of the wife does not squash her personality. A wife who sees her husband making unwise decisions should freely tell him so, with all respect and honesty. The judgment, insight, and opinion of a loving wife is a great asset to her husband. Women often have a better intuitive grasp of things than men, especially in spiritual matters. As Klaus Hess put it:

In physical life, the man begets new life while the wife bears it and brings it forth. In spiritual life this is often reversed: the woman begets a new vision, sees a new dimension of spiritual reality, and the man must then patiently bring it forth in its practical out-workings.

The only exception to the rule of submission is if your husband should ever require that you act contrary to God's commandments. Then he no longer acts with God's authority and you must obey God rather than him.

2. *Teaching Him*

The wife must help make her husband a lover she desires. No book can tell a husband what pleases a woman as precisely as can his own wife. A husband and wife are the best teachers of one another. A woman should be excited to inform her man about the one woman in the world whom he should intimately know. She should communicate freely how she feels, what gives her pleasure, what excites her. Tell him how he can best meet your needs during a crisis or when you are discouraged and down, especially when going through menstruation and pregnancy. Unless you teach him all this, he may never know.

3. *Studying Him*

If you are going to love your husband, share his life, take him as he is and adapt your personality to his, you must study him. You must learn everything about him. As Ruth Peale rightly said:

If I could give one piece of advice to young brides, and only one, it would be this: Study your man. Study him as if he were some rare, strange, and fascinating animal, which he is. Study him constantly, because he will be constantly changing. Study his likes and dislikes, his strengths and weaknesses, his moods, and mannerisms. Just loving a man is fine, but it's not enough. To live with one successfully you have to know him. And to know him you have to study him.

Look around you and decide how many of the best marriages you know are ones where a wife in a deep sense actually knows her husband better than he knows himself. Knows what upsets him. Knows what pleases him. Knows what makes him laugh or makes him angry. Knows when he needs encouragement. Knows when he's too charged up about something and needs to be held back. Knows, in other words, exactly what makes him tick.[5]

Although the basic characteristics of your husband may not change, studying him never stops. The wife who studies her man over the years will come to know him even better than he knows himself. She will be aware of qualities and potential in him that he himself may not be aware of.

4. *Helping Him*

A wife's primary role is to be a helpmate to her husband. She is to give of herself, her time, and her energy to her husband, children, and home. God has bestowed on women great talents and abilities. These abilities could be used as a tremendous help to their husbands.

One way to help your husband is to listen intelligently when he talks about his work. Many jobs are so competitive that there is hardly a person to confide in in a man's working world. If as a wife you can be a trustworthy, always-available sounding board, you will be making an enormous contribution to your husband's career. You don't need to have a business background or specialized knowledge of your husband's job to help him. You already have a specialized knowledge of your husband himself and that is all you need to help him.

You can help your husband in other areas as you see the need arise. When you learn to be your husband's helper, you make yourself indispensable to him. The result is closeness and harmony in your marriage.

Understand Your Husband's Needs

Many times women get hurt unnecessarily because they don't understand their men. When a man and woman marry, they commit themselves to exclusively meet certain intimate needs. If the man's needs go unmet, he becomes frustrated and unfulfilled. While some men never give in, some succumb to the temptation of an affair and go through the agonizing pain of infidelity. In order for your marriage to be affair-proof, you must be willing to discover the needs of your husband and learn to meet them. There are basically four things your husband needs:

- significance,
- sexual fulfillment,
- an attractive wife, and
- domestic support.

1. *Significance*

Significance comes first among a man's needs. Some marriage counselors would disagree with this and insist that sex is more important to a man than significance. They would prefer to place sex on top of the list of man's needs. But why does a man's job seem to have a higher priority to him than his marriage? Why would a man accept a job transfer from New York to California and leave his wife behind to join him later if sex is more important? An average man would rather keep his job than keep his marriage.

Men place significance high on their scale of values. This is evident by the fact that a man usually possesses a stronger ego than a woman. If he is not a man in his own eyes, he is nothing. To be a man, he has to provide for the needs of his wife and children; he has to strive for a place of prominence and significance in the society. This inevitably leads to a rigorous competition between his job and home. To achieve a balance between two areas of responsibility requires self-discipline and constant vigilance. This masculine need for significance is well documented by James Dobson in his *Straight Talk to Men and Their Wives:*

> *It isn't easy to implement a slower lifestyle. Prior commitments have to be met. Financial pressures must be confronted. The employer seldom asks if you want to accept a new assignment. Your business would fail without your supervision. Your patients have no other physicians to whom they can turn. Several of your church members are in the hospital and awaiting your ministerial visit. There seems to be no place to stop. Also, we must not overlook that ever-present masculine need to succeed . . . to push . . . to strive . . . to accomplish.*
>
> *Besides, isn't everyone else doing the same thing? Sure they are. I don't even know any men who aren't running at a breathless pace. My physician, my lawyer, my accountant, my handyman, my mechanic, my pastor, my next-door neighbor. There is symbolic sweat on the brow of virtually every man in America. Most of these husbands and fathers will admit that they're working too hard, but an interesting response occurs when this subject is raised. They have honestly convinced themselves that their overcommitment is a temporary problem.*[6]

As you understand your husband's need of significance, cooperate with him in meeting that need. He mostly needs your support and reassurance of your love during a time of defeat, when he has lost his job, when his business has just collapsed or when things are no longer at ease in his workplace.

2. Sexual Fulfillment

It is typical to hear women make the following remarks about their husbands:

"Jim has turned into an animal. All he ever thinks about is sex."

"I feel so used by my husband. When Bob wants sex, he wants it right now, at a moment's notice. We always end up in the bedroom. It's made me resist him physically."

"I don't love him anymore. When it comes to sex, he is damn inconsiderate and too demanding."

"All men are alike, and are born wanderers and adulterers." Comments like these only reveal that women are not aware of their husbands' need of something they cannot do without. Studies show that the male in all species of living creatures has the stronger sex drive. The sexual need of a man is well expressed by Tim and Beverly LaHaye in *The Act of Marriage*:

> *God designed man to be the aggressor, provider, and leader of his family. Somehow that is tied to his sex drive. The woman who resents her husband's sex drive while enjoying his aggressive leadership had better face the fact that she cannot have one without the other.*
>
> *To illustrate the physical cause of the male sex drive, let us introduce the scientific evidence that "each drop of*

(seminal) fluid is said to contain as many as 300 million sperms." Since it is possible for a man to have two to five ejaculations a day, depending upon his age, it is obvious that his reproduction system manufactures a supply of semen and many millions of tiny sperm daily. If unreleased through coitus, this can be very frustrating to his mental and physical well-being.[7]

To the typical man, sex is like air or water. He can't do without it. The sexual drive in man influences his behavior, personality, work, motivation, and almost every other characteristic in his life. Without it he would not be the man with whom she fell in love. If a wife doesn't understand the power of her husband's sex appetite, she will wind up with a tense, frustrated husband. It is a wise woman who cooperates with that need rather than fights against it.

Some women cheat their husbands out of their bodies or use their bodies as a weapon of control. Never be guilty of using sex as a weapon or bargaining tool, whether to punish your husband or to get something from him. When you do that, you are making a prostitute of yourself because you are selling your body in exchange for something you want your husband to give. Paul said:

For the wife does not rule over her own body, but the husband does; likewise the husband does not rule over his own body, but the wife does. Do not refuse one another except perhaps by agreement for a season, that you may devote yourselves to prayer; but then come together again, lest Satan tempt you through lack of self-control (1 Corinthians 7:4,5).

The only legitimate reason you have for denying your husband your body would be if both of you agree to fast and pray instead. If you place a price tag on your sexual relationship, your husband may feel that the price is too high and go shopping for a better deal. I recommend that you protect your marriage from affairs and divorce by making your body available to your husband on a regular basis.

3. An Attractive Wife

Most men find it hard to appreciate a woman for her inner qualities alone. Your physical attractiveness is of profound importance to your man. To have you look attractive is something he needs badly. You should endeavor to look something like the woman your husband married. After all, that was the woman he fell in love with. Isn't this an unrealistic expectation? Does it mean you must stay young for life? Getting older is no excuse for letting weight creep up, not fixing your hair or dressing sloppily. When you are not attractive to your husband, he starts thinking that your physical attraction he once enjoyed has gone forever. You make it easy for him to give in to temptation when Julie comes along nice-looking and giving him the eye. You can guard against this dangerous situation by making every reasonable effort to stay attractive. A simple test of your attractiveness is how much your husband wants to fondle you. When a man has an attractive wife, it means that he has the appeal and talent that deserve someone of her caliber. So make sure you are giving him the very best you can.

There are those who say that good grooming is worldly and that you are not spiritual when you are well groomed. They often quote 1 Peter 3:3 and insist that you should not care for your hair, wear jewelry, or dress attractively. They always stop in their reasoning before they finish the verse or they are forced to conclude that clothing is wrong. Good grooming is looking your best for Christ, not drawing attention to yourself.

You can enhance your attractiveness to your husband through:[8]

- cleanliness.
- well-balanced diet.
- enough exercise.
- enough rest.
- proper makeup.
- attractive hair.
- clean hands.
- carefully chosen clothes.
- proper posture.

Today's market abounds with books, videos, programs, and a host of other products to help you (and your man) look attractive. Of course, to be attractive takes time and money, but you can be attractive with what you already have.

4. *Domestic Support*

Every man has the fantasy of a home where his wife greets him lovingly at the door, the kids are well-behaved, and the home is well-maintained with no hassle. As mentioned earlier, man's need of significance has cost him overcommitment, overwork, and sometimes frustration. Most men are frustrated at work due to competition and they don't want to come home and be frustrated more. A man expects his wife to ease his life by cooking his meals, washing and ironing his clothes, attending to the needs of the kids, and maintaining the home.

Better is a dry morsel with quiet than a house full of feasting with strife.... It is better to live in a corner of the housetop than in a house shared with a contentious woman (Proverbs 17:1; 21:9).

When a man gets married, he sees his wife as making his life a lot easier because most of what he used to do alone as a bachelor is now taken care of by his wife. So he probably doesn't have to make his bed, wash his clothes, iron his clothes, wash dishes, and pick up everything he drops. Everything runs smoothly until the arrival of children. When the couple starts having children, domestic responsibilities increase and so do the expenses and the need for greater income. Now the man worries about making more money and consequently resents sharing household chores after a tough day. The problem becomes complex if the wife also works. This calls for understanding on the part of a husband and wife.

By saying that your husband needs your domestic support, we don't mean that you have to do all the domestic work. Of course it should not be the woman doing everything. It ought to be whoever does it best and whatever the couple is in agreement on. The couple should create a fair division of labor.

Table 5.1
Comparing his needs with her needs

	His Needs		Her Needs
Major:	Significance	Major:	Security
Others:	Sexual fulfillment	Others:	Love and affection
	An attractive wife		Conversation
	Domestic support		Financial security
			Honesty
			Companionship
			Family commitment

Understand Your Wife's Needs

Understanding and meeting your wife's needs is a golden key to a happy, successful marriage. By nature, women seem to be more complex than men. So they seem to have more needs, but her most dominant need is *security*, just a man's most dominant need is *significance*. (His need and her needs are compared in Table 5.1.) Your wife's need of security manifests itself in the form of basic needs, including:

- love and affection,
- conversation,
- financial security,
- honesty,
- companionship, and
- family commitment.

It is obvious that some of these needs are conflicting; an attempt to meet one need may jeopardize meeting another. Meeting these needs simultaneously may be asking for the moon. This is where balance is called for and wisdom must be exercised.

1. *Love and Affection*

Psychologists agree that all people have a basic need to be loved. This is generally more true of women than men. Women have a tremendous capacity to give and receive love. In their eyes, affection denotes security, protection, comfort, approval, and other vital things. It shows care, concern, and appreciation. Again and again, a woman needs to know that she is loved. She needs to know that she is very precious and valuable in your life, more important than your mother, children, friends, secretary, and job. As far as a woman is concerned, affection is the cement of her relationship with a man. She cannot do without it.

His Needs, Her Needs by Willard Harley[9] is must reading for every couple. According to Harley, affection is the environment of the marriage, and sex is an event. When it comes to sex and affection, you can't have one without the other. No wonder husbands are asked to love their wives (Ephesians 5:25; Colossians 3:19).

Since we will talk on love or affection at a greater length in the next chapter, it will suffice here to just mention a few ways you can let your wife feel, from time to time, that you really love her. Here are a few suggestions, and you may add more to the list.

1. Hug and kiss her on a regular basis.

2. Discover three ways each day to tell her you love her.
3. Take time to sit and talk.
4. Ask for her opinion and value what she says.
5. Learn to enjoy what she enjoys.
6. Compliment her often.
7. Pray for her and let her know that you do.
8. Give her gifts from time to time.
9. Send her cards or flowers once in a while as a surprise.
10. Go on romantic outings.

Put down this book now. Go, find her, and thank her for being her, and for being your woman.

2. *Conversation*

We have already discussed at length the vital role of communication in marriage. We want to emphasize here that it is important for a woman to be with someone who cares enough to talk with her. Hardly ever do you hear a man say, "My wife isn't talking to me anymore." Your wife needs you to talk with her. Sometimes she needs you as a sounding board to help clarify her thinking. Be available, patient, and understanding with her.

3. *Financial Security*

Common phrases such as "My wife thinks money grows on trees" reveal that women need financial security. They value the security of an adequate supply of money to provide for housing, clothing, food, transportation, utilities, and other basic needs. We don't encourage wives who live beyond their means by financing big homes, big cars, and expensive vacations. We don't support wives with unrealistic expectations, who are trapped in the habit of a higher standard of living. But when a woman marries, she at least expects her husband to earn sufficient money to meet her needs just as her father used to do, if not better.

4. *Honesty*

As we mentioned in the previous chapter, honesty is an important quality for a happy, successful marriage. Honesty is needed in communication as well as in other areas of the husband-wife relationship. Dishonesty is one of the most difficult problems in human relations. The married partner who is unfaithful is breaking the laws of God and man.

Although men and women have difficulties with honesty, it is usually the men who are afraid of opening up to their wives. To feel secure, your wife must be able to trust you for accurate information about your past, present, and future. She has a right to know when you go out and come in, where you are going, and what you are going for. She has the right to know how much you withdraw from your joint savings account and how you spend that money. We often think that it is the big, drastic things that break a marriage. But it is really the little things that cause the big things. If a husband and wife can get into the habit of never lying to each other, even in the smallest things, then they are very unlikely to deceive in large things.

Remember that the goal of a successful marriage is for her to become your best friend. That can't happen if you lie and hide things from her. Your marriage can't survive lack of honesty and lack of openness. Total honesty is the strongest defense against infidelity in your marriage.

5. *Companionship*

Obviously, we are social creatures and cannot tolerate solitude any better than Adam did before Eve was created as his companion. Women need men and men need women. We continually depend on each other for emotional stability. But men easily find social fulfillment outside the home. Men typically love sports and games, while women don't. Men find recreation in hunting, boating, fishing, and bowling, but women don't. Men like to fix things, build, and work in the garage. These things that interest most men don't interest most women. Women are not as successful in finding outside interests and activities as are men. Religious activities are perhaps the main outside interests that women enjoy. For whatever reasons, the world of women is typically more narrow than that of men. But few women enjoy solitude, loneliness, and boredom.

A woman looks upon marriage as perpetual companionship. Too often a man doesn't understand his wife's need of his companionship. If he realized this need in his wife, he would not allow his job to take him out of the home for long periods of time, he would spend less time in front of the tube, he would spend less time with the boys outside the home, and he would either reduce his recreation time outside the home or find mutual recreational interests and activities. Learn to stay more at home and enjoy wifely companionship. If you do, your wife will end up being your best friend—the goal of a happy, successful marriage.

6. *Family Commitment*

Children's development is the duty of both father and mother. The influence of a father on his children is profound and powerful. Most of us learned love, care, concern, and tenderness from our mothers. But we learned diligence, honesty, and the value of a dollar from our fathers. As a father, you can't leave your wife to raise your kids all by herself. She needs your commitment. She needs you to administer discipline to the children. A loving husband will not let his children get away with being disrespectful to their mother. He treats his wife with respect and protects her from hurtful situations.

So spend time with your children. Aim at family togetherness.

The Rewards of Understanding Your Spouse

Understanding your spouse and his/her needs helps your relationship to grow, mature, and become fulfilling. The rewards you derive from such understanding are too many to list here. We will touch just four of these rewards:

- happiness,
- an irresistible spouse,
- less friction, and
- fulfillment.

The Bible guarantees that a man or woman of understanding will be happy.

Happy is the man who finds wisdom, and the man who gets understanding, for the gain from it is better than gain from silver and its profit better than gold. She is more precious than jewels, and nothing you desire can compare with her. Long life is in her right hand; in her left hand are riches and honor. Her ways are ways of pleasantness, and all her paths are peace. She is a tree of life to those who lay hold of her; those who hold her fast are called happy (Proverbs 3:13-18).

Discretion will watch over you; understanding will guard you (Proverbs 2:11).

When a man and woman get married, they are irresistible to each other, i.e. they have an overpowering appeal toward each other. They either maintain that state of irresistibility or drift away from it and become incompatible due to selfishness, insensitivity, lack of communication and understanding, and so forth. Through understanding, however, the husband and wife know each other's needs. As they try to meet those needs, they remain or become irresistible.

Understanding one another's needs and roles tends to reduce friction in the home. Of course, it will not solve all major problems; it will not pay the bills or wash the dishes, but it does reduce minor irritations, which are usually caused by lack of understanding.

Another reward of understanding is fulfillment and contentment. When your needs are met within the home, you don't hunger for more outside. You become fulfilled, contented, and less vulnerable to temptations outside the home.

Finally, understand that it is selfish and unrealistic to expect your spouse to meet all your needs. Only the Lord can supply and meet all your needs according to His riches in glory

(Philippians 4:19). Your mate is human and limited and can only meet your basic needs. There is no greater torment and frustration than to expect so much and receive so little. You probably have seen a marriage go on the rocks because one partner was determined to change the other in order to meet the partner's needs and the other could not change.

Marriage is meant to be enjoyed. You can achieve a happy, successful marriage as you seek to effectively play your role of understanding and meeting your spouse's basic needs.

As Secret Number 5,

> Understand your spouse's basic needs and be willing to meet them.

Notes

[1] George D. McKinney, *Christian Marriage: An Act of Faith and Commitment* (San Diego, CA: Vision Publications, 1977), p. 12.

[2] Tim LaHaye, *How to Be Happy Though Married* (Wheaton, IL: Living Books, 1968), pp. 11-18.

[3] Larry Burkett, *The Complete Financial Guide for Young Couples* (Wheaton, IL: Victor Books, 1989), p. 22.

[4] H. Norman Wright, *More Communication Keys for Your Marriage* (Ventura, CA: Regal Books, 1983), pp. 123, 124.

[5] Ruth Stafford Peale, *Secrets of Staying in Love* (Nashville, TN: Thomas Nelson, 1984), p. 34.

[6] James C. Dobson, *Straight Talk to Men and Their Wives* (Waco, TX: Word Books, 1984), p. 138.

[7] Tim and Beverly LaHaye, *The Art of Marriage* (Grand Rapids, MI: Zondervan, 1976), p. 23.

[8] Daren B. Cooper, *You Can Be the Wife of a Happy Husband* (Wheaton, IL: Victor Books, 1986), pp. 128-133.

[9] Willard F. Harley, *His Needs, Her Needs* (Old Tappan, NJ: Fleming H. Revell Co., 1986).

CHAPTER SIX

THE SECRET OF
LOVE AND APPRECIATION

*Love is patient, love is kind. It does not envy, it does not boast, it is
not proud. It is not rude, it is not self-seeking, it is not easily
angered, it keeps no record of wrongs. Love does not delight
in evil but rejoices with the truth. It always protects,
always trusts, always hopes, always perseveres.
Love never fails
1 Corinthians 13:4-8, NIV*

Dr. Lawrence J. Crabb, a clinical psychologist and
marriage counselor, conducted research on a group of
people. He asked them to close their eyes and meditate on
these questions: What do I really want? What are my deepest
longings? What do I most desire that would bring me the
greatest joy? As they meditated, Dr. Crabb asked them to
choose one word that best expressed their longings. Among
the words they offered were *acceptance, meaning, love, purpose,
value,* and *worth.* Here is Dr. Crabb's comment on his
findings:

*Most of us, when we look within, can point our fingers on
a strong desire to love and be loved, to accept and be*

accepted. When we sense that someone genuinely cares about us, or when we ourselves sense a deep compassion for someone else, something profound is stirred within us. I suggest that our longing for love represents one set of needs that partly defines what it means to be a person or spirit.[1]

Love is a basic need of a man or woman. It is the key that guarantees a happy, successful marriage. In Ephesians 5:25, husbands are commanded, *Love your wives,* while in Titus 2:4, the elderly women are urged, *Train the young women to . . . love their husbands.* But why do we have to be commanded to love after marrying? Perhaps what we have termed love is not love at all. Love is not feeling, although feeling may follow love. Feelings are not dependable; they are up one moment, down the next. But you can count on love.

Love is the trademark of Christianity. Jesus announced:

By this all men will know that you are my disciples, if you have love for one another (John 13:35).

This is my commandment, that you love one another as I have loved you (John 15:12).

The same idea was picked up by the apostles when they wrote:

He who does not love does not know God; for God is love . . . And this commandment we have from him, that he who loves God should love his brother also (1 John 4:8,21).

By this we know love, that he laid down his life for us; and we ought to lay down our lives for the brethren (1 John 3:16).

Walk in love, as Christ loved us and gave himself up for us (Ephesians 5:2).

We notice from the foregoing quotations that the hallmark of Christianity is a sacrificing love.

The fact that we confuse love with lust or infatuation shows that we don't really know what love is all about. But love is something we can all learn. In this chapter, we will study love in a husband-wife relationship along the following lines:

- the characteristics of love,
- developing your love,
- how to love with words,
- how to love with deeds,
- appreciating love, and
- the rewards of love and appreciation.

The Characteristics of Love

There are at least three Greek words used for love in the Bible: *philia, eros,* and *agape.* Philia is the love that exists between friends, companions, or parents and children. Eros is the love that seeks sensual expression. It is the love that begins with attraction and eventually leads a man and woman to marriage. It is the sexual and romantic love. Agape is divine love. It is the self-giving love that keeps loving even when the other person becomes unlovable. Agape loves whether or not the other person deserves that love. It is not based on certain characteristics but on the fact that the other person exists. It is kind, sympathetic, thoughtful, and sensitive to the needs of the object of love. This is the kind of love God has for us

(John 3:16) and the one that the husband is commanded to have for his wife in emulation of Christ's love for the church (Ephesians 5:25). It is this kind of love that makes a marriage last. When philia and eros are low in a husband-wife relationship, agape can keep the marriage going. A Christian marriage usually have elements of philia (friendly love), eros (romantic love), and agape (divine love).

No discussion on Christian love would be adequate without reference to the Love Chapter—1 Corinthians 13. An outstanding work on 1 Corinthians 13:4-7 is *Love Within Limits: A Realist's View on 1 Corithians 13* by Professor Lewis B. Smedes.[2] The apostle Paul gave us a beautiful description (not definition) of love in 1 Corinthians 13:4-8:

> *Love is patient and kind; love is not jealous or boastful; it is not arrogant or rude. Love does not insist on its own way; it is not irritable or resentful; it does not rejoice at wrong, but rejoices in the right. Love bears all things, believes all things, hopes all things, endures all things. Love never ends.*

Paul was here taking a comprehensive view of love's outlook and attitude to life in general. We notice from this passage the twelve characteristics of love:

- patience,
- kindness,
- lack of jealousy or envy,
- humility,
- respect or courtesy,
- unselfishness,
- good temper,
- right morality,

- guilelessness,
- hopefulness,
- endurance, and
- immortality.

Before going over the twelve characteristics, let us make the following observations. First, we observe that there are other characteristics of love that are not included in this list. For example, other Scriptures teach that love is sincere or genuine (Romans 12:9; 2 Corinthians 6:6; 8:8; 1 Peter 1:22), love constrains (2 Corinthians 5:14), love builds (1 Corinthians 8:1), and love does not fear (1 John 4:18).

Second, no one naturally meets all these characteristics of love. One may be patient and generous by nature, but lack courtesy and good temper. Another person could be guileless and humble, but lack patience and generosity. It is the Holy Spirit who can supply us the power to bear fruits through which a complete supernatural love can be expressed (Galatians 5:22,23). Since God is love, 1 Corinthians 13:4-7 describes the attributes of God. God's goal for saving us is to conform us to the image of His Son so that we can have the same attributes.

Third, it may be helpful to examine what Paul said before presenting the characteristics. Paul had just given a synopsis of spiritual and administrative gifts. He admonished the Corinthians that the body of Christ has many members with different complementary functions and that one member should not try to do everything. Then he said:

> *But earnestly desire the higher gifts. And I will show you a still more excellent way. If I speak in the tongues of men*

*and of angels, but have not love, I am a noisy gong or a
clanging cymbal. And if I have prophetic powers, and
understand all mysteries and all knowledge, and if I have
all faith, so as to remove mountains, but have not love, I
am nothing. If I give away all I have, and if I deliver my
body to be burned, but have not love, I gain nothing* (1
Corinthians 12:31; 13:1-3).

It is evident from this passage that a person may have a great
gift of power for work, yet very little love. Thus we conclude
that:

LOVE IS A MOTIVE, NOT AN ACT

This is why love is so hard to understand—because we can
only judge an act; only God can judge the motive behind the
act. It is the act, what people do for you, that you respond to
as love. It is a common experience to see a person perform an
act of love, but with a hidden agenda. So what Paul was
saying is that you can render *acts* of love—patience, kindness,
giving, etc.—without love being the ulterior motive. But if
you have love, love characteristics are bound to manifest
themselves.

1. *Patience*

First of all, *love is patient.* Most of us would probably not put
this trait first and foremost. We would most likely consider
kindness as the number-one characteristic of love. But the
Holy Spirit knows better. Ponder for a moment on love as
being patient. It is difficult to understand this in our society,
where instant gratification is the order of the day. "Love is
patient" means that love can wait, that love is not in a hurry.

Love can wait for the other partner to make up his/her mind, to change and grow. Love knows that it takes time for the human mind to respond, to effect changes, and to grow. People who have not learned the secret of patience cannot wait for anything. But life makes them wait often enough, whether they like or not. It is such people who involve themselves in premarital sex and never learn what they should know in order to spend their lives together. Such people end up being frustrated, resentful, and depressed. So patience comes first because it is the strength that lovers must have if their relationship is to retain its vitality and last long.

2. Kindness

Second, love is kind. To be kind is to show mercy to others. It is to treat others nicely, not because they deserve the treatment. Few things are more attractive in life than being kind. Kindness is graciousness. It is a virtue that influences the heart at all times. God's loving kindness is the strong magnet that drew us to Him and binds us to Christ. God is kind; so must we be. If all believers would just be kind to all we meet daily, the whole world would be greatly blessed and a blessing would be poured out of heaven such that there would be no room to receive it.

What does it take to be kind? Kindness must show in our speech, look, work, and the way we treat others. Do I always say kind things about people, especially behind their back? Think about how ungodly Christians backbite other Christians, particularly friends. Unkind words never die. Therefore, before you say something about others, before repeating any story, honestly ask yourself:

Is it true?
Is it necessary?
Is it edifying?
Is it kind?

Remember:

> *The tongue is a fire. The tongue is an unrighteous world among our members, staining the whole body, setting on the fire the cycle of nature, and set on fire by hell. From the same mouth come blessing and cursing. My brethren, this ought not to be so* (James 3:6,10).

Kindness does not monopolize the conversation by a recital of its own views. It manifests itself in spontaneous and unsought consideration of other people's rights. It tries to recognize something to speak well of and to commend. Kindness will do what argument, opposition, and war may fail to achieve. Dr. Maclaren, of Machester, used to say, "Be kind! Everyone you meet is fighting a hard battle. Be kind!" And Paul said:

> *Be kind to one another, tenderhearted, forgiving one another, as God in Christ forgave you* (Ephesians 4:32).

3. *Lack of Jealousy or Envy*

Genuine love knows neither jealousy nor envy. (The Bible uses *jealousy* and *envy* interchangeably, so we will assume that the two words mean the same thing.) Envy is a subtle trait that even Christians can display. Keep in mind that Paul was writing to Christians. Do you rejoice with those who rejoice? Do you dislike intensely to hear others praised? Is your criticism of your friend objective, and not based on his outperforming you? Do you regard the praising of others as censure to yourself? Do you delight in pointing out the flaws in the work or character of others? Envy is working untold harm in the Christian community. It breeds suspicion, distrust, bitterness, resentment, and backbiting. It destroys the fabric of Christianity. It is sad but true that even Christian leaders envy each other's success and it shows in their talk. Some Christians are not love-motivated, but envy-motivated in their work for Christ. In every Christian group, you find men and women of small mind who delight in stirring up jealousy and envy. We must be vigilant against the seed of envy being sown into our mind by the enemy. We must nip envy in the bud. There are several reasons why envy or jealousy should not be given room in our lives.

First, envy is utter futility. There is nothing to gain by envy or jealousy. If I am jealous of my friend's success and try to rob him of the commendation he deserves, I am the loser because I don't allow my friend to tell me the secret of his success. It makes me mean and miserable and that shows in our relationship. When I try to underrate his prowess or undermine his reputation before others, I am displaying my smallness of mind. For sure, such action will not allow my friend to love me more.

Second, envy is self-destructive. It clouds your own sky and takes the sunshine out of your own life. Envy locks you up in a cage and prevents you from securing the very thing you envy in another. It is injurious to your health and character. Proverbs 14:30 says:

A sound heart is the life of the flesh; but envy the rottenness of the bones (KJV).

*A relaxed attitude lengthens a man's life; jealousy rots it
away* (LB).

Third, envy hurts God and His cause. God is love. Therefore, any trace of envy is not only damaging to the cause of
Christ, is not only hurtful to a godly character, but is a
deliberate accusation that God is not love. Envy also questions
His wisdom. It is a tactful way of questioning why God has
bestowed on others that which really ought to be ours. Since
envy hurts God and His cause, God cannot tolerate it in our
lives. We see God's judgment of envy at several occasions in
the Scriptures.

*When men in the camp were jealous of Moses and Aaron,
the holy one of the LORD, the earth opened and swallowed
up Dathan, and covered the company of Abiram* (Psalm
106:16,17).

Aaron and Miriam became jealous of Moses and were severely
punished (Numbers 12:1-16). Some disciples even tried to
move John the Baptist to envy Jesus, but John was too great
a man to give room to envy in his heart. He knew the remedy
for envy. He said:

He must increase, but I must decrease (John 3:30).

The cure for envy is seeing things from God's viewpoint.
We see this in the example of John the Baptist cited above.
We see it in the life of Moses. When two men were found
prophesying in the camp, Moses was asked to forbid them,
but he said:

Are you jealous for my sake? Would that all the LORD's people were prophets, that the LORD would put his spirit upon them! (Numbers 11:29).

Also, in Luke 9:49,50 we see our Lord Jesus Christ handle jealousy in the proper manner.

John answered, "Master, we saw a man casting out demons in your name, and we forbade him, because he does not follow with us." But Jesus said to him, "Do not forbid them; for he that is not against you is for you."

We must have the right mind and attitude toward our brethren and friends. We must let the love of God reign over and control us. When love dominates our heart, it becomes impossible for envy or jealousy to enter, and we will be able to say nice things about others, and rejoice and congratulate them when necessary.

4. *Humility*

Love is neither boastful nor arrogant. We just noticed this trait in the lives of Moses, John the Baptist, and our Lord Himself. If we are to be Christlike, which is what it means to be a Christian, we must be clothed with humility. We too must be meek, gentle, and lowly in heart. We must make no parade of ourselves or do things through vainglory. We must not be self-assertive, boastful or conceited. Rather,

In humility count others better than yourselves (Philippians 2:3).

Remember that meekness is not weakness, but power controlled and inspired by the love of God.

We must test ourselves in all sincerity to see if we harbor pride in our lives. Every gift we have, every virtue we possess, every success we achieve, every battle we win, and every righteousness we display are His and His alone. "For who sees anything different in you? What have you that you did not receive?", questioned Paul. "If then you received it, why do you boast as if it were not a gift?" (1 Corinthians 4:7).

5. *Respect or Courtesy*

Love is not rude. It is, rather, courteous, polite, and respectful. Respect or courtesy has to do with how we treat others in words or actions. How you say things is equally as important as what you say.

It is sad to note how marriage partners do and say things to each other that they would never do or say to anyone else. Partners who take each other for granted lack courtesy. Respect or courtesy is an essential element in a healthy marriage. It involves the willingness to listen to your spouse's opinions. It takes being able to recognize, accept, and value not only the ways you are alike but also the ways in which you are different. It involves respecting your partner's decisions and choices. Make every effort to put respect into action in your relationship because no marriage can survive without it. Respect has its own rewards. When you respect your spouse, you receive reciprocal respect in due course.

6. *Unselfishness*

Love does not insist on its own way. It is natural to be selfish. Even after giving our lives to Christ, there is the temptation to be selfish. An unknown author said:

There is a foe whose hidden power
The Christian may well fear.
More subtle far than inbred sin,
And to the heart more dear.
It is the power of selfishness,
It is the willful "I"
And ere my Lord can live in me,
My very self must die.

Probably the main reason we yield to the temptation of selfishness is that we often forget that we are no longer our own. We have been bought by Christ (1 Corinthians 6:19). Our goal then should be to promote His kingdom interests, not ours. Paul said:

Whether we are at home or away, we make it our aim to please him. . . . For the love of Christ controls us . . . he died for all, that those who live might live no longer for themselves but for him who for their sake died and was raised (2 Corinthians 5:9,14,15).

Are you living for yourself or to glorify Christ? The aim of a soldier is to satisfy the one who enlisted him (2 Timothy 2:4). As we allow Christ's love to dominate and control our actions, we can be unselfish like Christ.

Love is not selfish. It does not seek its own praise, profit, glory, or honor. Love's interest is to promote others' interests, its gladness is to make others glad, its pleasure is to give others pleasure, and its blessing is in blessing others. Its supreme joy is not getting, but giving. Love is willing to make way for others. It delights in championing the rights of others rather than insisting on its own rights. What a happy world, happy people, and happy marriages we would have if we would obey Paul's commands:

Let no one seek his own good, but the good of his neighbor (1 Corinthians 10:24).

Let each of you look not only to his own interests, but also to the interests of others (Philippians 2:4).

7. Good Temper

Love is not irritable or resentful. It is not easily provoked. It does not blaze out in passionate anger. It is not touchy and unwilling to hear criticism or suggestion. It is never angry without a cause. It is amazing that little things can provoke us if we let them. Someone merely looks at us and we get offended. Someone may laugh, and we think the person is laughing at us. One fails to catch what we say and we flare up. But love is not bad tempered. If annoying things are done innocently, without the intention of annoying us, we have no cause to lose our temper.

If any good comes out of our provocation, there would be reason to be angry. But bad temper injures everybody. Bad temper not only mars the comfort and contentment of all around, but has a terrible blighting effect on your own character. Everything vexes a bad-tempered man. Even if he gets what he is vexed about, he is so inwardly ashamed of himself that he takes further offense. Nothing pleases such poor, peevish folk. Solomon said:

Make no friendship with a man given to anger, nor go with a wrathful man (Proverbs 22:24).

Bad temper is made up of a number of grave sins—selfishness, impatience, anger, pride, hatred, touchiness, unforgiveness, unkindness, and lack of self-control. We must be self-controlled if God is to entrust us with His power. Only God knows how many souls we drive away because of our repulsive attitude. Psalm 119:165 says:

Great peace have they which love thy law: and nothing shall offend them (KJV).

Are we numbered among God's never-offending lovers?

8. *Right Morality*

Love does not delight in evil but rejoices with the truth (1 Corinthians 13:6, NIV). Each of us is susceptible to the danger of falling into the sin of thinking evil of others. It is hard to conceive of a Christian rejoicing at the fall of a friend or even of a rival. We sometimes easily suspect evil and harbor suspicions of others. Samuel Chadwick said, "I hate to think of the worst of others when I might think the best." And Paul said:

Love does no wrong to a neighbor; therefore love is the fulfilling of the law (Romans 13:10).

Let us remember that the person who dwells in the secret place of the Most High is:

He who walks blamelessly, and does what is right, and speaks truth from his heart; who does not slander with his tongue, and does no evil to his friend, nor takes up a reproach against his neighbor (Psalm 15:2,3).

You can tell where a person dwells by his/her speech. You cannot dwell in the secret place of the Most High and speak evil of your brethren. Tale-bearing makes us tools in the hands of the devil, the accuser of the brethren (Revelation 12:10). Therefore, take no evil thoughts of God's guidance or providence. Take no evil thoughts of His servants—your pastors, elders, etc. Take no evil thoughts of your neighbor, your friend or your spouse.

9. *Guilelessness*

Love bears all things, believes all things. Love is simple and straightforward. It is not that love is blind and does not face fact, but it is not suspicious. Love may be blind, but it does not live long if it stays that way. Those who love understand more of each other's true personalities because love helps them to see so deeply that they can accept and affirm each other. Real love can excuse the other and bear all things because it has a feeling for the imperfectness of human nature and existence. Eugene Kennedy well said:

> *A real lover can excuse his beloved precisely because he loves the other in reality and not in some idealized state. A wife, for example, can look deeply into her husband's life and understand, in a way that no one else could, why he behaves as he does. She knows all the secret hurts, the sensitive spots, and even the potential unrealized. She can take all this into account, and instead of standing outside of him and judging him harshly, she can add her strength to his. . . . The same thing works for the husband in relationship to his wife. He knows the inner landscape of her personality. Love bids him to keep exploring it with her,*

making his strength gently present, putting himself fully at her side with the sensitive understanding of all the things that make her the way she is.[3]

Life is more meaningful with those who strive to trust and believe and support each other through hard times.

10. *Hopefulness*

To be hopeful is to face the future with gladness, thankfulness, and a sense that the present is worth living because we can expect the future to bring what we desire. Hope, at its deepest level, is not focused on particulars. It looks beyond a change in character, a cure for disease, a solution for a problem, an escape from pain, for assurance from God that life has point and meaning in spite of character, disease, problems, and pain.

The power to love overcomes the urge to resign and lose hope. Because love bears all things, it can hope all things. It is easy for love to do that because love realizes that earth-wide possibilities are wrapped up in every heaven-born soul and because it recognizes that the one loved is created by God, whose love is the catalyst that can change all things. Love rejoices in the ultimate triumph of truth. So it never loses courage or hope. To influence people for good, we must not only love them, but believe in them and expect great things of them.

11. *Endurance*

Love endures all things. It means love puts up with trespasses against it. Love keeps no record of wrongs. It does not talk about other folks' failings and failures; it does not blaze them abroad. It covers a multitude of sins (1 Peter 4:8). We will talk more on endurance in Chapter 8.

12. *Immortality*

Love never ends. Since God is love and God is immortal, it is easy to understand why love never ends. This is a great mystery about Christian love that has never been captured by poets and artists. Love is not like food that provides temporary nourishment but does not permanently quench hunger. Love remains with us because it adds something to us that neither ebbs away nor separates from us at death. Love carries its effects on us and continues to be powerful well beyond the relationship in which it is experienced.

Since love is an imperishable commodity, we must learn to become experts in loving so that the whole world can be strengthened to put away its fears. We should make the lessons of loving a lifetime learning.

So faith, hope, love abide, these three; but the greatest of these is love (1 Corinthians 13:13).

Love is the greatest and strongest virtue in human relationship.

Developing Your Love

Willard Harley in his splendid book *His Needs, Her Needs* proposed the concept of the Love Bank. Harley believes that each of us has a Love Bank containing many different accounts, one for each acquaintance. Every experience you have with an acquaintance, friend or spouse is translated into a deposit in or a withdrawal from your Love Bank. We make deposits or withdrawals at the Love Bank each time we treat others depending on how we treat them. When Tom and Cindy get married, Tom's balance in Cindy's Love Bank may be 950 units while Cindy's balance in Tom's may be 1,000. If they fail to maintain and protect their love for each other, their Love Banks may diminish to the extent that they don't love each other anymore and opt for the wrong way of escape.

Love is a fragile thing. It must be maintained and protected if it is to survive with time. Love does not come from the blue. It must be planted, watered, nourished, and cared for. Because love has its problems, it must be weeded too. Love can die if left unattended. And whenever love dies, the marriage dies. However, since the Christian faith believes in resurrection power, love can be rekindled and a dead marriage can live again. To develop or rekindle your love for your spouse takes:

- loving yourself and
- loving others as Christ loves.

1. *Loving Yourself*

You cannot fully and freely love someone else until you have a proper self-image, a healthy and wholesome self-esteem. Developing your own self-esteem is foundational to love. Robert Schuller put it this way:

> *The person who does not love himself is too empty of love to give it away ... and feels too unworthy to accept it from God or from others.*

The quest for self-esteem remains of central importance for human beings throughout their lives. It motivates much of our activity in seeking satisfying relationships and meaningful work.

Your self-esteem is your overall assessment of yourself. High self-esteem indicates that you have positive feelings about yourself. You are glad to be what you are. You believe in yourself and consider yourself valuable. Low self-esteem causes you to feel inferior or be insecure, and be preoccupied with yourself. You erect defenses and tend to wear masks. While we must guard against pride, we must not be dominated by low self-esteem—an inferiority complex. Both pride and low esteem are false estimates of our worth. Seeing ourselves from God's perspective is the right measure of our worth—no more, no less.

How much are you worth? Are you glad for who you are? Do you really feel good about yourself? How you see yourself affects everything you do. Your self-image affects how you interact with your spouse, your friends, your co-workers, and God. Proverbs 22:7 says:

As he thinks within himself so he is.

It is the way you think of yourself deep down inside that motivates your actions.

You can love yourself and have a high self-image only when you see yourself from God's viewpoint. Do not allow ads or your emotions to dictate to and mislead you. The truest thing about you is what God says about you. Let us examine briefly what God says about you in His Word.

First, God created you in His own image (Genesis 1:26; 1 Corinthians 11:7). Because of this singular fact, God was compelled by love to redeem man after Adam's fall. Because you are so valuable and precious in His sight, God sent His only begotten Son to die for your sins. If someone should ask how much you are worth, you are worth what God paid for you—Jesus (1 Corinthians 6:20; 7:23).

Second, God has made you special and unique. You are a person of worth and value. As someone said, "God doesn't make junk." Don't go through life being like someone else. If you do, who is going to be like you? You are created to be you, uniquely and for a unique purpose.

Third, God loves you unconditionally. He accepts you just as you are.

I have loved you with an everlasting love; therefore I have continued my faithfulness to you (Jeremiah 31:3).

As a father pities his children, so the LORD pities those who fear him. For he knows our frame; he remembers that we are dust (Psalm 103:13,14).

God does not say, "I will love you when ...," "I will love you but ...," or "I will love you after ...." He loved you while you were yet a sinner, dead spiritually and insensitive to Him and His love (Romans 5:6).

Lastly, you belong to the royal family. You have the greatest heritage possible.

You are a chosen race, a royal priesthood, a holy nation, God's own people, that you may declare the wonderful deeds of him who called you out of darkness into his marvelous

*light. Once you were no people but now you are God's
people; once you had not received mercy but now you have
received mercy* (1 Peter 2:9,10).

Now that you know what God says about you, you need to
take three actions to develop your self-esteem.

First, stop putting yourself down. Stop allowing that
inferiority complex to dominate your actions, feelings, and
thoughts. You cannot help having self-debasing thoughts
coming to your mind. You cannot help receiving critical,
unkind comments from others who judge wrongly your
motives and intents. But it is entirely your choice to accept or
reject them. Don't allow what comes to your mind or what
people say about you depress you. Stop occupying yourself
with self-destructive mental activity. If God does not condemn
you, who can? If God is for you, who can be against you?
(Romans 8:31).

Second, accept yourself. This does not mean you should
not change, grow or improve. It means you discover some
good characteristics in yourself and cultivate them. Self-
acceptance is closely tied to the capacity to receive forgiveness
of your sins. The one who cannot accept himself is the one
who cannot forgive himself. You can accept yourself because
Christ has accepted you. Stop being somebody else. Be
yourself.

Third, start believing in yourself. You are a child of God.
God has a unique, wonderful plan for your life.

*For I know the plans I have for you, says the LORD, plans
for welfare and not for evil, to give you a future and a hope*
(Jeremiah 29:11).

You are filled with many exciting possibilities. Look for them and discover them. Apply yourself diligently to develop your unique talent and ability. In his excellent book *Be Happy You Are Loved* Robert Schuller said:

YOU have your own identity; none of us is exactly alike.
YOU have your own unique finger-prints;
YOU can make your own unique impression on the world!
YOU have an innate sense of dignity. Do not suppress it.
Cultivate it! Hold your head up high.
YOU have latent possibilities. Find a need and fill it. With all the hurt in the world today, there is no excuse for feeling useless. YOU have unique ability.
YOU can find it if YOU will look in the right places.
YOU have a divine destiny. YOU were created with a specific purpose in mind. God chose someone special—YOU!
He believes in someone special—YOU! God believes in YOU. YOU can, too.[4]

2. *Loving Others as Christ Loves*

Once you develop self-love or a positive self-image, you can overcome selfishness, the greatest enemy of a successful marriage. It will be easier for you to obey the Lord's command:

You shall love the Lord your God with all your heart, and with all your soul, and with all your mind. This is the great and first commandment. And a second is like it, You shall love your neighbor as yourself. On these two commandments depend all the law and the prophets (Matthew 22:37-40).

The second commandment becomes a reality in your life when the first is obeyed.

God is love (1 John 4:8,16). We must love as Christ loves (John 15:12). As mentioned earlier, 1 Corinthians 13:4-7 may be regarded as a description of Christ. As suggested by Josh McDowell,[5] substitute your name in the word *love* and see how you measure up:

- Is Matthew patient with Chris?
- Is Matthew kind to Chris?
- Is Matthew envious of Chris?
- Is Matthew proud or boastful?
- Is Matthew rude to Chris?
- Is Matthew selfish, or does he seek his own interests?
- Is Matthew angry with Chris?
- Does Matthew do Chris wrong?
- Is Matthew truthful to Chris?
- Does Matthew hope the best for Chris?
- Is Matthew enduring with Chris?

As you measure yourself by 1 Corinthians 13:4-7, you discover your strong points and weak points. You discover areas of your life you need to allow the Holy Spirit to work on.

Having developed our love, how do we express it to others? There are two avenues by which love can be manifested: by words and by deeds.

How to Love with Words

There are at least four avenues by which your love can be expressed to your spouse with words:

- compliments or praise,
- kindness,
- entreaty, and
- acceptance.

1. *Compliment or Praise*

Love builds up (1 Corinthians 8:1). One way of building up your mate is to compliment him/her. Look for something, small or great, that you admire in your spouse and compliment him/her about it. It does your spouse good to get a compliment as often as possible. We all need to be told over and over again that we are appreciated. We do not praise each other because it is easy to take things for granted, rationalize things or feel that praising will spoil others.

Your loving support and admiration are valuable to your mate. A compliment acts as a stimulus and is a source of encouragement, whereas a complaint acts as a depressant and is a source of discouragement. You compliment your husband, for example, by bringing attention to his commendable qualities, by praising him, honoring him, and giving him proper distinction. Of course, you discover those hidden qualities in him through proper study as we discussed in the previous chapter. As you honestly praise your husband, you may help him discover those traits, interests or strengths he may not be aware of himself.

Giving compliments at appropriate times influences someone's feelings toward you. When most people are praised for their action or behavior repeatedly, they are motivated to perform better and wind up with a sense of self-worth and self-confidence. Words of compliment draw family members together, create a positive sense of well-being, encourage interdependency, provide a powerful incentive for growth and develop the tremendous potential for achievement. Giving compliments at home amounts to saying:

"You are important."
"You belong here."
"We value you."
"We believe in you."

2. Kindness

Love is kind (1 Corinthians 13:4). Kindness has to do with how you speak. It means you should not be caustic, sarcastic or cutting in your speech. Every time you say something to your spouse, ask yourself, "Was that kind?" If not, you should apologize.

A soft answer turns away wrath, but a harsh word stirs up anger (Proverbs 15:1).

Let your speech always be gracious, seasoned with salt, so that you may know how you ought to answer everyone (Colossians 4:6).

To be kind is to be uncritical of each other. Criticism is a destroyer of love. It destroys love as cancer destroys healthy cells. More than anything else, it kills the desire to love.

Criticism never accomplishes what we want it to. Where criticism fails, kindness succeeds.

To be kind in spite of your negative feelings takes God's help and your willingness. We must seek God's grace to be kind to one another.

3. *Entreaty*

Love does not insist on its own way (1 Corinthians 13:5). Rather it entreats: "Could you do this for me?" "How do you feel about this?" "How about that?" "Is this a convenient time to ...?" These are words of entreaty rather than command.

Entreaty and persuasion are closely related. Every wife thinks that she is married to a stubborn man. The same could be said of every husband. Therefore, we must master what Ruth Peale, in her book *Secrets of Staying in Love*, has called a "subtle and tricky art," the indispensable art of persuasion. Ruth Peale said:

> *Have you ever stopped to think how essential this thing called persuasion is, not only in marriage but in life? It's involved in just about everything that matters. You can't force anyone to be your friend. You can't make anyone love you or marry you. You can't compel anyone to hire you, or give you a raise. No matter how much authority you may have, you can't just bark orders and hope to get things done. There has to be a winning of acceptance, of agreement, of cooperation. There has to be successful persuasion—and there are certain rules for accomplishing this.[6]*

Ruth Peale gave the four rules of the art of persuasion as timing, others' interest, creating a climate of compliance, and patience. A typical illustration of the art of persuasion is found in the parable of the widow and the judge (Luke 18:1-8).

4. *Acceptance*

> *Love ... is not irritable or resentful ... Love bears all things, believes all things, hopes all things, endures all things* (1 Corinthians 13:5,7).

We all long to be accepted by others, particularly by those closely related to us. Sometimes we feel it is asking for too much to accept one's spouse the way he/she is. You must learn to accept others, including your spouse, by following the steps of Christ:

> *While we were yet sinners Christ died for us* (Romans 5:8).

> *He hath made us accepted in the beloved* (Ephesians 1:6, KJV).

God loves and accepts you unconditionally. You must do the same. As you love your spouse unconditionally, without ultimatums, you will see him/her draw to you like a magnet.

Acceptance may mean tolerating the other person. Tolerating or accommodating your partner's quirks, occasional forgetfulness, different viewpoint, and disagreeable moods means you allow him/her to be human just as you are. When you need to communicate your displeasure, do it in a way that helps rather than hinders your relationship.

Many marriages go on the rocks because one partner seeks to remake the other in his/her image. It is only immature love that makes you like just one or two areas of your mate and dislike the others. You must accept your mate as total person.

There should be an ongoing practice of warmth and acceptance in your home so that there is an opportunity for both of you to be healed from the hurts experienced from the often cold and cruel world we live in. Everyone needs a place to go for warmth and acceptance, without criticism and pulling down. When love is expressed in words of acceptance, it acts like a cement, a bond that holds a marriage together.

How to Love with Deeds

Loving with words is good but not enough. Loving words are insignificant unless they are placed in the context of loving actions. "Action," they say, "speaks louder than words." We must couple our loving words with loving deeds. The beloved apostle John said:

Let us not love in word or speech but in deed and in truth. (1 John 3:18).

Real love must be backed with action. There are numerous ways you can put your love into action; you are limited only by your imagination, creativity, and will. Flowers, going out for dinner, letters, vacations, courtesy, phone calls, and cards are but a few ways to express your love. Besides this, there are at least three major ways to love with deeds:

- giving and sharing,
- caring, and
- making selfless decisions.

1. *Giving and Sharing*

Love is giving. Love is sharing. Acts of giving or sharing are one of love's strongest voices. Love is giving—giving of oneself to another. Giving is fundamental to the Biblical concept of love. According to James 2:14-17, your love or faith is impractical and useless if it is not put into the action of giving. We see love demonstrated by God Himself. The divine love prompted the act of giving.

*God so loved the world that he **gave** his only Son* (John 3:16, emphasis mine).

*The Son of God ... loved me and **gave** himself for me* (Galatians 2:20, emphasis mine).

You must express your love to your spouse by giving. Sometimes this may involve spending money. But you can also give your time and effort. Every member of the family can give. The husband particularly is expected to set the pace, to lead in this act of love. You must give yourself, your money, your interest, and your time. Why not plan to do something specific for your spouse each day of this week? Act on the plan right away.

2. *Caring*

Love is caring. Love must reach out with sympathy and understanding, being able to cry when your spouse cries, rejoice when your spouse rejoices (Romans 12:15). Showing interest in another person's activities and well-being can be a form of caring. Giving somebody a ride and calling somebody by phone could be acts of caring. It helps when you ask someone: "How did you make it to work yesterday in spite of the storm?" It shows you are interested in the person's welfare, that you share in the person's burdens and problems, that you care. Caring could also take the form of hospitality and entertainment (Hebrews 13:2).

So we see that caring has many faces. As Lewis Smedes put it:

> *Care is love's investment in another person's needs.*
> *Care is love's permission for the other to walk to the beat of a different drummer.*
> *Care is love's gratitude for the other's unexpected gifts.*
> *Care is love's flexibility to go where another needs to go.*
> *Care is love's firmness to stay close by when the other cannot move.*
> *Care is love's generosity to give when the other speaks of needs.*
> *Care is love's presence when being there matters most.*
> *Care is love's power to survive the death of desire.*[7]

3. *Making Selfless Decisions*

Love is unselfish. It looks out for the interest of the person loved. In making decisions, your love for your spouse should compel you to consider his/her interests. A loving husband should make his decisions with the family's best interest in mind. Before you decide on accepting that job offer, before you accept that transfer to California or New York, before you make that major purchase, consider your family's best interest. In case you cannot decide and come to total agreement, wait. Give your spouse time to think and adjust to the decision.

Appreciating Love

This chapter would be incomplete if we failed to mention appreciation. Love and appreciation are twins; they go hand in hand. They are like the transmitting and receiving ends of a transmission medium. Love is at the sending or transmitting end, while appreciation is at the receiving end. It is important that we show love; it is equally important that we receive love. Love does not become effectual until it is received and appreciated by the object of love. God loved the world and gave His Son to redeem it, but the love of God is only actualized in the lives of those who have received and appreciated the love.

Taking things for granted is the opposite of appreciation. You have heard people say, "I deserve that. It is my right. Why should I be grateful for it?" What a sad perspective! To express appreciation, to be grateful, to say thank you, to affirm, to make attempts to show love are all part of providing a healthy environment where people and marriage can blossom.

Appreciation is a way of reciprocating love. If a wife does not express her appreciation of her husband's acts of love, she will have a dissatisfied mate. To show appreciation involves having a grateful attitude and giving compliments. A grateful heart is one of the qualities of an emotionally stable person. *Be thankful—appreciative, giving praise to God always* (Colossians 3:15, AB). Be thankful, grateful when your husband gives you a gift. Never reject his gift, whether small or big. Be grateful at least for his thoughtfulness, which is more important than the gift. Therefore receive what he gives you with sincere appreciation. Your gratitude and appreciation will motivate him to do more.

Like love, appreciation must be communicated. And, like love, appreciation speaks many languages and a husband and wife do not necessarily speak the same one. For an effective communication of appreciation, you must take the time and effort to learn a language that your spouse can understand. Here are twenty-five languages of love and appreciation:

1. Meeting material needs.
2. Meeting emotional needs.
3. Helping.
4. Sacrificing—spending or giving.
5. Caring.
6. Being committed.
7. Saying words—giving ample praise and compliments.
8. Listening.
9. Being patient.
10. Keeping silent sometimes.
11. Being a friend.
12. Being fair, frank, and firm.
13. Writing a little note.
14. Presenting a flower.
15. Giving honor.
16. Touching.
17. Being on the same side.
18. Bringing out the best.
19. Setting priorities.
20. Praying.
21. Giving each other freedom to grow.
22. Providing acts of kindness, hospitality, and service.

23. Cooperating.
24. Supporting.
25. Fulfilling the other's dreams.

People are different. What may work for one person may not work for another person. For example, some families or individuals are not comfortable with physical contact due to cultural differences. To such individuals, expressing love and appreciation by touch is a foreign language. From these twenty-five languages of love and appreciation, you can find at least four that your spouse understands. Cultivate the habit of using these practical ways to communicate your love and appreciation to your spouse from time to time. Don't use the same language all the time. "Variety," they say, "is the spice of life."

The Rewards of Love and Appreciation

When you follow the path of love and appreciation, God's plan for your life in general and marriage in particular, you will be rewarded in many ways. First, love or appreciation in any form, at any time, brightens anyone's existence. The brightness is often reflected back to you. The spirit of giving and receiving love brings a new atmosphere into your home. It is an atmosphere that creates a climate conducive to happiness and growth. Love makes your spouse feel accepted and secure; it makes life worth living. Appreciation increases the hope of success in your marriage and enhances the motivation for your mate to express love, to try to change or improve. Your loving kindness and appreciation of your spouse will stimulate the highest and best in him/her.

Second, every human being will respond to love. As your spouse begins to sense your love and appreciation, he/she will respond with love and appreciation. Because of the principle of reciprocity, the principle of reaping what you sow, loving will bring you love.

For whatever a man sows, that he will also reap (Galatians 6:7).

Do to others as you would have them do to you (Luke 6:31, NIV).

As Gary Smalley rightly said:

Remember, you are the one who gains when you strive to have a loving relationship with your wife. My wife has told me dozens of times that when I treat her right I'm the one who wins. My loving care motivates her to do extra things for me, to respond gladly to my needs and desires, but this has never been my main motivation. The strongest motivation for me has been the challenge and rewards of living my life as outlined in Scripture .... And I always try to remember that love is a choice. I choose to care about my relationships. The same choice leading to great rewards can be yours.[8]

Third, you enjoy inner peace and stability when you practice love and appreciation. When your wife is fully loved as Christ expects of you, when she knows that she means more to you than anything or anyone else, she is fully under your control. When you accept your husband as he is, admire him, and care for him as Christ instructs you, you will receive rewards from Christ because He has promised to reward those who obey Him. When your love is based on scriptural principles, you will receive both earthly and eternal rewards. Love is a decision, not a feeling or infatuation. You can decide to put into practice what you have learned from this chapter and love your spouse deeply.

As Secret Number 6,

> *Above all, love each other deeply, because love covers a multitude of sins* (1 Peter 4:8, NIV).

Notes

[1] Lawrence J. Crabb, *The Marriage Builder* (Grand Rapids, MI: Zondervan, 1982), p. 28.

[2] Lewis B. Smedes, *Love Within Limits: A Realist's View of 1 Corinthians 13* (Grand Rapids, MI: W. B. Eerdmans, 1978).

[3] Eugene C. Kennedy, *A Time for Love* (Garden City, NY: Image Books, 1987), p. 129.

[4] Robert H. Schuller, *Be Happy You Are Loved* (Boston, MA: G. K. Hall & Co., 1988), p. 81.

[5] Josh McDowell, "Nonverbal Communication: What It Can Say" in *Husbands and Wives* (Wheaton, IL: Victor Books, 1988), Howard and Jeanne Hendricks (eds.), p. 298.

[6] Ruth Stafford Peale, *Secrets of Staying in Love* (Nashville, TN: Thomas Nelson, 1984), p. 99.

[7] Lewis B. Smedes, *Caring and Commitment* (San Francisco, CA: Harper and Row, 1988), p. 30.

[8] Gary Smalley, *If Only He Knew* (Grand Rapids, MI: Zondervan, 1988), p. 19.

CHAPTER SEVEN

THE SECRET OF COMMITMENT

A house divided against itself will fall
Luke 11:17, NIV

The Christian life is a life of commitment. You become a member of God's family through a deliberate commitment of your will. The same goes with Christian marriage. Commitment is a promise by a husband and wife to make the marriage operate as it should. It means that the couple are willing to change and lend a helping hand to each other.

Commitment is what the marriage vows are all about. In exchanging your wedding vows before the minister, you committed your wills to each other in the presence of God and many witnesses. Although vows may vary, the husband said to his wife words like:

I, Mike, take you, Jane, to be my wedded wife, to have and to hold from this day forward, for better or for worse, for richer or for poorer, in sickness and in health, to love and to cherish, till death do us part.

Here Mike was committing himself to spend the rest of his life with Jane. By the statement "till death do us part," he was committing himself to stick with his wife irrespective of what happens. This is indeed a venture of faith and an act of commitment.

The same goes with Jane. She responded by saying words like:

> *I promise before God and these witnesses that I will love Mike, comfort him, honor him, and obey him in sickness and health. In forsaking all others, I will perform unto him all the duties that a wife owes to her husband until God, by death, separates us.*

Jane's vow is a pledge that embraces an act of faith and a commitment of the will. It is not a shallow emotional act. It is a conscious decision of the will without escape clauses. It is a deliberate commitment to work at the marriage and make it succeed.

Wedding is an action, while marriage is a process. In a marriage, commitment is what maintains the husband-wife relationship, even when the fires of love have burned low or are threatening to go out. Commitment is what keeps you going, never giving up or quitting. It is what makes you keep trying and adjusting because you rule out other alternatives, including divorce.

Professor Nick Stinnett of the University of Nebraska at Lincoln conducted research on family strengths. He and his team studied strong white families, strong black families, strong ethnic families, and strong single-parent families. The studies were not limited to the U.S., but were extended to strong families in South America, Switzerland, Austria, Germany, and South Africa. They interviewed Christian as well as non-Christian families. They had only one criterion for being included in the sample of strong families: the families had to rate themselves very high in terms of marriage happiness and in terms of their satisfaction in parent-child relationships. They wanted a profile of information about these families to discover what makes them strong. Their findings are best expressed in Dr. Stinnett's words:

> *All together, we studied 3,000 families and collected a lot of information. But when we analyzed it all, we found six main qualities in strong families. Strong families:*
>
> * *are committed to the family,*
> * *spend time together,*
> * *have good family communication,*
> * *have a spiritual commitment, and*
> * *are able to solve problems in a crisis.*[1]

From these research findings, it is evident that commitment plays a double role in a happy, successful marriage. Whenever there are commitments to the family and to the Lord, the marriage is bound to succeed.

Commitment is essential to the success of any group, whether it is a football team, a business organization or a family. Our Lord understood the importance of commitment in selecting His disciples. He said:

> *If any one comes to me and does not hate his own father and mother and wife and children and brothers and sisters, yes, and even his own life, he cannot be my disciple.*

Whoever does not bear his own cross and come after me,
cannot be my disciple.... So therefore, whoever of you does
not renounce all that he has cannot be my disciples (Luke
14:26,27,33).

Here Jesus was not talking about literally hating ourselves and
our relations. Rather He was talking about commitment. To
be His disciples, we must be so committed that it appears as
though we hate our fathers, mothers, wives, etc.

To a family, commitment means the family comes first.
The ultimate glue in a marriage is not love, sex, feeling,
children, or law. It is commitment—the conscious decision to
stay together through thick and thin, to make the family
healthy and loving, and to make the marriage work.

In this chapter, we will examine:

- enemies of commitment,
- ingredients of commitment,
- commitment to family goals, plans, and priorities, and
- the rewards or benefits of commitment.

Enemies of Commitment

Before we look at what commitment entails, it may be helpful
to first consider those things that pose as enemies to your
family commitment. These enemies are not only against your
commitment to your family, they also work against your
commitment to God. They can be subtle or blatant, but they
are enemies every couple must be aware of. They include:

- overcommitment to other things,
- adultery,

- selfishness,
- materialism,
- a decadent environment,
- fear, and
- lack of family goals and priorities.

1. *Overcommitment to Other Things*

We are living in an age when it is hard to implement a slower lifestyle. We have many things to do and they all seem to be equally important. While all these things, from jogging to cooking, have their place, we must constantly resist the temptation of overcommitment. We must not let commitment to other priorities thwart commitment to our marriage.

According to Dr. James Dobson, overcommitment is the number-one marriage killer. Dobson noted:

We live our entire lives in the fast lane, hurtling down the road toward heart failure. We have deluded ourselves into believing that circumstances have forced us to work too hard for a short time, when, in fact, we are driven from within. We lack the discipline to limit our entanglements with the world, choosing instead to be dominated by our work and the materialistic gadgetry it will bring. And what is sacrificed in the process are the loving relationships with wives and children and friends who give life meaning.[2]

We must learn to prioritize our commitments—God, family, job, and others in that order. When we talk about the commitment to God as the number-one priority, we do not mean church or social activities. We mean your daily, personal devotion and fellowship with God. Your marriage should be given priority over commitments other than your commitment to God. Learn to schedule time with your family. Have time to talk and listen to your spouse. Have time to be with your children, to let them express their love and feelings.

2. *Adultery*

The desire for extramarital sexual relations, which may eventually lead to an affair, is an enemy of commitment. Adultery is one of the destroyers of marriages. It shakes the very foundation of marriage—trust—and shocks the heart. It represents the ultimate dishonesty and deceit. You never find a case of adultery that does not involve some form of deception. No normal wife will be bold enough to flaunt her infidelity publicly and no normal husband will do the same. There is always a conspiracy to hide the truth. The long-term effect of infidelity is heartbreak and tragedy.

To protect your marriage from affairs and the divorce that may result, be aware of the following facts. First, you must endeavor to meet the needs of your spouse as explained in Chapter 5.

Second, remember that your sexual relationship with your spouse is exclusive. If a wife is a good cook, an attractive woman, an intelligent speaker or a dedicated nurse, her husband is not the only one who enjoys those talents. If a husband is a diligent business man, a good orator or a devoted believer, his wife is not the only one who shares the benefits of those gifts. But behind their closed doors, a couple enjoys an exclusively intimate union, not shared with anyone else on earth. This is what God intends sex to be—exclusively for a married couple.

Third, if your marriage has become stale or boring, do something about it to enliven it. Don't be afraid to get help from your pastor or a marriage counselor. Don't wait till it is too late.

Fourth, remember that God holds the husband responsible for the marriage. Proverbs 5:15-20 tells us that the burden of loyalty and fidelity lies on the shoulders of the husband, and provides four ways to escape the trap of infidelity:

- Rejoice in the wife of your youth.
- Be satisfied at all times with her breasts.
- Be excited with her love.
- Refuse to find sexual satisfaction with others.

Lastly, adultery is a sin against God. It is a gratification of the lust of flesh. It is yielding to Satan's trick and foul suggestion. We must be careful and watchful because it is easy to be in love with a person other than our spouses. For sure, there will be moments when other men or women appear to be more interesting to you than your spouse. There is always someone more beautiful, smarter, more successful, wealthier. But that is alright because your sexual relationship is not based on that. When you have a problem with your wife, instead of humbling yourself and finding a biblical solution to the problem, you may give in to Satan's deception and believe his lie about sensuality. You begin to have pity on that pretty secretary who has serious emotional needs. She offers you an easy way out of your problem. You become emotionally involved with her, and illicit sex results. But what a price you and your lover will pay for the illicit relationship. Both of you will have to face the spouses you have betrayed, the children you have abandoned, and the God you have disobeyed just because of the fleeting pleasure. Remember David's affair with Bathsheba and the consequences they both suffered (2 Samuel 11). Husbands and wives, evaluate the material you allow to come before your eyes. For your family's sake, guard your heart from uncontrolled passions.

Above all else, guard your heart, for it is the wellspring of life (Proverbs 4:23, NIV).

When you are tempted with adultery, read Proverbs 5:1-23; 6:20-35; 7:1-27. These passages helped me to obey God before I got married and they are still helpful.

3. *Selfishness*

Selfishness is another enemy of family commitment. It is one of the biggest problems in marriage. It attacks the very foundation and heart of the home. It defeats God's purpose for marriage, which requires that a husband and wife complement each other since we all are dependent creatures.

As it was well noted by Paul Steele and Charles Ryrie:

Selfishness motivates one to take another man's car, another man's life, or another man's wife, and selfishness fills the courts of our land with thieves, murderers, and adulterers ... If the divorce courts had a rule that only unselfish people could get divorces, it would sound the death knell for divorce. Why do people divorce?

"I want my rights!"
"He has no business treating me that way!"
"I have to think of my happiness!"

"If she is going to do her thing—I'm going to do mine!"
"I can't take it any more."

I. Me. My. Mine.[3]

Selfishness is a sign of immaturity, as we shall see in the next chapter. It is the fruit of carnality. In Galatians 5:19, Paul wrote about the deeds of the flesh and listed fifteen selfish qualities:

- Self-centered sexual life—immorality, impurity, sensuality.
- Self-centered spiritual life—idolatry, sorcery.
- Self-centered social life—enmity, strife, jealousy, anger, disputes, dissensions, factions, envy, drunkenness, carousing.

He contrasted these with nine unselfish qualities:

- Unselfish sexual life—faithfulness, self-control.
- Unselfish spiritual life—love, joy, peace.
- Unselfish social life—patience, kindness, goodness, gentleness.

Selfishness is a do-your-own-thing syndrome. You want to keep all the options open. But the deep fulfillment that comes out of a husband-and-wife relationship never surfaces unless the couple are fully committed to each other. You cannot just push to get your own way and expect to have a happy, successful marriage. The best medicine for selfishness is offered by Paul:

Walk by the Spirit, and do not gratify the desires of the flesh. For the desires of the flesh are against the Spirit, and the desires of the Spirit are against the flesh; for these are opposed to each other, to prevent you from doing what you would (Galatians 5:16,17, emphasis mine).

4. *Materialism*

It is difficult to commit yourself in a society where careers, self-actualization, pursuit of wealth, and materialism command more respect than commitment to family. Materialism and a focus on things, money, worldly possessions, and comfort keep us from godly commitments and ruin our family life. We must remember Lot and his wife (Genesis 19). They were so preoccupied with worldly possessions that they lost their touch with God. Their lives ended in shame.

Of course, we must have food, clothing, and housing to exist. To be comfortable and decent, we must have furniture and furnishings, education, training, jobs, cars, and all these things that seem important in life. Jesus knew how important these "things" were to the people of His day when He warned His disciples against materialism in Matthew 6:25-34. Our lives are more important than these "things." Since things occupy so much of our time and thinking, we followers of Christ must guard against their taking first place in our lives. We must set our priorities right. We must not allow the enemy to deceive us with temporal things and rob us of things of eternal value and consequences.

5. *A Decadent Environment*

In our society today, it takes so little to be accepted in the world and in the church. Our permissive society allows open marriage and easy divorce. Commitment is almost a foreign word. The common philosophy is that everybody is doing it.

So why bother? Even churches condone acts of immorality. How seldom do we hear of someone being disciplined because of unfaithfulness to his/her marital vows? Societal permissiveness has a way of weakening our commitment.

6. Fear

We fear the consequences of total commitment in our relationship with God and with our spouse. There are several reasons people are edgy about commitments. You fear that your commitment may result in a loss. You never want to enter that "ultimate prison" of never turning back. So you enter marriage with easy escape clauses. We fear that things may change that will make our partners change their minds. We fear being abandoned.

Fear is of one of the tools of the devil, as discussed in Chapter 3. The only way to eliminate fear in your commitment is to be sure you build your marriage on a solid foundation as discussed in Chapter 1. If Christ is the focus of your marriage, you need not fear committing yourself to the marriage. God promises blessings to those who are fully committed to His plan and obey Him.

7. Lack of Family Goals and Priorities

Without a clear vision and purpose in life, we drift on the ocean of life. We lose focus and bypass the real issues of life. A couple that lacks family goals and priorities cannot be fully committed to each other. We will discuss this more later in this chapter.

Ingredients of Commitment

A happy, successful marriage needs commitment from both the husband and wife. As mentioned in Chapter 5, a wife needs her husband to be committed to the family. All commitments in life cost something—money, time, energy or one's very life. Parenting takes times—lots of time—and requires family commitment. For your marriage to be happy and successful, there must be: •

- commitment of the mind, heart, and will,
- spiritual commitment,
- commitment of time,
- sacrifice,
- responsibility,
- communication of commitment, and
- commitment to family goals.

The last issue will be discussed separately in the next section.

1. *Commitment of the Mind, Heart, and Will*

Commitment deals with three essential aspects of your life— your mind, heart, and will. The relationship between commitment and the mind, heart, and will has been graphically explained by Jerry White:

> *Mind. Heart. Will. These aspects of the whole person are inseparable and essential for Christ-centered, biblical commitment.*
>
> *The mind is the seat of intellect and knowledge, resulting in theology.*

The heart is the seat of belief and affection, resulting in a desire for God.

The will is the seat of decision and obedience, resulting in a holy life.

What happens when some are missing?

Mind only leads to an intellectual theology devoid of real life.

Heart only leads to unstable emotionalism without true biblical basis and without the life of obedience to accompany it.

Will only leads to legalism without the knowledge of the Word and without depth in the life.

Mind and heart only lead to commitment that never gets applied to the real issues of life.

Mind and will only lack the joy of relationship and loving service to God.

Heart and will only lead to aberration of commitment without a biblical basis.[4]

It must be stressed that commitment is a choice. Commitment is the volition of our will, our deliberate decision and determination to make things work. In Luke 14:26,27,33, quoted above, Jesus asked people to make a choice between Him and others if they wanted to be His disciples. So we see that commitment is of the will.

For your marriage to be happy and successful, you must decide to be committed even when things are rough. Choose to be committed to the pledge you once made to make your marriage work. Decide to be committed to the idea that God ordained your marriage and that He wants your marriage to grow and deepen as the years go by.

2. *Spiritual Commitment*

As Dr. Stinnett's research indicates, spiritual commitment plays a major role in the life of strong families. For a family that is spiritually committed, religion is a personal, practical, day-to-day experience rather than a routine of life. If you are a spiritually committed husband or wife, you will see God as having a definite purpose for your life. God is the source of joy and strength for your family and for you as an individual. Your conscious awareness of God in your day-to-day life will help you to be patient with your spouse and kids, help you get over anger quickly, help you to be supportive of your spouse, and help you see life as meaningful and worth living.

To be spiritually committed means you are devoted to God as a family. You read the Bible and pray together. Someone has said, "You can't quarrel with the woman you pray with every day." Many couples have acknowledged that they feel closer to each other after prayer or family devotion than before it.

Spiritual commitment is not limited to domestic activity. It extends to frequent church attendance and involvement in a local church. Although not everyone is called to full-time "Christian service," all of us are called to minister (Ephesians 4:12). Every Christian has one or more gifts (Romans 12:6-8) and needs to use them to benefit other believers. This may mean participating in Sunday school, nursery, "netcare" ministry, soul winning, music ministry, tape ministry, youth ministry, prayer and fasting ministry, placing Bibles, prison and hospital visitation, ushering, missions, and so forth.

Besides these personal and church-related ministries, there are hundreds of civic, environmental, and parachurch organizations in which you may be led to be involved. Just remember to keep your priorities straight: God, family, job, and then outside ministry.

Spiritual commitment promotes family strengths and serves as a preventive measure against divorce. There are values that the Christian faith emphasizes such as love, humility, tolerance, kindness, and unity. When these values are put into action, they tend to enhance the emotional wellness of the family.

3. *Commitment of Time*

Our commitment in marriage is manifested in the way we spend our time, the priorities we live by, the attitudes we communicate, and the sacrifices we are willing to make. Spending time together as a family is vitally important because it reflects the first step of commitment to one's family.

Parenting involves time commitment. It involves all kinds of interactions that are necessary in order for the child to develop into a mature human being. But little of that complex process can take place unless the parent is there physically and emotionally, unless the parent makes a commitment of time.

In a family where there is little or no commitment of time, both the husband-wife relationship and the parent-child relationship suffer. The husband and wife feel unimportant to each other. This leads to an inferiority complex. People who feel inferior are easy victims of affairs because of their feeling that having others of the opposite sex fall for them makes them feel temporarily significant. An affair becomes a way to seek significance and cover an inferiority complex. Also, children who are not well attended to by their parents, who spend little or no time with their parents, are easy victims of drugs—PCP (Phencyclisine hydrochloride), cocaine, heroin, marijuana, etc. Such children become involved in drugs at early age.

In spite of my busy schedule as a professor and writer, I have committed myself to spending thirty to sixty minutes every working day to teach my daughter, Ann. While her mom reads her Bible and prays with her before going to bed, I teach her reading, math, etc. and make sure she does her homework. I derive joy in doing this and take it as a matter of commitment, not of convenience.

To have a healthy, happy, and successful marriage, you need to spend a lot of time together. But how do you go about spending time together with your family? Here are some helpful ideas:

1. Make a project of spending time together.
2. Make it a time for fun.
3. Make it individual-oriented as well as group-oriented.
4. Remember incorporating grandmoms and granddads who can make children feel special and offer them wisdom.
5. Spend time with your spouse alone.
6. Plan and enjoy your vacation.
7. Give compliments, give affection, give attention, listen, and build up each other.

4. *Sacrifice*

To be committed sometimes means to sacrifice. To sacrifice may mean doing things that are not so convenient. An athlete does not excel without making some sacrifices. An artist does not create great paintings without struggle. A marriage does not last without a commitment to invest in other members of the family or without making sacrifices.

Sacrifice may mean meeting the needs of your spouse and your marriage. Chapter 6 already covered your spouse's needs and how you can meet them. It may take sacrifice to meet those needs.

Sacrifice may mean doing things for your spouse that you know will please him/her. It may mean listening to him/her when you don't particularly want to hear what he/she needs to verbalize. It is to share in your spouse's joy, laughing, weeping, and pain. As a husband, make it a point to sacrifice and to fulfil your wife's desires for you and the children. Start to do things for your wife that you know will please her. Work on that vacuum cleaner she complained about. Remember your promise to wash dishes and mow the lawn. As a wife, begin to do things that you know your husband will like. Make supper on time. Sew on that button he has been talking about for a while. Bake that pie he loves.

At the heart of sacrifice is the willingness to put the interests of the family ahead of self. It is the unselfish attitude that is willing to cut out activities, civic involvement, or work demands in order to enhance family life. It is not enough to give your family the leftover time. If leftovers don't produce a successful athlete or musician, why do we expect them to produce a successful marriage?

Love without sacrifice is not genuine love. God loved and He gave—His Son, many promises, etc. Commitment without sacrifice is meaningless. As Josh McDowell rightly said:

Sacrifice is the mouth-piece of commitment. We know our mate is committed when he or she is willing to sacrifice on our behalf, not only by what he or she says, but by what is done as well. Unless you are sure that your mate is committed to the relationship and is willing to sacrifice for it, you cannot abandon yourself to the other person as God intended. You will always be holding back. As a result, you will be robbed of the intimacy and oneness in the relationship you were designed to enjoy.... Research indicates that when a couple demonstrate commitment to each other, mutual attraction grows—the perception of the mate changes, and the individuals become more loving toward one another. One such study reveals that a growing commitment and the willingness to sacrifice and work on the relationship is the key to a long-term, happy marriage.... Let there be no doubt: Mature love is characterized by a commitment that is willing to sacrifice.[5]

5. Responsibility

Responsibility has a twofold role to play in family commitment. Members of the family must be willing to share household responsibilities and must be responsible or dependable in carrying out their assigned responsibilities.

In a home, job roles must be shared and job responsibilities have to be handed out. Certain things must be done for the family to function properly, and if someone fails to pull his/her weight, too much weight will fall on others. There must be things the husband does, things the wife is best at doing, and things the children must do. Sometimes the family may need to pay someone outside the home to do certain things. Some of the problems in family relationships are caused by people failing to carry their weight. They let the burden fall on others, and sooner or later things begin to fall apart due to overburdening of others.

For your marriage to succeed, you must commit yourself to sharing in household responsibilities. This is particularly important for men who have the traditional conception that household chores should be done by their wives. Believe it or not, your wife alone cannot do the thousand and one household chores. She needs your help in sharing the responsibility. Listen and benefit from Gary Smalley's experience:

> *I learned the greatest lesson in my life not in college or graduate school but right in my own home. In one single lesson, I gained a deep understanding of what my wife goes through every day of her life. If every husband in America could undergo my experience, the wives in America would be enthroned as queens. What was the lesson? My wife had major surgery and spent two weeks in the hospital. During that time I took care of all three of our children. I cooked the meals—all forty-two of them, not counting the eighty-four snacks in between. And I attempted to fulfill the thousands of household responsibilities in my "spare time." I soon realized it would take all I had just to keep up with the kids and do "surface" cleaning. I couldn't do half the work my wife normally did. One day she asked, "Have you been able to clean out the closet?" Clean the closet? Good grief, I had been stuffing things in the closet just to get them out of the way! Once I even lost one of the kids and found him lodged between the basketball and the dirty clothes! "Honey, I haven't had time to clean out the closet. I'm exhausted!" I responded. All those additional tasks she*

crammed into her schedule made me realize how frustrating and exhausting housework can be without help.

I'm sure you realize the average husband gets up Sunday morning, dresses himself, expects breakfast and glares because his wife isn't ready on time for church—while she's supervised dressing the children and everything else that goes into the preparation.[6]

Not only do you need to share household responsibilities as a family, you need to be responsible and dependable in pulling your weight. Mature love involves responsibility. Unfinished jobs and broken promises show lack of responsibility and dependability. Without commitment and responsibility, a marriage union is nothing but two self-centered individuals living together. There is no such thing as sex without responsibility or intimacy without commitment. So be committed and responsible.

6. *Communication of Commitment*

The Scriptures provide two ways of communicating your commitment: written and verbal. God's covenant with His people on Mt. Sinai was written down (Exodus 20). Nehemiah led his people to make a written commitment (Nehemiah 9:38). Joshua and Samuel made a verbal commitment with the Israelites (Joshua 24:24; 1 Samuel 12:23). It helps sometimes to communicate verbally or in writing your commitment to your spouse and children.

Not long ago, I was thinking about my wife while in a plane. It occurred to me to reassure her of my commitment to her. So I opened my diary and wrote down the commitment: "Chris, I will do everything possible to support and bring the best out of your potential." When I got home, I verbalized the commitment. Several months later, Chris was looking for something in that diary and came across that statement of commitment. She told me later what that statement meant to her.

From time to time, set aside some time to join hands with your spouse and communicate your commitment in words like these:

"I made a vow before God and I'm not going to break it. I'm pledged to this marriage. I will deal with our problems one day at a time. With the Lord's help I want to work at this marriage and make it happy and successful. I want this home to be exemplary. I want it to be the kind that will bring God the maximum glory and us the maximum good."

If you do this on a regular basis, you will find that no conflict is unsolvable. God put His commitment to us in writing. Learn to put yours in writing as well.

Commitment to Family, Goals, Plans, and Priorities

To enhance commitment, a family must have:

- goals,
- plans, and
- priorities.

1. *Goals*

Commitment has no meaning without goals. Besides obedience to God, goals are motivation to the long-term commitment that a happy, successful marriage takes.

As a husband, not having goals or plans for the future makes your wife insecure. Remember that security is her most significant need, as discussed in Chapter 5. Having common goals as a husband and wife encourages commitment by giving you direction and purpose in life. Sometimes a goal may be the strength of the family, a glue that makes the family stick together. Commitments live on goals. Goals give the energy to move on when life gets tough.

Without goals, we drift in life and accept whatever comes by. Having goals keeps you focused and purposeful as a family and serves as a powerful motivator to commitment. Goals have power to lift your eyes from the present situation toward a better future. Goals are important to a family psychologically, physically, socially, and spiritually. Psychologically because goals give a sense of fulfillment and contribution to life and help you to answer puzzling questions commonly asked: "Who am I? Why am I here? Where am I going?" Physically because goals help allot your time and energy appropriately. Socially because goals will prevent you from joining the crowd and losing focus. And spiritually because goals help you think about the future as you live in the present (Philippians 3:13,14). Every couple must set goals for their time.

A goal is a statement about what could be or what should be. A goal is a future idea which is accomplishable and measurable. A family goal must be a clear vision or call of what God has meant for the family to accomplish. What is that specific ministry God has for you? You may not have an answer for this right now, but you should seek the Lord's face for an answer. It may take years to discover your ministry, but you must discover it. Your life is a waste if you don't accomplish your mission in life. A husband and wife may have different but complementary ministries so long as their ministries do not conflict.

Each person has some gifts and an assignment from God to use those gifts to benefit others. Romans 12, 1 Corinthians 12, and Ephesians 4 discuss spiritual gifts given to each of us to build the body of Christ. If your gift is not musical, refuse any invitation or temptation to sing in the choir. If your gift is administrative, do not refuse leadership position. You should serve where you can use your gifts. I have discovered that one of my gifts is writing. That is why I wrote this and other books. Discover your gifts, develop them, and use them to the glory of God.

2. *Plans*

While a goal is what you believe you need to be, a plan is what you need to do to be what you need to be. Goals are destinations, while plans are journeys to reach the destinations. If you are going to reach your goals, you must decide how you are going to do it. Planning is figuring out how to achieve your goals. Planning saves time in that it seeks alternatives and optimizes your resources to reach your goals.

Biblical men and women believed in planning. The wise man advised:

> *Commit your work to the Lord, and your plans will be established* (Proverbs 16:3).

The virtuous woman described in Proverbs 31 is committed to planning. Jesus taught His disciples to count the cost of discipleship just as a builder would calculate the cost of building a watchtower (Luke 14:25-30). Paul planned his work (2 Corinthians 1:17).

3. *Priorities*

Having goals and plans is not enough. We must have priorities. It is one thing to have a destination in mind, but it is quite a different thing to get there. Every day there are distractions in your journey toward a destination, beckoning your attention and asking for your commitment of time and effort: Do this. Buy that. Go here. Eat ours. Be involved in this. If you heed the distractions, you will not reach your destination. Priorities will help you avoid the distractions of life.

Once you set your family goals, cut back on those things that will not help you achieve those goals. Drop what you don't have time, desire, or ability to do well. Learn how to W.I.N., that is, how to say, "What's Important Now?" Since you can have too many goals, setting priorities helps you determine which goals are more important.

In setting your priorities, keep the three levels of commitment in mind: God, family, and other tasks including jobs and ministries, as shown in Figure 7.1. If you do not set your priorities in this order, you will be out of balance.

You also need to keep in mind the two kinds of commitment: short-term and long-term commitments. Short-term commitments may include helping someone with math, hobbies, being in a conference planning committee, leading a Bible study group, and being a choir director. Long-term commitments would include your life vision, developing personal character, and pursuit of holiness. Short-term

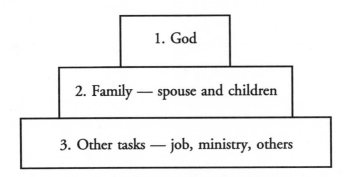

Fig. 7.1 Three levels of commitment.

commitments are usually many, while long-term commitments should be few. Most of our time and energy is spent on short-term commitments. Since long-term commitments involve a large part of your life, they should not only be few, but significant and rooted in Scripture. Finally, be careful not to make the following common mistakes concerning lifetime commitments:[7]

- Committing too quickly.
- Committing before you are mature.
- Having unrealistic expectations.
- Committing while drunk on romantic love.
- Having a wretched self-image.
- Not knowing how to communicate.
- Not sharing the same faith or values.

The Rewards of Commitment

Commitment to your family pays its dividends. There are at least four ways by which your family commitment pays. Commitment:

- meets your needs,
- builds your relationship,
- serves as a preventive measure against divorce, and
- brings you fulfillment and glorifies God.

Commitment promotes each other's happiness and wellness. Members of a committed family know for sure that other family members are for them and would be right there to help if necessary. They meet the needs of each other.

Commitment builds relationships between husband and wife and between parents and children. You need to know that people who promise to be with you are there when you need them. If we all lived as free-floating, self-seeking individuals, we would all be left hanging in the vacuum of each other's undependability. Commitment creates small islands of security for us in our ocean of insecurity. It is the invisible fiber that binds a family together as an invisible entity. Acts of commitment instill lasting memories, help mutual attraction grow, and help family members become more loving toward one another. When your mate and children know that you are committed to the family, there is a great feeling of security, love, and closeness. The relationship built through commitment eventually leads to intimate friendship—the highest level any human relationship can ever reach. The best friend you should have, besides your friendship with Christ, is your spouse. That takes commitment.

Commitment is a sure preventive measure against divorce. There are times in every good marriage when you don't like your spouse very much. Emotions come and go. Commitment is the ultimate glue in marriage. It is braced against the inevitable storms of life. People who are not committed to their marriage see divorce as an easy alternative to all degrees of conflict in marriage. They make insufficient effort to work out the conflicts. They fail to realize that even the most successful marriage has conflict from time to time. Lack of family commitment eventually leads to divorce and family disintegration. And disintegration causes the children and adults to suffer intense loneliness, isolation, and a feeling of failure. As the Lord said:

A house divided against itself will fall (Luke 11:17, NIV).

An uncommitted family will eventually break up. To ensure that your family lasts long, is happy, and is successful, you must be committed. Commitment is the price you must pay to avoid family disintegration. The price is worth it because you will be better off when you are committed to your family.

Lastly, commitment brings you fulfillment and glorifies God. Life offers no greater reward than the deep fulfillment of a life that is committed to God and family. Paul, as a committed Christian, described the Christian life as that of a soldier, an athlete, and a farmer (2 Timothy 2:4-6)—each living a life of commitment in his profession. Paul felt happy and fulfilled at the end of his life because he was committed to what God had commissioned him to accomplish (2

Timothy 4:6-8). A committed life and family bring glory to God.

As Secret Number 7,

> Commitment to your family builds lasting memories and relationships with your spouse and children, the people you are most responsible for.

Notes

[1] Nick Stinnett, "Six Qualities that Make Families Strong," in *Family Building: Six Qualities of a Strong Family,* ed. George Rekers (Ventura, CA: Regal Books, 1985), pp. 35-50.

[2] James C. Dobson, *Straight Talk to Men and Their Wives* (Waco, TX: Proven Word, 1984), p. 139.

[3] Paul E. Steele and Charles C. Ryrie, *Meant to Last* (Wheaton, IL: Victor Books, 1983), p. 79.

[4] Jerry White, *The Power of Commitment* (Colorado Springs, CO: Navpress, 1985), p. 29.

[5] Josh McDowell, *The Secret of Loving* (Wheaton, IL: Living Books, 1989), pp. 310-312.

[6] Gary Smalley, *For Better or For Best* (Grand Rapids, MI: Pyrange Books, 1988), pp. 135, 136.

[7] Lewis B. Smedes, *Caring and Commitment* (San Francisco, CA: Harper & Row, 1988), p. 77.

CHAPTER EIGHT

THE SECRET OF MATURITY

Be babies in evil, but in thinking be mature
1 Corinthians 14:20

Let us ... go on to maturity
Hebrews 6:1

Maturity is essential if a marriage is to be happy and successful. Maturity is basically unselfishness. Selfishness is a killer of marriage. To be selfish is to seek one's own welfare or advantage without due regard for others. It is seeking one's pleasure at the expense of others. We see babies as notoriously selfish; they are oblivious to anything but their own well-being. However, we expect babies to change, grow up, and become mature physically, intellectually, and emotionally. It is unfortunate that while many people mature physically and mentally, their emotional growth lags far behind. Emotional babies don't make good marriage partners.

Growing old does not necessarily imply that we are growing up. There is no credit due you for growing older; that just happens. Growing old is a process we cannot escape. But to grow up and become mature in thinking is a credit to you because it takes some effort on your part. Maturity is reflected in your ability to work effectively with others, including your spouse. It is a state of mind, not a date on a calendar.

The apostle Paul compared carnality to babyhood (1 Corinthians 2:14-16; 3:1-9). From his comparison, we can infer that there is a parallel between spirituality and maturity. A believer is either spiritual or carnal to the degree that he allows the Holy Spirit or his own sinful flesh to control his life. A carnal believer is one who has received Christ, but still lives in defeat because he trusts in his own efforts to live the Christian life. In such a life, self is on the throne. Interests are directed by self, often resulting in discord, misery, and frustration. The carnal life is void of abundant and fruitful living. In contrast, a spiritual believer submits to the Holy Spirit and allows Him to take charge of more and more specific areas of his life. He shows evidence of growth and spiritual adulthood. Thus the mature Christian is not a blameless, insipid kind of person, out of touch with real life, but rather a wise, spiritually grown-up kind of person; one who is always moving on, and finding more in life, in people, and in God. He becomes increasingly capable of building a happy marital relationship.

Trivial matters irritate immature people and cause them to lose control, act immaturely, and make selfish, emotional decisions. A mature person is not easily disturbed, irritated or upset. He maintains his self-control when things do not go his way. He understands that all things work together for good for those who love God. He therefore sees an unfavorable situation as God's design for his good and His glory.

God desires that we change, grow up, and become mature. He has given us His Spirit and gifts to this very purpose. In Ephesians 4:11-14, we read:

> *His gifts were that some should be apostles, some prophets, some evangelists, some pastors and teachers, to equip the saints for the work of ministry, for building up the body of Christ, until we all attain to the unity of the faith and of the knowledge of the Son of God, to mature manhood, to the measure of the stature of Christ so that we may no longer be children, tossed to and fro and carried about with every wind of doctrine ....*

As we submit to the Holy Spirit, He helps us to become mature. As we submit to those God has placed in our lives (husband, wife, pastor, etc.), we yield, change, and become increasingly capable of building a happy, successful marital relationship. A couple therefore should aim at maturity, help each other and their marriage to mature, and after many years together they will not only be as happy as they were on their wedding day but their love will be incomparably richer, deeper, and more satisfying.

To grow up and be mature, you must work on areas of your life that reflect immature behavior. A mature person possesses certain specific characteristics, including:

- willingness to change,
- self-discipline,
- humility,
- patience, and
- endurance.

These qualities enrich the lives of a couple and their union.

Willingness to Change

The presence or absence of spiritual maturity is never more noticeable than in one's willingness to change or adapt to the changing circumstances of life. There can be no growth or development in the life of a person, nation or family unless there is change. The spiritual life is a life of growth. We are called to grow unto the measure of the stature of the fullness of Christ. The end of growth is perfection, meaning both purity of heart and maturity of character. But there can be no growth without the desire to change. Change in us produces maturity and maturity is a key to a happy, successful marriage. The great thing about human beings is that they can change. This is the underlying assumption in this book. Habits can change. In a sense, life consists largely of making habits and breaking habits, for we are all creatures of habit. A husband and wife who live together must change and adapt to each other in the depths of their being. You are not the same person you were five or ten years ago, are you? You are changing, perhaps for the better.

Christianity has always been change-oriented. Changing lives is Jesus' business. He has changed the rich and the poor, the mighty and the meek. We hear sermon after sermon every Sunday and study the Bible to effect changes in our way of living, our attitude, our perception, etc. We are to continue to change and grow spiritually throughout our Christian lifetime. God's purpose is to change us and conform us to the image of His Son (Romans 12:2). Warren Webster, a missionary who spent fifteen years in Pakistan, once said:

> *If I had my life to live over again, I would live it to change the lives of people, because you have not changed anything until you have changed the lives of people.*[1]

It is strange that we spend so much time looking for the right person, one who possesses most of the qualities we hold dear, and just after marrying the person we mentally enroll him/her in our school of marital reform. We want him/her to change, and he/she would want us to change. Of course, there is nothing wrong in asking our spouse to change if we too are prepared to change. It is natural to desire variety and seek more in our mates. These are legitimate reasons. But if our method of requesting the change is wrong, it will not effect the desired change. Applying the right approach will surely remake our spouse into an ideal mate we so much desire. So we will examine the wrong and right ways to change our spouses.

There are at least three wrong ways people use to effect change in their spouses:

- comparing,
- manipulation, and
- criticism and nagging.

1. *Comparing*

Comparing our mates to other men or women is a wrong way to change them. Your mate is a unique creature of God, with unique ability and potential. Your mate can never be like the others you are comparing him/her with. God never requires that we compare ourselves with others. He only requires that we compare ourselves with Christ and that we imitate what is good in others (1 Peter 3:21,22; 3 John 11). If you see your neighbor doing something you would like your spouse to imitate, suggest it to him/her, but you must resist the temptation of comparing apples with oranges.

2. *Manipulation*

Manipulation is the tool of the flesh we use to get what we want from others. To get our way, we use words such as "If you loved me, you would ... ," "You better do this or else I will ... ," "I will change if you ...." For women, the favorite manipulative tools are sex and tears. For men, money and authority are common manipulative weapons. Although manipulation can work, it is a risky approach. It can backfire and sound like a power play. No one likes to be dominated or threatened by another person.

3. *Criticism and Nagging*

Men often resort to cutting comments or sarcastic remarks as a way of effecting change, while women employ nagging, assisted by occasional ridicule. It is a common experience that neither cutting comment nor nagging works.

You may have tried to change your spouse using one or all of these approaches, but nothing has worked. You have tried to remake your spouse yourself and the results have been far less than you anticipated. It is high time you do it right. The right ways to change your mate include the following:

- let God do what you can't do,
- use prayer,

- initiate the change,
- be an encourager, and
- be cooperative.

1. *Let God Do What You Can't Do*

There are certain things only God can change in a person. Don't try to do God's work by trying to change your spouse. You lack the power and resources to do it. Let the indwelling Spirit of God remake your spouse in the image of Christ. The Holy Spirit is the divine teacher and He will convince your spouse of sin, righteousness, and judgment (John 16:8).

God is at work in you, both to will and to work for his good pleasure (Philippians 2:13).

2. *Use Prayer*

Let Christ carry all your burdens. He wants you to come to Him and share your problems with Him in prayer. Talk to Him about what you want Him to change in your spouse. Since He knows what is best for you and your spouse, don't limit God by telling Him when and how to answer your prayers. Let Him work out the change according to His plan and timing.

3. *Initiate the Change*

To be honest, we are far from guiltless, but we try hard to get the splinter out of our spouse's eyes while ignoring the log in our own (Matthew 7:5). We should first concentrate our attention on our own faults, thinking on how we can improve ourselves. Our prayer should be:

*Lord, change me—not my husband [wife], not my child-
ren—just me!*[2]

The emphasis should be on changing *me*, not anybody else.
Recognize that you are responsible for the outcome of your
marriage, its success or failure. Try as you may, you can do
nothing to change your spouse that will not be destructive;
you can change only yourself. Become ruthless with yourself
and never permit yourself to say, "I can't." If you yield to the
Lord, He can change you through His Spirit, Word, circumstances, people, etc. Change is contagious. When you are
changed, your spouse and children will change.

As the head of the home, the man should initiate the
change. He must be a pacesetter in initiating change as an
example to the rest of the family. To be effective, change must
come from the top. This principle is applicable to the
corporate world, the church, and the family. The man must
change and grow so that his family can change and grow. The
man must set the example. We cannot expect the women to
read books and attend seminars on how to be good wives
while we remain unchanged. A rehabilitated and reformed
wife will only be frustrated in a home with an unchanged
man. The change should start with the man, the head of the
home.

4. *Be an Encourager*

After you have prayed for your spouse about what you want
God to change in him/her, concentrate on his/her positive
traits. Fix your mind on whatever is pure, honorable, and
praiseworthy about your spouse. We are called to be encourag-
ers (1 Thessalonians 5:14; Hebrews 3:13).

5. Be Cooperative

If you want your spouse to change a sloppy habit, your cooperative support is needed. For example, Tom is always leaving his clothes all over the house and Valerie doesn't like that. Valerie needs to cooperate with Tom to effect habitual change by giving him some suggestions, ideas, and alternatives. If your partner is ignorant about certain things, give him/her the necessary information to effect the change. If the change involves quite a lot, start out slowly so that it is easier to effect. It is normal for your spouse to fear and resist change because human nature is conservative. But in a family where trust, intimacy, and cooperation exist, a spouse may view the request for change as a way to improve and achieve even greater intimacy.

Self-Discipline

Self-discipline is a mark of maturity. Someone has said, "There is something about maturity that comes through adversity. If you don't suffer a little, you will never stop being a kid!" Self-discipline is self-denial.

Self-discipline is the ability to regulate conduct by principle and judgment rather than impulse, desire, pressure or social conformity. Perhaps the best synonym for self-discipline is self-control, which is the fruit of the Spirit (Galatians 5:23). Self-control is one mark of growth and maturity in the Christian faith. It is the control of one's self, the governing of one's desires, the ability to avoid excesses, and to stay within reasonable bounds. It is to say, "No," to sin as it tempts one's appetites, "Yes," to righteousness, and, "I will," to obedience to the Lord. It is the exercise of inner strength under the direction of sound judgment that enables us to do, think, and say what is pleasing to God. It is to honor God with your body, to take captive every thought, and to curb your emotions. An undisciplined man is a poor risk no matter how warm his wife is; a self-disciplined man will keep himself pure even if it means total abstinence for the rest of his life.

Self-discipline is not an end in itself, but a means to an end. The purpose of self-discipline is that we may be trained for God to use as His instruments in the way He chooses. A by-product of this goal is the enrichment of one's marital relationship.

As Jerry Bridges well noted:

Self-control is the believer's wall of defense against the sinful desires that wage war against his soul. Charles Bridges has observed that the person without self-control is easy prey to the invader: "He yields himself to the first assault of his ungoverned passions, offering no resistance.... Having no discipline over himself, temptation becomes the occasion of sin, and hurries him on to fearful lengths that he had not contemplated.... Anger tends to murder. Unwatchfulness over lust plunges into adultery."[3]

In Proverbs 25:28, Solomon said:

A man without self-control is like a city broken into and left without walls.

So far, we have talked about self-discipline in relation to life as a whole. We now turn to the particular because self-discipline is a very particular matter. First of all, we need to remind ourselves that all undisciplined behavior begins in the *mind* and springs from three sources: the desire of the flesh, the desire of the eyes, and the pride of life. This three-fold desire is characteristic of the world with its self-indulgence, superficiality, arrogance, and conceit. In order to counteract this three-fold desire, we need a practical habit of self-discipline that will cover every area of our lives. The desire of the flesh is an uncontrolled love of pleasure. Pleasure itself is not evil; we are supposed to enjoy life to the fullest. But when the desire for pleasure becomes a craving and it must be satisfied at all costs, it becomes undisciplined.

Self-discipline must affect five aspects of our lives:

- the body,
- the mind,
- the heart,
- the tongue, and
- use of our resources.

1. *The Body*

Discipline of the body is the ability to subordinate the body and its appetites to the service of the mind. Greediness and overindulgence in food and drink are signs of undiscipline. However, discipline of the body does not mean a rigorous asceticism. It does mean obedience to the laws of health, the right use of sleep and rest, exercise and fresh air. Paul said:

I buffet my body and make it my slave, lest possibly, after I have preached to others, I myself should be disqualified (1 Corinthians 9:27, NASB).

2. *The Mind*

Discipline of the mind is a measure against the desire of the eyes, which covers a great deal. We are all aware of the dangers of day-dreaming, of picturing ourselves in situations we know do not glorify God. Discipline of the mind is the ability to resist the temptation of filling one's mind with trifles, with sordid and unloving thoughts. Sometimes even a look at a certain picture that has lowering suggestions can do great harm to the inner life. We cannot prevent flies from flying, but we can prevent them from building their castle on our heads. Useless, foolish, and unholy thoughts must be brought into captivity to the obedience of Christ (2 Corinthians 10:3-5).

To counteract the desire of the eyes, we must pray like the Psalmist:

> *Turn [away] my eyes from looking at vanities* (Psalm 119:37).

3. *The Heart*

Discipline of the heart is a measure against the pride of life. The pride of life covers most of what we mean by "pride" in the modern sense of the word: pride of family, of birth, of a good name; pride of nation, race or color; pride of knowledge, strength or physical skill; pride of achievement, position and the effort to attain it. The pride of life may infect a believer.

The discipline of the heart is the ability to control the emotions and affections. It is difficult to detach our desires from what we want most when we see clearly that this way, achievement or relationship is not for us. Only through God's help can we subordinate our emotions to reason and our affection to control.

A disciplined character has learned that emotions may not immediately obey the will, but actions must. Like Paul, we must let the love of Christ be the controlling factor in our lives (2 Corinthians 5:14).

4. The Tongue

A self-disciplined person not only subordinates the physical appetites for food and sex, he subordinates his emotions, moods, and tongue. He does not live by the creed "I can't help it" and similar expressions of moral flabbiness. Nothing does more irreparable harm to our family, neighbor or even our own spiritual life than the uncontrolled use of the tongue. It is no wonder that James said, "The tongue is a fire."

Discipline of the tongue is the ability to bridle one's tongue. This may involve the discipline of silence. If we know how to keep silent at appropriate times, we will save ourselves from a lot of self-invented troubles. A biting remark about an absent person may destroy a relationship and may lead to moral or spiritual disaster. A truly disciplined character means mastery of moods and bridling of tongue.

To put a check on the use of our tongue at every occasion, we must pray like David:

Set a guard over my mouth, O LORD, keep watch over the door of my lips! (Psalm 141:3).

5. *Use of Our Resources*

As we will fully discuss in Chapter 9, we are stewards or managers of the resources God has entrusted to our care. God's resources are time, treasure, and talent.

We need discipline in the use of our time because it is God's gift. So many people get nervous and irritable because they are always in a hurry. Others keep up a senseless and unbalanced schedule because they are ambitious and want to get on, to make a name, or to make money, or to achieve some self-centered purpose. All these ways of living are living without God. God can teach us how to use time aright and to put our priorities in the right order. All of us have twenty-four hours a day to work with; it is how we use the time that differs from individual to individual. Paul counseled the Ephesians and Colossians to redeem the time (Ephesians 5:16; Colossians 4:5), to buy opportunities for time is opportunity. Use of time is God-given stewardship for which we must render account (2 Corinthians 5:10). All attainments and achievements are conditioned by the proper use of time. The ideal use of time is a balanced use of it (Ecclesiates 3:1-8). As one unknown author suggested:

> *Take time to work; it is the price of success.*
> *Take time to think; it is the source of power.*
> *Take time to play; it is the secret of perpetual youth.*
> *Take time to read; it is the fountain of wisdom.*
> *Take time to be friendly; it is a road to happiness.*
> *Take time to dream; it is hitching your wagon to a star.*
> *Take time to love; it is the privilege of redeemed people.*
> *Take time to look around; it is too short a day to be selfish.*

Take time to laugh; it is the music of the soul.
Take time for God; it is life's only lasting investment.

No discipline is more important than regular personal fellowship with God, which involves a deliberate choice of time for thinking God's thoughts. As Paul instructed Timothy:

Spend your time and energy in the exercise of keeping spiritually fit (1 Timothy 4:7, LB).

Discipline yourself for the purpose of godliness (1 Timothy 4:7, NASB).

It takes discipline to resist the temptation of indulging whimsical desires and wasteful spending. As Pat Robertson, president of the Christian Broadcasting Network, once said:

Lack of self-control is our No. 1 problem. For the individual, it takes the form of wasteful spending, leading to debt, gluttony, absenteeism, drunkenness, divorce, free sex, drug abuse, violence, and crime. For the city, state and nations, it comes as deficit spending and a "printing press mentality" whereby we print money to pay for our profligacy.[4]

In order to spend our money wisely, we must follow some disciplinary principles. We must learn to avoid the indulgences of life. We must be able to discern the difference between needs, wants, and desires in every purchase we make.

Take heed, and beware of all covetousness; for a man's life does not consist in the abundance of his possessions (Luke 12:15).

He who loves pleasure will be a poor man; he who loves wine and oil will not be rich (Proverbs 21:17).

Not only do we need discipline in our use of time and treasure, but in our talents also. What are your gifts and special talents? What would God want you to accomplish in your lifetime? Are you accomplishing God's will in your life? How can you best use your talents to serve God? Why were you born? Your answers to these and related questions will help you assess the use of your talents.

Humility

Humility is another mark of maturity. It is a trait that manifests itself in our relationships:

- toward God,
- toward ourselves,
- toward others,

and in our attitude toward trials and blessings that come our way or abilities and achievements with which we are blessed.

1. *Toward God*

Pride and humility are used in the Scriptures primarily to speak of our relationship with God. Pride is always referring to one who is independent of God; humility speaks of one who realizes his dependence on God. That is why 1 Peter 5:5,6 said:

"God opposes the proud, but gives grace to the humble."
Humble yourselves therefore under the mighty hand of God,
that in due time he may exalt you.

Whether we are living independent of or dependent on God
will show in our relationships with others. Thus when we are
exhorted to be humble with others (Romans 12:16; 1 Peter
5:5), we are urged to exercise mutual humility because we are
dependent creatures.

Humility toward God begins with a high view and fear of
God's person. We are humbled before God as we see Him in
His majesty, awesomeness, and holiness. Like Moses falling to
the ground, Isaiah crying, "Woe is me!" Ezekiel falling face
down, and John falling as though dead, a mature believer
humbles himself in the presence of God.

One is not truly humble before God if one is not humble
toward God's Word.

This is the one I esteem: he who is humble and contrite in
spirit, and trembles at my word (Isaiah 66:2, NIV).

We must develop a spirit of humility toward the Bible in
regard to our conduct and doctrines.

Spiritual maturity is never attained until we submit to the
Lordship of Christ. The key question that determines whether
or not He has been given that place of authority in your life
is: "Who makes the decisions?" Is Christ in control or in
charge of your life? Submission to authority is a mark of
maturity and it takes humility to do that. Learn to submit not
only to God, but to your wife or husband, your pastor and
elders of your church, your boss, and the civic government.

2. *Toward Ourselves*

This has to do with our self-evaluation, how we think about ourselves. A mature believer does not brag about his own gifts, abilities, and attainments. He does not think of himself more highly than he ought to (Romans 12:3). He acknowledges that all that he is and all that he has come from God (1 Corinthians 4:7). Like Paul, he realizes that he is what he is by the grace of God (1 Corinthians 15:10).

Boastful pride is simply a futile attempt to put ourselves on a pedestal above others. We may vaunt ourselves by monopolizing a conversation, assuming that others desire to listen to us. Or we may be puffed up because of our knowledge. Even beauty may puff up. We must be humble lest the suspicion of boasting enter in. Rather than exalting ourselves, we should aim at elevating others, praising them, and cheering them so as to add to their pleasure and comfort.

The saddest form of pride is spiritual pride. When a Christian begins to boast about his successes, real success disappears. Every vestige of success is due to God, and to Him alone because it is He who provided the means and power to achieve. The higher God places us, the lower we should esteem ourselves, and the more we should glorify Him. We must decrease so that He may increase (John 3:30). Remember that we are but mirrors to reflect the glory of God; a mirror never calls attention to itself unless there are flaws in it.

3. *Toward Others*

A mature believer is not only humble before God and about his own gifts, he is humble toward other people. In 1 Peter

3:8, Peter emphasized five attitudes that can bring vitality to any relationship, especially marriage: harmony, sympathy, brotherly love, compassion, and humility. Thus humility is an important trait that must exist in any relationship we have with others, particularly with our spouses. There are four ways by which we demonstrate humility toward other people: submission to others, serving others, honoring others, and submission to authority.

To submit to others out of humility is to be teachable or to be humble enough to admit that we have erred when another person corrects us. Unsolicited suggestion or correction of others is difficult for immature hearts. Immature people try to find excuses for their failures and shift blame onto others. When they are corrected, they take it as a personal affront. They are more concerned about protecting their own egos than about growing. On the other hand, a mature person accepts correction and suggestions from others. He sees corrections and suggestions from others as a part of God's design to bring him to maturity.

Jesus is our greatest example and pacesetter in the area of serving others in humility. He said He did not come to be served, but to serve others (Mark 10:45; Matthew 20:25-28). Humility in serving others requires the grace of God. When immature people serve others, God does not get the glory; they do and their reputation is enhanced. But when mature people serve others, God is glorified (1 Peter 4:11; Matthew 5:16). Through God's help, those of us who are not natural servants can learn to serve one another.

Another way we demonstrate humility toward others is by honoring them. An immature person seeks and demands respect and honor from others, while a mature person gives respect and honor to and commands respect and honor from others. We are to honor others above ourselves (Romans 12:10). We are to place others above ourselves in matters of position, concerns, and needs.

Submit to one another out of reverence for Christ (Ephesians 5:21, NIV).

Clothe yourselves with humility toward one another, because "God opposes the proud but gives grace to the humble" (1 Peter 5:5, NIV).

Do nothing from selfishness or conceit, but in humility count others better than yourselves. Let each of you look not only to his own interests, but also to the interests of others. Have this mind among yourselves, which is yours in Christ Jesus, who, though he was in the form of God, did not count equality with God a thing to be grasped, but emptied himself, taking the form of a servant ... (Philippians 2:3,7).

The final hallmark of humility toward others is the ability to assimilate imposed discipline with grace and profit. In most of life's normal circumstances rebellion is stupid, destructive, and childish. Habitual rebellion is a sign of immaturity. An immature person will assert loudly, "No one can tell me what to do and how to do it," but a mature person readily accepts and submits to authority. Submissiveness is characteristic of the wisdom that comes from heaven (James 3:17).

A humble attitude toward God, about ourselves, and toward our spouses will surely relieve tension and conflict in marriage.

Patience

There is no such thing as instant maturity. It is not attained overnight. It is a dynamic process that continues throughout life. If you leave your marriage just because you want to avoid the necessary steps that require maturity and growth, you do yourself as well as those in your life a great injustice. You simply postpone facing the very same maturation requirements in any subsequent marriage. Then they usually come sooner and more intensely. Why not endure and learn the lesson right now? It will involve some diligence and discipline, as does a college course, if we are to graduate in the school of God. As Wilmont Buxton once said:

> *No great work is ever done in a hurry. To develop a great scientific discovery, to paint a great picture, to write an immortal poem, to become a minister, or a famous general—to do anything great requires time, patience, and perseverance. These things are done by degrees, "little by little."*

It takes time to mature and we must be patient with each other.

As mentioned earlier, habits can be changed. But change takes time and we must be patient with each other to let the change take its full course. Impatience is a tool of the flesh and a mark of immaturity. An impatient partner is hard to live with. However, an impatient person can change if he/she desires. If we allow Him to, the Lord will work mighty changes in us. Patience is the fruit of the Spirit. The characteristics of patience include:

- tolerance,
- waiting on God, and
- waiting on others.

1. *Tolerance*

We cannot help but come across people whose behavior affects, irritates or disappoints us. Impatience with the shortcomings of others often has its roots in pride because our attitude shows that we consider ourselves better. If we have the proper attitude toward the shortcomings or mistakes of others, we can relax rather than get irritated. To help us tolerate others, we must walk around imagining we have a sign on our back reading:

PLEASE BE PATIENT
I'M UNDER CONSTRUCTION
GOD'S NOT FINISHED WITH ME YET

We must understand that God is working on each of us, to change and conform us to the image of His Son. This should help us to bear with others who are equally under God's construction. It will help us to accept other people just as they are without imposing our way on them. This was what Paul had in mind when he wrote:

Accept him whose faith is weak, without passing judgment on disputable matters.... Who are you to judge someone else's servant? To his own master he stands or falls. And he will stand, for the Lord is able to make him stand (Romans 14:1,4, NIV).

Admonish the idlers, encourage the fainthearted, help the weak, be patient with them all (1 Thessalonians 5:14).

To tolerate people is to accept them the way they are. It is treating them the way God treats us. If God would not tolerate us and accept us just the way we are, He would not call us His people or hear us when we pray. We must learn to act like our Father.

A patient partner is confident of the potential growth of the other. Growth can't be forced. It is nurtured by providing time and a conducive environment for the other to think, feel, do, become, and be. In short, the patient partner gives the other room to live and grow.

2. *Waiting on God*

We need to exercise patience in the outworking of God's schedule for our lives. We are often tempted to speed up God's agenda or substitute an alternative solution as Sarah and Abraham did with Ishmael, only to end up with sorrow instead of joy.

It is a mark of maturity to be able to wait on God after we have prayed several times on a particular request. Immature believers are "microwave Christians" who want instant salvation, instant sanctification, and instant glorification, who want God's blessings right now. They live for the here and now, insisting on their own way in every situation. They do not want to take the time, exercise the patience, or pay the price to go through God's fire for perfecting their lives.

The cure for impatience with the fulfillment of God's timetable is to believe His promises, obey His will, and leave the results to Him.

3. *Waiting on Others*

Most often we want others to do what we want when we want it. But this is an immature attitude. You can't always expect to have your wishes and hopes granted instantly. You may have to just plant the seed of an idea, and then wait. If you insist on an instant reply, you will most likely get a negative one because most people don't like to be backed into a corner.

Love is patient, we are told in 1 Corinthians 13:4. Love can wait on others to grow, change their views or accept our position. People who do not understand the meaning of patience find it difficult to allow others to grow at their own pace. They meet delay with resentment and frustration. Life makes them wait often enough whether they like it or not. It always pays to be patient, especially with your spouse.

Consider the case of Laura and Ben, who had been thinking of buying their own house since they were married four years ago. Laura felt it was high time to start looking for a house of their taste, but Ben flatly said no and gave all sorts of reasons. Laura had the choice of either waiting and remaining calm or arguing and flaring out with Ben. Laura chose to wait until Ben got convinced. It took almost a year before Ben saw the need to buy a house. Not only were they able to save more money toward the purchase, houses became cheaper so that they were able to afford a better home. Laura was happy that she waited and that they hadn't bought the previous year. They were both glad they got a better house. It always pays to be patient. Don't expect too much too soon.

Endurance

There are many things you would like your spouse to be doing right now that he/she is not doing. If you are patient enough and are willing to cooperate, he/she will learn to do some of those things and you will both be happy. However, there are certain things that will not change in your spouse no matter how long you wait. You must learn to endure and bear with him/her. We must be patient with what can be changed and endure and accept what cannot be changed. We must make Reinhold Niebuhr's prayer ours:

O God, give us serenity to accept what cannot be changed, and courage to change what should be changed, and wisdom to distinguish the one from the other.

Accepting your spouse the way he/she is and enduring what cannot be changed in him/her can free you from worry and dissipation.

You need endurance when the going gets tough, when one or both of you are passing through a rough time—financial problems, unemployment, disappointment at your place of work, sickness, etc.

To endure, it is vital that you both know God's will concerning a particular situation; otherwise you will not see any reason for enduring. It is also important that you have faith that God is able to fulfill whatever He has promised to accomplish. Endurance was hard for the Israelites in the wilderness. The golden calf is evidence of how difficult it was for them to endure God's invisibility and intangibility. For sure, God promised to take them to the Promised Land, but the stark reality of the present made the promise seem out of reach. Jesus endured the cross, despising the shame of it, because He knew God's will for the situation (Hebrews 12:2). Paul and Silas were able to endure and praise God even in prison because they knew God's will for their lives (Acts 16:25-34). Remember, quitters don't win and winners don't quit.

As Secret No. 8,

Marriage is a companionship in which each partner helps the other to grow to maturity.

Notes

[1] Charles R. Swindoll, *Growing Deep in the Christian Life* (Portland, OR: Multnomah Press, 1986), p. 151.

[2] Evelyn Christenson, *"Lord, Change Me!"* (Wheaton, IL: Victor Books, 1977), p. 5.

[3] Jerry Bridges, *The Practice of Godliness* (Colorado Springs, CO: Navpress, 1983), pp. 161,162.

[4] Neil Gallagher, *How to Save Money on Almost Everything* (Minneapolis, MN: Bethany Fellowship, 1978), p. 6.

CHAPTER NINE

THE SECRET OF FINANCIAL STEWARDSHIP

For where your treasure is, there will your heart be also
Matthew 6:21

M oney ranks high on every family counselor's list of problem areas in marriage. How we handle money is the best outside reflector of our true inner values. It is a true index of our Christian testimony. The husband and wife whose finances are a fiasco are a poor testimony to the wisdom and guidance of God.

Although money is not everything in life, its significance should not be slighted. To many, money represents power, love, status, and many other things, such as security, opportunities for oneself and one's family, and confirmation of one's worth. There are some who will say, "Give me all the money I need, and I will find everything else I want." We all spend most of our time either making money or thinking about how to spend money. We worry with money, and without it. Families are paralyzed with the fear of poverty, while some are destroyed from the stress of having too much money. Most family friction and frustration are caused directly or indirectly by money.

Money is like fuel. It gives you the power to function and do many things in life. Money in some form is necessary for our survival. It is needed to support God's work. But making and spending money is not easy in our competitive world. The lack of knowledge of how to use money wisely has crippled many marriages. There are proper and improper ways of using money. We need to learn what God's Word says on this subject of financial management.

The fundamental position of the Scriptures on money is that of stewardship. We are stewards of all God has entrusted to our care—talent, treasure, and time. By a steward, we mean one who manages *another's* property. God is the owner; each of us is a steward or manager. Since God is the original supplier of all our possessions, we are accountable to Him for the wise use of the resources He gives us. It is not the amount of our resources but our faithfulness that is important in stewardship.

It is [essentially] required of stewards that a man should be found faithful—proving himself worthy of trust (1 Corinthians 4:2, AB).

As stewards, we are responsible to use in the very best manner all that is entrusted to us. Sound planning, buying, saving, investing, and giving are all a part of our stewardship.

Sad to say, only a few Christians have accepted God's financial plan as their own, and they stand out as giants among their brethren. Many Christians withhold this area of their lives from God and consequently struggle with the world's financial system with all its frustrations, worries, and anxieties. Those who have not surrendered to God in the area of finances have not learned the simple lesson that God owns everything. As Paul said:

We brought nothing into the world, and we cannot take anything out of the world (1 Timothy 6:7).

As related in Matthew 25, God will withdraw His resources from the unfaithful stewards and give them to the faithful stewards. In order to be good stewards, we must learn the basic principles God has established for the management of possessions. God will not force His will on us. But once we accept His will in the area of finances, He will entrust more and more to us (Luke 12:48). It is how we manage money that determines how we will manage greater things if entrusted to our care.

In this chapter, we will examine essential ingredients that will help in your financial stewardship as a family. There are basically six principles of financial stewardship that we must apply to achieve God's best in the area of finances:

- giving God and government their parts first,
- laying aside for savings,
- staying out of debt,
- budgeting and keeping records,
- investing wisely, and
- setting goals, plans, and priorities.

Learning these principles for managing money is essential for marital oneness.

Giving God and Government Their Parts First

The Christian attitude toward human government should be positive. As mentioned in Chapter 3, God has established government at home, at church, and in the community for our own good, to maintain peace and orderliness, and to curb human excesses, lawlessness, and rebellion instigated by the enemy. A Christian is therefore urged to submit to authority.

Let every person be subject to the governing authorities. For there is no authority except from God, and those that exist have been instituted by God.... For the same reason you also pay taxes, for the authorities are ministers of God, attending to this very thing. Pay all of them their dues, taxes to whom taxes are due, revenues to whom revenue is due, respect to whom respect is due, honor to whom honor is due (Romans 13:1-7, emphasis mine).

For those of us who work for others, our taxes are usually taken out of our paychecks before we ever get them. We are forced to pay government first whether we like it or not. Christ mentioned that we pay the government:

Render to Caesar the things that are Caesar's, and to God the things that are God's (Mark 12:17).

It is therefore against God's will to evade taxes. This applies to all of us, particularly to those who own their business or work for themselves.

After we have paid our government the taxes, we must pay God our tithes. Every Christian family should establish tithe as the minimum testimony of God's ownership. This is an essential step in financial breathing. Tithe is a spiritual investment. It is basic to financial health and freedom. As Edwin Cole well said:

> *Tithing is necessary, whether you believe it or not, because it is only for those who tithe that God promises to rebuke the devourer. Men cannot outgive God. God will be debtor to no man. Giving to God without His giving more in return would essentially make God a debtor to the giver. That can't be done. Of course, God doesn't always give back the way men do. When you are tithing and obeying Him, God will give health so doctors' bills don't devour your income. He will give you favor in buying a car so that it is not a "lemon" and devour your income on repairs, or keep you constantly in debt—so your debts devour you.*[1]

Of course, we should never limit our giving to a tenth of our income. Beside tithes, we must give our offerings for the Lord's work. While tithes are compulsory, offerings are optional. Our offering is to be proportionate to God's blessing. Our offering is important to the Lord's work. The most important thing on earth is God's work and it must occupy a first priority in our lives. The work of God languishes, missionaries are sent home, and God's servants cannot afford a decent living because Christians are frugal in their giving. An external evidence of a family that is internally committed to God is the willingness to surrender to God a portion of their treasure.

> *Honor the LORD with your substance and with the first fruits of all your produce; then your barns will be filled*

with plenty, and your vats will be bursting with wine
(Proverbs 3:9,10).

One man gives freely, yet grows all the richer; another
withholds what he should give, and only suffers want
(Proverbs 11:24).

Laying Aside for Savings

As mentioned before, God owns everything we have, not just
the amount we give to His work. We are responsible for how
we spend the rest of our income after deducting the taxes,
tithes, and offerings. It is biblical that we lay aside a portion
of our income for savings. Why? There are at least five reasons
why a Christian must learn to save or accumulate wealth.
These reasons parallel why God intends that His people
prosper financially. Savings is the process by which we become
financially independent.

First, it is God's desire that you enjoy His provision. God
created the world and all that is in it—gold, silver, oil,
animals, cars, etc.

The earth is the LORD's and the fulness thereof, the world
and those who dwell therein (Psalm 24:1).

If God created the world, is it meant to be enjoyed by
robbers, prostitutes, drug pushers, etc.? The provision of God
is for the enjoyment of His people. Abraham, Jacob, David,
and Solomon were men of prosperity. Jesus came that we may
have life and have life more abundantly. Part of that abundant
life is meant to be enjoyed here and now. Also, God promised
His people that there would be no poor among them because

He was going to so bless them that they would lend and not borrow (Deuteronomy 15:4-6). Savings is a right step in the direction of enjoying God's provision.

Second, throughout the Scriptures, the wise man is the one who plans ahead to meet the needs of his family, business or other endeavor.

A prudent man foresees the difficulties ahead and prepares for them; the simpleton goes blindly on and suffers the consequences (Proverbs 22:3; 27:12, LB).

Planning ahead financially involves savings and investment. To fail to save a part of one's income is poor planning. The couple who saves a percentage of their income regularly will not only have the reserve funds they need for emergencies, but will also prove to be good stewards to whom God can entrust more.

Third, savings is a way of providing for the children and leaving a valuable inheritance for them. There are those who believe that leaving an abundant inheritance to children and grandchildren can wreck their lives and that those children should be allowed to earn their way. But inheritance is only a trouble for the recipients when they are not trained in the use of money (Ecclesiastes 7:11). Inheritance provides the recipients an edge in this highly competitive world, where it is very difficult to survive if one were to start from scratch. God's Word teaches that godly parents leave an inheritance for their children (Proverbs 13:22; 1 Chronicles 28:8; Ezra 9:12; Psalm 17:14). Savings is a way of providing for your family within reason.

Fourth, a couple who discipline themselves by saving regularly will eventually become rich and can do more for the Lord. We can do greater things for the Lord, embark on greater projects if we have more at our disposal. God has an agenda for this world and that agenda is clearly stated in Matthew 28:18-20. God's agenda is twofold: evangelization of sinners and edification of the saints. God's will is that the whole world be filled with His knowledge (Isaiah 11:9) so that His will can be done on earth as it is done in heaven. God depends totally on His people to carry out His mission. God understands that money plays a major role in the world system: *Money answers everything* (Ecclesiastes 10:19). This is why God promised to provide money for His people (Haggai 2:8) that they may use it to further His mission.

Lastly, God supplies a surplus to a Christian family to be able to provide for the needs of others. It is true that wealth comes with the gift of giving. God promises to bless those who give freely and to curse those who hoard, steal, covet or idolize. Although God intends that His people be rich, many of His people are poor because of:

- ignorance of God's will (Ephesians 5:17; Deuteronomy 15:4,5),
- disobedience to God (Deuteronomy 8:17-19; 11:26-29; 28:1-68),
- laziness (Proverbs 10:4; 26:13-15), and
- lack of goals, plans, and priorities (Proverbs 16:1,3).

One may be regarded poor when one finds it hard to meet one's basic needs. In spite of the fact that poverty is a choice, God is gracious enough to ask the rich to remember the poor

(Deuteronomy 15:7-11). God will provide a ministry for Christians attuned to His plan and purpose for this world. But it is a ministry of sharing, not of selfishness. An appropriate philosophy on giving for a family is:

NO FAMILY IS TOO POOR TO HELP OTHERS.

Almost everyone in America has the potential and opportunity to accumulate a surplus through the discipline of saving.

Having provided five reasons a Christian family should save, we now look into how to save money. It is very difficult to save in a system such as ours where every commercial seems to be saying that you are not okay unless you wear this special brand of clothes, live in this kind of house, drive this kind of car, use this kind of deodorant. The invention of the MAC card makes it harder for one to save. With the money machine at almost every corner, the temptation to withdraw your money is high. It takes discipline to resist this temptation to spend. In order to save, we must follow these disciplinary guidelines:

- learn to conserve,
- avoid indulgences,
- avoid unwise use of credit cards,
- plan and think before buying, and
- shop with sense.

1. *Learn to Conserve*

Saving is essentially conserving part of your income. Learn to conserve part of your income on a regular basis by eliminating expenditures that are not essential. There are many things we can do without. Most of us can reduce our expenditures substantially without reducing our standard of living. Obligate yourselves only for the absolute essentials. The necessities of life are relatively few. They can be met by a portion of your present income. As a wife, learn to make the dollar stretch by finding bargains, cooking economical dishes, eating more at home, learning to sew, and making other necessary efforts as described in Proverbs 31:13-14. As a husband, consider the interest of your wife and children before you make that financial decision. Do you really need that kind of car? As husband and wife, buying at sales will help you get more for your dollar. There are excellent books that will help you stretch your money. Four such books are by Gallagher,[2] Burkett,[3,4] and Quinn.[5] Take time to read one or two of them or books of similar nature as part of your financial stewardship.

2. Avoid Indulgences

In order to be able to save, one must learn to avoid the indulgences of life. One must be able to discern the difference between *needs, wants,* and *desires* in every purchase one makes. Needs are items that are necessary for your very survival and existence. These will include items such as food, clothing, home, car, and medical coverage. Wants are things you need, but you can do without them right now. Desires are items you wish to have or you want, but you cannot have without the cooperation of others. Needs are things you must have right now, while wants and desires can be met later. To illustrate the difference between needs, wants, and desires, suppose Andrew and Mary intend to buy a car. Based on their total income, the need of a car may be met by buying a used

Volkswagen; their want may be satisfied by a Pontiac; and their desire may only be met by buying a brand-new Cadillac. If the couple choose to fulfill their desire, their savings and other things may suffer. If, on the other hand, they decide to meet their need, they will be able to live within their means, and have their want and desire met later in life.

To avoid indulgences in your purchases, it may be helpful to ask yourself the following questions. Do I really need this item? Can I wait till a more convenient time to buy it? Does my lifestyle fit within the price range? Am I buying it for ego and power? Am I willing to trust God to provide so that I don't owe to own it? Will I ever regret buying it? Is this the sign of responsible stewardship? Did I plan to purchase this item before I entered the store? What substitutes are there? Honest answers to these questions will help you think before you buy and also to distinguish between luxuries and necessities. Although God wants us to live comfortably, He does not condone indulgences and lavish living.

> *Take heed, and beware of all covetousness; for a man's life does not consist in the abundance of his possessions* (Luke 12:15).

> *He who loves pleasure will be a poor man; he who loves wine and oil will not be rich* (Proverbs 21:17).

You will never save if you are never willing to sacrifice and deny your impulses.

3. *Avoid Unwise Use of Credit Cards*

Credit has been defined as goods or services received with payment deferred. It is basically possessing now and paying later. The use of credit has become widely accepted and an integral part of the American economy. We are bombarded at every corner with the media screaming, "Buy now and pay later." What you are not told is that if you buy now without cash, you will pay much more later and *you* will be the loser. Credit is a privilege for which you must pay. Interest on charge accounts varies between eighteen and thirty-six percent, but many couples fail to read the small print. Credit is a good servant but a bad master.

The best advice on credit and the use of credit cards is perhaps given by Larry Burkett, the founder and president of Christian Financial Concepts. According to Burkett:

> *Lenders promote the idea that you should establish credit early. Obviously so; that's how they earn their living. But the longer you can go without credit (and credit cards), the less you will depend on it later. Whatever you do, don't use credit for consumable items such as clothes, food, vacations, or repairs. We're the only generation in history to borrow significant amounts of money to buy consumables. Our grandparents didn't borrow the way we do. They lived on what they earned, saved, and then bought. Today, it's buy and pay back on debt. Only sometimes couples buy beyond their ability to repay.*
>
> *Another common myth is that credit cards can be used wisely. Don't be deceived. They can be used less foolishly, but rarely, if ever, wisely. Credit cards are not problems, but they certainly can lead to problems. A credit card, if managed properly, can be useful. But virtually everyone will buy more using a credit card than if they used only cash.*[6]

If you have to use a credit card, limit its use to things you need right away, and keep proper records to ensure that you don't overspend. If you don't overspend, you won't get in debt. If you are not self-disciplined or you are already in debt due to misuse of credit cards, limit the number of credit cards in your possession to one or two or avoid credit completely. Through the use of credit cards, we often limit God's ability to provide for our needs and place ourselves under unnecessary financial bondage. I agree with Larry Burkett's belief that every credit card should read:

DANGER!
USE OF THIS CARD CAN BE INJURIOUS
TO YOUR MARRIAGE

Credit leads to debt and debt has crippled many marriages. It is important that we understand God's attitude toward debt.

The rich rules over the poor, and the borrower is the slave of the lender (Proverbs 22:7).

Owe no one anything, except to love one another (Romans 13:8).

4. Plan and Think Before Buying

To be able to save, you will need to plan and think before buying. Never buy an item on the spur of the moment; you may later regret it. Take time to think about it and evaluate it in light of your needs and the possible indebtedness you may incur. Before any purchase, ask yourself the following questions: Is it a necessity—a need or is it a want or desire?

Does it reflect responsible financial stewardship? Is this the best possible buy I can get with the same amount?

Remember that spending and saving is a family affair. So you will need to analyze your plans and thoughts with your mate and children. Include them in the decision-making process so that you all work together as a team. Also, remember whenever you are buying that you are running a business. If your business loses money, you lose money. As is true of any business, you must plan and think to succeed. This may involve preparing a list of items that you need. It may mean buying your groceries and similar items once or twice a month to reduce your visits to the supermarket and avoid the temptation to buy what you really don't need. It may mean buying certain things in bulk rather than in small quantities.

Planning and thinking before you buy will help you sort out your needs from your wants and desires. It will also help you avoid impulsive, wasteful purchases. It does not require any effort to spend impulsively. It takes discipline to save impulsively.

5. *Shop with Sense*

To be safe and follow your plan as closely as possible, you need to shop with sense. Remind yourself *what* you are shopping for. Otherwise you will end up buying wants instead of needs. Know *when* and *where* to shop. Otherwise you will be sucked into sales that are not sales. When a store advertises sales, they only do so on a few things. Their intention is to lure you in so you will buy other items that are not on sale. Buy ahead of time. Remember *why* you are shopping. It is to buy necessities. Don't buy merchandise out of keeping with your lifestyle.

Staying Out of Debt

The third principle of financial stewardship is to live within the rest of the income and stay out of debt. Debt is a serious issue in a marriage relationship. Financial bondage saps your emotional energy and can cause you pain and sorrow. Being in debt is a serious problem and very damaging to the well-being of your marriage and family. It has a devastating effect on marital happiness and has ruined many marriages.

Debt is simply your inability to meet an obligation you agreed upon. It is easy to get in debt these days; we must find a way to get out of it. When does a family fall into debt? You are in debt when your payments are due and you can't meet them or when the amount owed (liability) exceeds the value (asset) of an item. When you buy something on credit, you are under a contract and not in debt. You are in debt when you fail to meet the terms of the contract. Debt occurs when you let your expenses exceed your earning. If you can't make your payments, you are in debt and should do whatever is necessary to get out of debt as soon as possible.

There are several causes of indebtedness. Uncontrolled use of credit cards always leads to debt. "Keeping up with the Joneses" is a common trap. We want to have what others have without caring whether or not we can afford to have the same things. As Will Rogers said:

Too many people spend money they haven't earned to buy things they don't want, to impress people they don't like.

It is a common problem among couples to live beyond their means and sacrifice basic necessities at the altar of luxuries. Closely related to that is greed. What we see, we want to have. Another cause of indebtedness is lack of family goals, planning, and priorities. To stay out of debt, we must guard against these causes.

First, we must avoid the unwise use of credit cards as mentioned above. It has been found that clothing is the credit card user's favorite purchase, made most often with a credit card offered by a department store. It's easy to buy impulsively. Learn to save impulsively. Refuse to buy anything that will cause your expenses to exceed the funds available.

Second, a Christian life should be free of greed and covetousness. Covetousness is a sin (Exodus 20:17; Luke 12:15). Covetousness and discontentment go hand in hand. Either or both can ruin a marriage. A discontent wife who is not satisfied with the things in her home will soon become dissatisfied with her husband for not being able to provide her with the things she desires. Her marriage is headed for serious trouble and may eventually wind up in divorce. Learn to be content with what you have. Be satisfied with your home, furniture, car, clothes, etc.

There is great gain in godliness with contentment; for we brought nothing into the world, and we cannot take anything out of the world (1 Timothy 6:6,7).

Keep your life free from love of money, and be content with what you have; for he has said, "I will never fail you nor forsake you" (Hebrews 13:5).

Not that I complain of want; for I have learned, in whatever state I am, to be content. I know how to be abased, and I know how to abound; in any and all circumstances I have learned the secret of facing plenty and hunger, abundance and want (Philippians 4:11,12).

Lastly, a family must have a financial goal, a plan to reach that goal, and a prioritization of their needs. This principle of financial stewardship will be fully discussed later. It will suffice to say here that family goals, plans, and priorities help people stay out of debt. A family without goals drifts financially and finds it difficult to understand where their money goes. A definite plan for handling the family money is important to have control over how money is spent and avoid debt.

If you are already in debt as a family, you can get out of it. You must decide to get out of debt because it does not glorify God. The very purpose of your existence is to glorify God and indebtedness nullifies and defeats that purpose. You need to get out of debt by taking the following steps.

The first step is to repent and confess to God that you have been a poor manager of the resources He entrusted in your care. After you have repented, you must make some adjustments in your lifestyle; otherwise your repentance is not genuine. Genuine repentance is always backed up by taking appropriate actions. If you have not been faithful in giving your tithes and offerings, begin to practice giving to God first. You cannot afford to rob God. You cannot sacrifice God's part. Choose a portion of your own expenditures to sacrifice. If you keep on robbing God, your income will never be enough and it will be difficult to get out of debt. If misuse of credit cards is the cause of debt, stop using them altogether.

Commit yourself to buying solely on a cash basis. It is tempting to run to another financial institution to borrow money to pay off the first. This robbing-Peter-to-pay-Paul approach will not get you out of debt; it will only worsen the situation and eventually lead to a crackup.

Second, have a definite, written plan on how you dispense your funds. Have a written plan of all expenditures and their order of priority. You cannot have it all. Prioritizing your expenditures is crucial because it helps you differentiate between your needs, wants, and desires.

Third, inform your creditors of your problems. Explain why payments may be late and how much you intend to pay on a regular basis. If possible, send a check with your letter of explanation. If you delay getting in touch with your creditors until payments are overdue, they are likely to resent any arrangements you suggest. It is better to call creditors before they call you.

Fourth, practice saving by applying the principles for saving discussed above. Use the savings to pay your debt.

Finally, you may need financial counseling. Seek the counsel of a Christian financial advisor. You can find one by asking your pastor or checking your phone directory.

Budgeting and Keeping Records

The principle of budgeting and keeping records is crucial to financial stewardship. Many people are in debt because of failure to apply this principle in handling their finances. A family who fails to live on a budget and maintain a good record of their income and expenditures is not managing their money efficiently. Most of us look at budgeting as a "necessary evil" because we do not want to be restricted in the use of our money. However, a budget should not limit but free us to get the best for our money. Some think they are operating on faith by not living by a budget. This is nothing but operating on presumption. Sloppy, haphazard handling of our finances will lead to much marital disharmony, which does not glorify God.

To apply the principle of budgeting and keeping records to your marriage, you must understand:

- the purpose of a budget,
- how to develop a budget, and
- how to keep records of your expenditures.

1. *The Purpose of a Budget*

A budget is essentially a flexible, workable plan for spending money to the greatest benefit of the persons involved. Notice the words *flexible* and *workable*. A budget must be flexible, otherwise it becomes a master rather than a servant. It should not restrict your spending, it should define it. It must be workable, otherwise it does not meet the family's needs or help them get the most for their money. A budget serves at least four purposes in a family's financial stewardship.

First, a well-planned budget helps the family get the most for their finances. It allows the family to invest in those things they value most. Without a budget, a family may get frustrated as their money is "leaking" away and they have no idea where it has gone.

Second, a budget provides a family with a realistic view of their income and expenditures. A budget helps control your spending in that it helps you decide whether or not you can afford a purchase. It can help you trust God and free your mind of financial anxieties. It can also help a family to stay out of debt.

Third, the process of developing a budget provides an opportunity for every member of the family to communicate and contribute to their financial goals and plans. It builds self-esteem in every family member. It allows them to discuss together their lifestyle, needs, and desires. The budget is essentially a statement of their values.

Lastly, a budget promotes oneness and reduces tension between a couple because it provides a financial plan accept-able to both of them. The budget allows them to work together as a team toward a common goal. The budget becomes a cooperative plan for the husband and wife rather than a weapon to attack the spending habits of each other. When a couple realizes the limits of their ability to spend, it will bring peace and reduce conflicts.

2. *How to Develop a Budget*

It is not possible to come up with a budget plan that will suit every family. Your family is unique and has special needs. What is presented here should only be regarded as a guideline. Your family budget should give expression to your present and future aspirations. It is a division of your income, a prioritiza-tion of your needs, and a means of controlling your expendi-tures.

It has been said earlier in this chapter that saving a portion of your income is an important principle of financial steward-ship. To achieve this, a family must keep two budgets: One is a twelve-month plan, the other is a one-month plan. At the beginning of each year the family should develop their annual budget based on their goals for that year. For example, consider James and Jane who are newly married. They plan to buy their home five years down the line. Part of their financial goal this year is to save $6,000. They intend to save $500 each month, at least on the average. At the end of the year, they want to put $4,000 in a fixed deposit for their down payment, they plan to spend $400 for Christmas presents, and so on. All of these goals should be reflected in their annual budget. Of course, this budget will vary from year to year.

Budgets are best handled on a monthly basis, although some bills are paid bimonthly, quarterly, or even annually. For these infrequent bills, take the annual total, divide by twelve, and budget for that amount each month. The budget for each month should be done as soon as the income is received and should reflect the annual budget.

To develop a monthly budget is simple. All it takes is allocating a certain percentage of your income to different items. You should first set aside ten percent (as a minimum) of your gross income for tithing to your local church. You can expect the government to take fifteen percent or whatever for income tax. It is recommended that the remaining amount be allocated as in Table 8.1. Of course, the categories and percentages will vary from family to family, depending on the family's age, size, plans, goals, priorities, and preferences.

It may be helpful to comment briefly on each of the categories listed above. Housing takes a major part of almost every family's income. Most family counselors recommend that young couples should avoid making long-term commit-

Table 8.1
A Typical Family Budget

Item	Percentage of Income
Housing	25%
Rent/Mortgage	
Property taxes	
Utilities	
Repairs	
Food	20%
Transportation	15%
Car loan/Transportation fare	
Fuel	
Repairs	
Clothing	5%
Insurance	10%
Life	
Health	
Car	
Entertainment	5%
Recreation	
Vacations	
Conferences/Retreats	
Savings	10%
Miscellaneous	10%
Offering/Donations/Gifts	
Allowance/Job-related expenses	
Education/Training/Child care	
Emergencies, etc.	

ments (buying a house, car, etc.) based on his and her incomes. All monthly expenses should be based on the husband's income alone because something will inevitably happen to interrupt the wife's income. The wife's income should be used for single purchases. A young couple must exercise caution in buying a home. Take time to save, take time to learn as much as you can about buying a home, and take time to shop around for locations and interest rates. Unless they are absolutely certain that they can afford it, a young couple should not venture into getting loans for a brand-new car. A good used car less than three years old beats the per-mile cost of a new car by more than forty percent.[7]

It is recommended that you have a menu plan and do your shopping accordingly. Buy what you need, not what is on sale. Notice that eating out should be part of the entertainment category, not of food.

Buy clothes of quality; they may be more expensive, but they last long.

You should select the insurance plan that fits your family needs, not a salesman's.

A lot has already been said on savings. If your family is in debt, what is in the savings category could be used to pay off your debt.

The miscellaneous category is the one that is easily overlooked by most couples. But this is the part that seems to drain your pocket and you can hardly account for it. An essential part of this category is the allowance or pocket money. Every family member—parents as well as children—must have some allowance or personal money to be spent without accounting for it. An allowance teaches children how to live within their means and relieves adults on a budget of having to account for every single daily expense. For example, as a professor I usually want to buy a lot of books. Although we have some allocation for book purchases in our monthly budget, that can hardly satisfy my interest in books. So I spend a large portion of my allowance to buy books that the budget doesn't cover. My wife, on the other hand, loves eating out and buying clothes. So she spends most of her allowance on those things. This idea of an allowance was introduced to us by Reverend Samuel Leigh[8] during a counseling session prior to our wedding and has greatly helped to reduce tension on financial matters.

In developing your budget as family, you are advised to keep it simple. Nothing prevents you from transferring funds allocated to one item into another category, but at least you know that a sacrifice is being made, and that is what the budget is meant for—to be your servant, not your master. Also, if your children are old enough, you can include them in your budget discussion. They should know what is going on and how it is going to affect them. It will make them feel they are part of the team (and they are) and tend to cooperate.

Finally, as a Christian family, commit the budget to the Lord in prayer after it has been completed. Pray for His help in implementing the budget.

3. *How to Keep Records of Your Expenditures*

While budgeting is the executive, decision-making task, bookkeeping is the secretary-treasurer's task. It is impossible to manage your finances efficiently without keeping good records. Someone should be responsible for writing the checks, balancing the check register, and seeing that the funds are spent according to the budget or an agreed modification of the budget. Although every member of the family should be involved in developing a budget, only one person should do the bookkeeping, to avoid confusion. In over eighty percent of families, the wife is the bookkeeper. This should be expected since women tend to pay more attention to details than men. The couple should decide who is best in keeping records. It may be the husband or the wife. The bookkeeper may be changed later if there is a need. As in other areas, the husband is ultimately responsible for the financial well-being of the family. He should therefore take a "hands-on" approach if a financial problem develops.

Whoever does the bookkeeping should understand or learn the basics of bookkeeping. The person should be committed to keeping it up to date. Prompt payment of bills and good recordkeeping require the cooperation of both husband and wife. It is helpful to have a regular time each week or month to discuss details of income and spending. This also can be a time to renew your goals and plans.

Investing Wisely

The parable of the pounds as taught by Jesus in Luke 19:11-27 is a graphic illustration that God wants us to profit with the resources He has entrusted to our care. The principle of the parable is that hoarding causes loss, while investing brings profit. God has given us three things to invest: time, talent, and treasure. The proper use of these things is to prosper and profit by them. It is true that time wasted is existence; used, it is life. You invest your talent in your profession as a lawyer, accountant, teacher, engineer, doctor, nurse, pastor, etc. In the same way, the treasures or riches God has given you must be invested wisely for you to prosper by them. Where you invest your money shows where your life is invested. Some practical principles for investing wisely include:

- investing for the future,
- investing in producers,
- letting your investment be in writing,
- investing in yourself, and
- investing in God's kingdom.

1. *Investing for the Future*

The Bible teaches that we should have long-term investments. A typical illustration of this is found in Joseph's days in Egypt (Genesis 41). In order to meet the needs of the Egyptians during the expected seven years of famine, Joseph saved for seven years. Our lives and marriages will be better off if we apply Joseph's principle. The future belongs to those who save now and buy later, not to those who buy now and pay later.

A son who gathers in summer is prudent, but a son who sleeps in harvest brings shame (Proverbs 10:5).

A good man leaves an inheritance to his children's children (Proverbs 13:22).

The ants are a people not strong, yet they provide their food in the summer (Proverbs 30:25).

Cast your bread upon the waters, for you will find it after many days (Ecclesiastes 11:1).

These and other verses remind us of the importance of wise investment for the future. We must learn to invest for the future and guard against the unexpected. Your family needs to have the security of financial support in case of your disability or death. Investments such as life insurance and health care are fundamental in terms of wise investment.

2. *Investing in Producers*

When you invest, you really invest in the corporate officers, the people making up the company, not in the company itself. A company is only as good as those officers managing it. So before you invest, investigate the people in the company. Ask for the owner of the company, the president, and those who will run it. Are these people faithful and trustworthy? If you don't know these people, don't invest in the company.

Watch out for risky investments and promises of immediate success and prosperity. Avoid those who promise a get-rich-quick plan, those who promise the "secrets" of making lots of money with no work, no risk, and no education. Beware of anyone who tells you that something is "surefire" or that it "can't miss." This get-rich-quick attitude, an attempt to make money with little effort, only leads to financial disaster. The old axiom "no pain, no gain" is probably as true now as when it was first uttered. Remember Proverbs 28:20:

He who hastens to be rich will not go unpunished.

In his excellent book *Communication, Sex, and Money,* Edwin Cole gave some excellent principles of wise investment. Cole said:

> *The man who does the least talks the most. Doers don't waste time or cover their deeds with conversation.*
> *Invest your time with men who inspire.*
> *Invest your money with men who produce.*
> *Invest your talent with men who create.*
> *"Iron sharpens iron ... " is the biblical principle for surrounding yourself with those whose sharpness of mind and character will sharpen your own.*
> *Don't be fooled by men who talk. Invest in men who produce.*[9]

Although you may seek godly counsel and wisdom from those who love the Lord and are concerned about biblical principles, do not allow others to make your financial decisions for you. Be in the driver's seat when it comes to controlling your destiny. Evaluate every investment decision in the light of your commitment to Christ and your goals. Often speculative schemes can cause you to lose your testimony, your credibility, and your money. So avoid them.

3. *Letting Your Investment Be in Writing*

Never venture into any investment or purchase unless it is in writing and signed. Putting things in writing helps to avoid misunderstanding, the tool of strife. Don't leave room for the devil through misunderstanding. There is a limit to which we can rely on our memory. Poor memory causes misunderstanding and undermines trust in a relationship. Writing down your agreements on paper never diminishes your trust, but allows you to transcend poor memories and misunderstandings and to have a harmonious relationship. God put His covenants, promises, and agreements with us in writing. Learn to do the same.

4. *Investing in Yourself*

The greatest investment you can make is in yourself. You invest in yourself when you develop your skill by going to a college, taking correspondence courses, training, reading, attending seminars or conferences, etc. Each of us is endowed with gifts, talents, and potential, but we act like the one-talented man (Matthew 25:14-30). His sin was doing nothing with what was given him. You must invest in yourself to be able to tap that unused potential, develop those unpolished gifts, and activate those dormant talents. Invest in such a way that you will prosper in your relationships with your spouse, children, friends, church, job, and community.

5. *Investing in God's Kingdom*

We have already mentioned the importance of giving for the Lord's work in terms of tithes and offerings. It must be stressed here, however, that investing in the kingdom of God is an investment in eternity and is the wisest of all investments. Our Lord said:

> *Do not lay up for yourselves treasures on earth, where moth and rust consume and where thieves break in and steal, but lay up for yourselves treasures in heaven, where neither moth nor rust consumes and where thieves do not break in and*

steal. For where your treasure is, there will your heart be also (Matthew 6:19-21).

There are basically three ways to invest in God's kingdom: giving tithes and offerings, investing in the gospel, and helping others, particularly those of the household of faith. Tithes and offerings are meant for the local church, for its support and expansion. Just as with our tithes, our offerings must be in proportion to our income. Rather than comparing our giving with others', we should apply the principle demonstrated in the widow's offering. Dr. Milton Grannum, expressed the principle as follows:

NOT EQUAL GIFTS, BUT EQUAL SACRIFICE.

Investment in the gospel (another form of offering) may go to the local church or to other ministries who propagate the gospel. This may include domestic radio, TV ministries, and foreign missions. In giving to these ministries, again, it is your responsibility as a good steward to find out about the lives of people involved because you are investing in those people. Just because a person calls himself a "minister" does not mean he is working for God or has a godly character. There are some workers who seem to run ahead of God and are involved in many huge projects all in the energy of the flesh. However, there are many works that count for eternity. It is wise that you find out about the organization before you give. Bearing the burdens of others is part of your Christian calling (Galatians 6:3,9,10). No family is so poor that it cannot give and help others.

When you invest in God's kingdom, you share in the rewards with those who are directly involved in the ministry (Matthew 10:41,42; 25:45). As Dr. Frederick Price noted:

> *Even though you may not be one of those set in the church to be a minister, you can be the support of a minister. Then for everything that minister accomplishes in the ministry, you will get credit for if you have been supporting it....*
>
> *If you place your tithe in your local storehouse, give regularly to the support of that ministry, pray for it, and are involved with it in any way, you get credit for every person who responds to the invitation to come to Christ.*[10]

Lastly, when you invest in the kingdom of God, remember what Jesus said:

> *Give, and it will be given to you; good measure, pressed down, shaken together, running over, will be put into your lap. For the measure you give will be the measure you get back* (Luke 6:38).

Two principles are mentioned in this verse. The first one teaches that the more you give, the more you get. You are the one who controls the blessings by what you give out. If you have not been receiving anything, it is probably because you have not been giving anything. God is always faithful in doing His part. The other principle is better rendered in the King James Version: *shall men give into your bosom.* It teaches that the blessings or rewards of your giving will come to you through the hands of men. We should not expect God to drop the blessings out of the sky. God will cause men to bless you.

Setting Goals, Plans, and Priorities

The last principle of financial stewardship is setting goals, plans, and priorities. This principle applied in a family helps the couple use their resources (time, talent, and treasure) wisely. Without goals and priorities, we waste life. In order to maximize opportunities and profit with the resources God invested in us, we must have specific goals. We must make plans and be determined to accomplish the goals.

1. *Setting Goals*

A goal is an aim in life. It is a specific, measurable activity to be done within a certain period of time. Goal setting is important in a family for at least three reasons. First, goal setting helps you determine your top priorities in life and make daily choices accordingly. When you have conflicts of interest, it helps to decide what is most important and to say yes or no to the opportunities as they come along. Second, goal setting provides you feedback and helps you measure your performance. This is particularly significant for those who do not receive evaluation on their performance—fathers and mothers, for example. Goals can help you judge and measure progress when there is no grade for a test, no sales records to show productivity, or no crown at the end of the race. Finally, goals help you discern the difference between what you want to do, what you ought to do, and what you really intend to do.

In a family situation, there are usually several kinds of goals: personal goals, family goals, and financial goals. Also, there may be long-range goals, mid-range goals, and short-range goals. These goals must be communicated to avoid conflict. To avoid selfishness every family member should be considered in making the goals. You cannot achieve your goals and not be selfish about it without the cooperation of the rest of the family. Through communication and commitment, personal goals can be achieved without jeopardizing family or financial goals.

For your goals to be effective, certain principles must be applied. First, your goals must be written down. "The palest ink," they say, "is better than the strongest memory." People who have written goals realize them far more than those who don't. Writing down your goals as a couple will help you avoid misunderstanding and strife. In writing down your goals, think in terms of specific periods of time in which you want to achieve your goals. Second, your goals must be honest, reasonable, and realistic. If you don't intend to follow a particular goal, it is not worth writing down. Lastly, your goals must be measurable. This is where a goal is different from a purpose. A purpose is the direction in which to move, but it is hard to measure. For example, my purpose may be to spend some time with my family after work each day. That purpose becomes a goal if I decide to spend one hour each day after work. A goal must be measurable. It is true that a goal is a dream with a deadline. Avoid operating in generalities. Don't be vague; be specific.

A Christian family must align their goals with God's Word and will for their lives. God's general will for us is that:

- we live for Christ (2 Corinthians 5:9,14,15; Philippians 1:21; Galatians 2:20; 1 John 4:9),

- we profit and bear fruits (John 15:5,8; Luke 19:13; Isaiah 48:17),
- bring glory to God (John 15:8; 17:4; Ephesians 1:12; Job 1:8-10), and
- we do good works (Ephesians 2:10; Titus 2:14; 3:8; Revelation 14:13; Galatians 6:9,10; 2 Corinthians 5:10).

In setting your personal or family goals, you must seek God's specific purpose for your life. Why were you born? What are your gifts and special talents? What would God want you to accomplish in your lifetime? You may not have answers to these questions right now, but you should keep thinking about them until you discover the answers. As you seek to answer the questions, you will discover God's specific purpose for you in life, and a goal, dream or vision will come out of that. The Bible says:

Where there is no vision, the people perish (Proverbs 29:18, KJV).

Without a goal or purpose, life is mere existence.

2. Making Plans

Once you have your goal set, the next step is to plan how to achieve your goal and then take concrete steps in that direction. It's one thing to know where you are going, but it's another thing to know how to get there. Your goals are what you intend to achieve or become. Your plans grow out of your goals. They are what you intend to do to achieve your goals.

Planning is doing things today to make us better tomorrow. Planning is necessary in order for persons in business to be successful, for teachers to be systematic, for pastors to be organized, and for virtually all of us, in every walk of life. Failing to plan is planning to fail in life. The future belongs to those who make hard decisions today. The future belongs to the creative, those who dream and work at their dreams, those who transform their potentiality into actuality.

In making your plans, some vital scriptural principles must be borne in mind. First, you must put God first; otherwise things will be out of order. We must let the interest of His kingdom be a priority over our personal interest (Matthew 6:33). It is what we do for Christ while we are alive that really lasts and counts (Revelation 14:13). Second, commit your plans to God. It is He who can spare your life and enable you to achieve (Proverbs 16:3; James 4:13-15). Allow God to guide you and help you carry out your plan. This means you must be flexible and sensitive to His guidance. Being flexible does not mean compromising your Christian principles. We must be rigid when it comes to holy living. But when it comes to God's guidance we must be flexible. Third, we are to make the most of time (Colossians 4:5; Ecclesiastes 3:1-8). Although we don't want to be time nuts, how we spend our time is vital. Lastly, no plan comes to fruition in an easy way. So you must be determined. You must persevere (Philippians 4:11-13).

3. *Setting Priorities*

It is not enough to have goals and plans; we must have priorities. Our life span is short and we want to achieve many things while still alive. Since we can't have it all, we must set some priorities on the use of our time, talent, and money. Having priorities in life helps you to be focused, to keep your life on target. It helps you to stay balanced. It helps you reject from day to day that great army of possible activities that clamor for your precious, limited energy and time, those activities that would prevent you from doing more important things. If your life is to be fruitful and purposeful, you must learn to say no to this and yes to that.

Time is life. To waste your time is to waste your life. To place priority on how you spend your time is to master your life and make the most of it. Of course, you don't want to become an overorganized person, an overdoer, or a time nut. But you want to be effective in selecting the best task to do from all the possibilities available and then do it the best way. The main secret of getting more done each day is to make a To Do list. Keep it visible and use it as a guide to action as you go through the day. It is not effective to keep To Do list in your head. Why clutter your mind with what can be written down? It is better to write all your To Do items on paper and leave your mind free for creative pursuits. Sometimes, it is hard to achieve all the items on the To Do list. This is where priority comes in. Much time that is not actually wasted is spent on things of secondary importance. We must learn to omit altogether or give very minor attention to things of little importance. A fool has been described as a person who missed the proportion of things.

Pursuit of material success must not be an end in itself and must not be your first priority. Remember that materialistic achievement does not pay beyond the grave, whereas whatever is done for the Lord will pay eternal dividends. We must not allow the good things of life to deprive us of the best God intends for us. God's interests, advancing His kingdom and dominion, must always be our number-one priority. A proper setting of our priorities will surely lead to divine dividends.

I believe that the Bible gives us three broad levels of priority. First, our commitment to God, which involves maintaining a close, personal relationship through daily devotions and prayer. Second, our commitment to our family, which includes husband/wife, children, and extended family. Third, our commitment to other tasks God assigns us involving people, church, neighbors, job, ministry, the world, etc. You will notice that each of these commitments naturally flows out of the one that comes before it. If we fail to set our priorities in this order, we will be out of balance.

As mentioned earlier, you need to be flexible and sensitive to God's leading. From time to time, you may have to redefine your priorities as God leads you to new territories or wants you to reevaluate your life.

4. *Making a Will*

A good plan must include a will. A wise steward of God's resources must prepare a will. Every year a lot of people die without leaving a will. To shrink from making a will is to endanger the comfort and well-being of your loved ones. Whether you own little or much, it is important that you prepare a will as a couple. If you don't have your own will, the state has made one for you.

A will is necessary in order to designate who will raise your children in the event that both parents should die. A couple may think that everyone in the extended family knows what to do if they die, but strange things happen after a death. Death is trauma enough without leaving the survivors legal problems as well. The problem of allowing your family to suffer unnecessary agony in the process of the court handling your estate could be avoided if you prepare a will. When you have a will, it insures that your spouse and children will be cared for as you desire.

A will is a person's written declaration of how his/her property is to be distributed after death. It is the instrument by which you express your intention regarding distribution of your property. A will is a financial-planning device to control who gets what, how much the person gets, and how much is to be held in trust for whom after your death. In order to be valid, it must comply with Statutes of Wills, which vary from state to state. In Pennsylvania, for example, anyone above the age of eighteen can make a will.

To prepare a will is not hard. A will may include the following ingredients: payment of debts, payment of administration expenses, burial expenses, disposition of the body, beneficiaries, and gifts. It must be signed by you, two attesting witnesses, and notarized. You can prepare one yourself or get a lawyer to do it for you. A will is relatively inexpensive. Shop around for lawyers' services.

Rewards of Good Financial Stewardship

God wants us to profit with whatever He has given us. As related in Matthew 25, God will withdraw His resources from poor stewards and give them to good stewards. If you are found a faithful steward in whatever God has entrusted to your care, He will entrust more.

If you follow the principles of financial stewardship explained in this chapter, your bills will be paid on time, your testimony will be protected, your marriage will be happy and successful, and your Savior will be highly honored.

As Secret No. 9,

> The proper use of money is to prosper and profit by its use.

Notes

[1] Edwin L. Cole, *Communication, Sex and Money* (Tulsa, OK: Honor Books, 1987), p. 182.

[2] Neil Gallagher, *How to Save Money on Almost Everything* (Minneapolis, MN: Bethany Fellowship, 1978).

[3] Larry Burkett, *The Complete Financial Guide for Young Couples* (Wheaton, IL: Victor Books, 1989).

[4] Larry Burkett, *Your Finances in Changing Times* (Chicago, IL: Moody Press, 1982).

[5] Jane B. Quinn, *Everyone's Money Book* (New York, NY: Delacorte Press, 1979).

[6] Burkett (1989), pp. 38, 39.

[7] Burkett (1989), p. 78.

[8] Samuel M. Leigh, *Marriage Meant to Be Enjoyed* (Ibadan, Nigeria: Scripture Union Press, 1988), p. 34.

[9] Cole, pp. 208, 209.

[10] Frederick K. C. Price, *High Finance* (Tulsa, OK: Harrison House, 1984), p. 166.

CHAPTER TEN

THE SECRET OF PARENTING

Do not provoke your children to anger, but bring them up in the discipline and instruction of the Lord
Ephesians 6:4

Parenting is one of the most difficult assignments God has given humanity. It is demanding and sometimes frustrating. It is demanding because it requires effort, sacrifice, and time. It is frustrating because by the time we figure out the proper techniques of parenting, our kids are gone.

Being a parent has never been an easy task. And today it is harder than ever. However, we can all improve by learning the basic ingredients essential to good parenting. Nothing in life is free. If we want to be good parents, we must be willing to change. We cannot afford to make the mistake of rearing our kids the way we were reared.

Good parents are needed more than ever. They are usually loving, welcoming, and capable parents. They provide the privilege of a child being born and raised in a home where there is a safe and nurturing environment. The need for good parenting is best illustrated in a study which compared two families and recorded by Charles Swindoll:

The father of Jonathan Edwards was a minister and his mother was the daughter of a clergyman. Among their descendants were fourteen presidents of colleges, more than one hundred college professors, more than one hundred lawyers, thirty judges, sixty physicians, more than a hundred clergymen, missionaries and theology professors, and about sixty authors. There is scarcely any American industry that has not had one of his family among its chief promoters. Such is the product of one American Christian family, reared under the most favorable conditions. The contrast is presented in the Jukes family, which could not be made to study and would not work, and is said to have cost the state of New York a million dollars. Their entire record is one of pauperism and crime, insanity and imbecility. Among their twelve hundred known descendants, three hundred ten were professional paupers, four hundred forty were physically wrecked by their own wickedness, sixty were habitual thieves, one hundred thirty were convicted criminals, fifty-five were victims of impurity, only twenty learned a trade (and ten of these learned it in a state prison), and this notorious family produced seven murderers.[1]

Parenting has so many facets that this chapter can hardly do it justice. On the other hand, there is virtue in simplicity. This chapter therefore focuses on:

- the duties of parents,
- the father's role and the mother's role,
- understanding your children,

- understanding your teenagers, and
- the rewards of good parenting.

The first two sections deal with understanding your responsibilities as a parent. The next two sections address the needs of your children as kids and as teenagers and how to meet those needs.

The Duties of Parents

We often hear that children are gifts from God, but gifts are yours to keep. Children are not. They are really on loan and one day they will leave our roof. Perhaps the gift is the opportunity to play a significant role in the process of "weaving the child into an adult," as Patricia Rushford called it. Rushford said:

> *Someday others, whether you want them to or not, will come to insert threads of immorality, greed, arrogance, and disobedience, just to name a few. We must then weave quickly and with wisdom. We will want to weave in an abundant supply of threads called love, joy, patience, kindness, goodness, faithfulness, gentleness, and self-control. The child's weave should be thick and durable so that when the others come with teachings of immorality, confusion, and wickedness, our child will be able to stand strong and well-disciplined against them.*[2]

We sometimes shift the responsibility of taking care of our children to the school, the church or the society. But certain things are best done by parents. Being a good parent to your children is one job that no one else can ever do as well as you can. Your duties as a parent toward your children are to:

- love them,
- teach them,
- train them,
- provide for them,
- guide them,
- discipline them, and
- pray for them.

1. *Love Them*

The first duty or responsibility of parents is to love their children. Besides the basic physical necessities of life, there is no need more fundamental than the need to be loved. Every person has a longing for love and affection. The home is the best place to show, grow, develop, and exercise love and affection. When love is present, other shortcomings are minimized. When it is absent, everything else seems out of place. When you show and express love to your children, you help them develop in a healthy manner and enable them to sidestep many problems in life. Although a lot has been said about love in Chapter 6, it is emphasized here in relation to expressing it to children. There is a difference between loving your spouse and loving your children. But how do we express love to our children?

First, love involves giving and sharing. God loved the world and He gave His only Son (John 3:16). Giving of yourself and your time, talent, and treasure is what love is all about. Love is demonstrated in the act of giving. Sharing life experiences with your children is another way to express your love.

Second, love must be expressed in words. Let them know that they are loved and special to you. Expressing your love in words is particularly needed when you administer discipline. As you discipline your children, express your affection as well.

Third, love must be expressed in actions. If you tell your children that you love them but your actions, attitudes, and behavior show the opposite, they will not believe you. One way to express love in your actions is to remember special occasions such as their birthdays, graduations, and anniversaries. These are moments to show that they are special to you. The gift of touch is a unique way to express your love. Children need to be touched or cuddled, even as newborns. Another way to communicate love in action is to love your spouse. It is true that the best way a father can love his children is to love their mother. The same can be said of a mother loving her children's father. Let your children see love being practised between you and your spouse. Love is a learned response. The best place for a child to learn love is at home, between his father and mother. Love between parents affects a child's ability to love and receive love. Be a model of love for your children.

Lastly, love involves discipline. Genuine love involves the willingness to incur the child's displeasure in the short run in order to bring about more desirable results in the long run. You correct your child's behavior because in the long run such correction will benefit the child.

2. *Teach Them*

The primary responsibility of teaching children belongs to the parents, not to the church or school. Through Moses, God gave specific instructions to Israel to teach the young generation. The teaching was to be deliberate.

> *These words which I command you this day shall be upon your heart; and you shall teach them diligently to your children, and shall talk of them when you sit in your house, and when you walk by the way, and when you lie down, and when you rise* (Deuteronomy 6:6,7).

This is a strong command. It expresses God's desire that parents embark on a deliberate, conscious, and consistent transfer of godly principles and values to their children. It also expresses the fact that teaching must go on all the time, in all events of life, in order to transform a child into a godly adult.

The importance of teaching our children was expressed by Charles Swindoll when he quoted Dr. Albert Siegel as saying:

> *When it comes to rearing children, every society is only 20 years away from barbarism. Twenty years is all we have to accomplish the task of civilizing the infants who are born into our midst each year. These savages know nothing of our language, our culture, our religion, our values, our customs of interpersonal relations. The infant is totally ignorant about communism, fascism, democracy, civil liberties, the rights of the minority as contrasted with the prerogatives of the majority, respect, decency, honesty, customs, conventions, and manners. The barbarian must be tamed if civilization is to survive.*[3]

But what exactly do we have to teach our children? You can't teach them everything they need to know. Yet the most important teaching—the teaching that shapes the child's personality, values, attitudes to life, and relationship with God—ought to come from parents. If you fail to teach your children these important things, they will pick up something else. Life abhors a vacuum. If you don't sow godly values in them, you are by default sowing wind, and you will reap whirlwind (Hosea 8:7). Things you ought to teach your children include basic things, values and attitudes, and Christian truths.

First, you teach them the basic things, including the language. You must begin teaching your children at an early age. Most of this teaching can be informal. Remember that the child's world is small and that parents are the most important persons in that world. Your influence on your child cannot be overestimated.

Second, you teach them values and attitudes. The real strength of a family is derived from its spiritual and moral values. But values just don't happen; they must be taught to your children. You need to teach them about honesty, integrity, respect for constituted authority, responsibility, love for mankind, self-discipline or self-control, humility, kindness, trustworthiness, truthfulness, modesty, courage, forgiveness, faith, and devotion to God. You need to teach them good work habits and how to have godly attitudes to situations. They need to know not just what these true values mean, but how to apply them in daily living. Sometimes it is pedologically beneficial to teach these values and attitudes in the form of stories, which children always enjoy and tend to remember. Children who learn these values and attitudes early in life enjoy great peace, stability, and prosperity in their adulthood (Isaiah 54:13).

Third, you teach them basic Christian truths. The principles of Christianity are liberating and powerful. The most valuable contribution a parent can make to his child is to instill in him/her a genuine faith in God. Children are inquisitive. They often ask questions about life and death, the nature of God, the location of heaven, etc. After a quick prayer for help, a parent can usually find some simple explanation that satisfies children's curiosity while helping them grow in the knowledge of God. Even small children have the capacity to understand simple explanations of truths about the Trinity and Jesus' birth, death, and resurrection. If you fail in teaching your children the truth, they become easy prey to error, to all kinds of false gods and philosophies.

Furthermore, remember that children learn best by example. You can't teach your children about a way of life that you are not actually living. Your teaching will lose much of its useful impact if your behavior is inconsistent with it. Children see their parents very close up, and are greatly influenced by what they see. If their parents' behavior does not square with the principles the parents teach, they will not take those principles seriously. Your attitudes and values are caught by your children more than your teaching. Do your children see you taking time to study God's Word? Do they see you react terribly when things go wrong? Do they see you submit to the police when you are caught for breaking a traffic law? What do you communicate to them concerning your attitude toward material possessions, toward neighbors, toward people of different color, toward spiritual matters? Be that yourself which you would like your children to be. Remember that each day, you are consciously or unconsciously making deposits and withdrawal in the memory banks of your children. Like Paul, every parent should be able to say to his/her children:

Follow my example, as I follow the example of Christ (1 Corinthians 11:1, NIV).

Finally, planned teaching may be needed in dealing with persistent behavioral problems. Here it is especially important that parents work as a united team. They need to talk together about what each child needs to learn and the best way to teach it.

3. Train Them

Most of the training of children these days is not done by parents, but by schools, television, and peers.

While teaching mainly involves instruction, training involves putting some aspects of the teaching into practice. One may consider teaching as the theory, while training is the practice or application. For example, you may teach your child the importance of prayer and how to pray. But until you train the child to pray, the teaching may not have much impact. Or you may teach your child that it is a good habit to save money. That habit may never be cultivated until the child is trained to save. Of course, not everything we teach requires training.

The scriptural basis for training is found in Solomon's words of wisdom.

Train up a child in the way he should go, and when he is
old he will not depart from it (Proverbs 22:6).

It says that you should train your children in the way they
ought to go, not the way they want to go. We all know how
easy it is to do what is wrong, and how hard to do what is
right. To do what is right is not natural to any child. Ask
your child if he/she wants to go to church, and the answer
may be no. They need to be trained to do the right things.
You can tell the adults who were trained. The man who
comes home and dumps his clothes anywhere he finds, he
expecting his wife to pick them up like his mother used to do,
was not properly trained.

Training must begin early in life. It may be training in
table manners, in picking up shoes and toys, in tying shoes,
brushing teeth, etc. Even little children can learn to help
around the house. Children feel significant when given the
opportunity to work and render useful service. Take the time
to explain why each chore is important, and how to do it
right. Although it takes parents longer time to train a child to
do a chore than to go ahead and do the work themselves,
training makes children feel competent in their work.

Training requires practice. A child who is assigned complex
chores without any training will not do a good job; he/she
may grow up feeling incompetent about any work at all. Take
time to figure out which chores will really be best for each
child—what will challenge them without exceeding their
abilities—and teach them how to do their work. Rather than
explain the job only once, work with each child for the first
few times until the child can do the work alone. The time
you invest in the beginning pays off later. When your child

first sees how something is done properly and knows what your standards are, you are helping him/her avoid failure.

In training children, we must bear in mind that each child is a unique individual. There never has been one just like him/her, and there never will be. Although all parents recognize that their children are different from one another, very few are really aware of how important these differences are. If certain long-range goals and values are to be attained, they will have to be attained along pathways compatible with the child's own unique nature. Each child comes to the world with a unique set of talents and abilities, which parents should help discover, recognize, and develop. So, study each child and decide how best to train the child, enforce rules, motivate, and reward the child in terms of his/her individual needs.

4. *Provide for Them*

God's Word teaches parents to lay up an inheritance for their children. Besides leaving an inheritance, they are to provide for the needs of their children. This may sound like saying the obvious, but we have seen some parents who ignore this responsibility and allow their children to suffer or struggle through life. Some provide little and expect their children to take care of them later in life. God's Word says the exact opposite.

> ... *children ought not to lay up for their parents, but parents for their children. I will most gladly spend and be spent for your souls* (2 Corinthians 12:14,15).

You brought those children here, whether by plan or accident. They are here, and you are responsible for their survival.

Good parents should want their children to have it better than they do; not easier so that it makes them lazy, but better. The best you can do for your children is to provide for their education and training to a level at which they will be financially independent. So provide for their education, whatever it costs. You will be glad you did.

5. *Guide Them*

Children need to be guided when growing up. They enter life with great potential for good and evil. They are naturally bent to selfishness, evil, rebelliousness, and lawlessness (Psalm 51:5; Proverbs 22:15). They can go terribly wrong without proper guidance at home. The best counseling services in the finest school cannot make up for lack of guidance from a good father and mother. Wisdom exercised in guiding your children is one of the best measures of how much you really love and value them.

Your children need threefold guidance—in facts, behavior, and attitudes. Children come to the world without information, attitudes or established ways of behavior. They have to acquire a sane view of life, sex, and people. You guide them in facts when you teach, and they get other facts from school, church, etc. It is guidance in behavior and attitudes that they especially need at home. Children are impulsive and immature. They need parental guidance to function well and feel secure.

To be able to guide your children, you must be willing to talk to them, listen to them, and try to understand them. Especially during adolescence, parents should take the time to listen to their children because they could really be hurting and having problems. This way, many problems could be solved or avoided before it is too late.

Lastly, parents must learn to keep secrets, especially with teenagers. If you go out and tell others a secret your child has shared with you, you are destroying his/her confidence in you.

6. Discipline Them

God holds parents accountable for the discipline of their children. He punished the house of Eli, the priest, for failing to discipline his two sons (1 Samuel 3:13,14). You must back up your love, teaching, and training with discipline.

Human beings, including children, prefer doing things in their own way. If left unchecked and undisciplined, we become restless, selfish, frustrated, and unhappy. Discipline is necessary to keep a child on the right track.

Folly is bound up in the heart of a child, but the rod of discipline drives it far from him. Do not withhold discipline from a child; if you beat him with a rod, he will not die. If you beat him with the rod you will save his life from Sheol (Proverbs 22:15; 23:13,14).

The word *discipline* has many meanings. In its broadest sense it encompasses all the training and formation a child receives. Here we use it in the corrective sense. Discipline has a specific role in teaching a child the consequences of not heeding parental instructions. Thus the goal of discipline is to help the child form acceptable standards of behavior and develop self-discipline. The objective is to make your children feel bad about their wrong behavior but to feel good about themselves. The purpose of discipline is to give wisdom

(Proverbs 29:15; Ephesians 6:4), to avoid shaming the parents (Proverbs 29:15), to keep the child from hell (Proverbs 23:13,14), and to avoid ruining the child's life (Proverbs 19:18).

In the process of disciplining your children, certain principles must be applied. First, discipline must begin early in the life of a child. In Proverbs 22:15, cited above, we are told that *folly is bound up in the heart of a child.* Starting early to shape that foolish will is appropriate and wise. If you wait to discipline the child, it will only get harder.

Discipline your son in his early years while there is hope. If you don't you will ruin his life (Proverbs 19:18, LB).

This verse suggests that there is the possibility of running out of hope. If a child is not disciplined at an early age, there will come a time when it is hopeless to try to discipline him/her. No wonder we have adults who are not useful to their home or community. Such adults end up in prison or on the streets. If you don't spare your child's crying now, *you* will not have to cry later. If disciplined early enough, he/she will give you rest later (Proverbs 29:18).

Second, in disciplining your child, allow for logical and natural consequences for his/her behavior. This is the principle of sowing and reaping, of cause and effect. It is a way to discipline your child effectively without the usual hassle involving parental power and force. In using logical consequences as a way to discipline your child, you must be involved in determining the consequence of misbehavior, but in using logical consequence you let nature do its job. For example, a good logical consequence for studying is no TV until homework is completed or no gift for poor grades. Let your child learn that there are logical consequences for every wrong act. Logical and natural consequences are for everyone, children as well as adults. A typical example of natural consequences is the story of the prodigal son in Luke 15:11-24. The son of a wealthy farmer became a bum as a natural consequence of his behavior. The importance of natural consequences is well expressed by Henry Wadsworth Longfellow:

> *The laws of nature are just but terrible. There is no weak mercy in them.... The fire burns, the water drowns, the air consumes, the earth buries. And perhaps it would be well for our race if the punishment of crimes against the law of man were as inevitable as the punishment of crimes against the laws of nature—were man as unerring in his judgment as nature.*

When we allow nature to run its course, we completely avoid a power struggle and conflict. Don't be afraid to let your children suffer to some degree as a result of making wrong choices. It is not being mean, but being realistic about life.

Third, discipline must be aimed at controlling outside behavior. A spanking is to be reserved for dealing with disobedience, rebellion, and stubbornness. Stubbornness is one of the most dangerous of all human traits. It is the trait you find in every addict and gang member. A child who willfully disobeys a clear command of his/her parents should be spanked. Children need to learn that their parents are in charge. However, your spanking will change only your child's actions. God alone can effect a change in the inner life. You must strive to do your best and trust God to fill in the gaps.

Fourth, you must stay balanced in administering discipline. There should be verbal correction along with physical pain.

The rod and reproof give wisdom, but a child left to himself brings shame to his mother (Proverbs 29:15).

The rod is corporal punishment, while reproof is verbal correction. We must endeavor to maintain balance between reproof and punishment. In spite of its painfulness, discipline is an expression of love. We see this in the way God administers discipline to His own:

For the Lord disciplines him whom he loves, and chastises every son whom he receives. It is for discipline that you have to endure. God is treating you as sons; for what son is there whom his father does not discipline? . . . For the moment all discipline seems painful rather than pleasant; later it yields the peaceful fruit of righteousness to those who have been trained by it (Hebrews 12:6,7,11).

As you apply discipline, express your affection as well.

Fifth, you must be consistent. If there is any principle all experts on child rearing agree on, it is consistency. Some stress the importance of this principle to the point of recommending that if you don't do anything else, be consistent. As Tim LaHaye beautifully put it:

Lack of consistency is even more pronounced when children come along. After years of observation, I have concluded that our church's best young people come from either consecrated Christian homes or nonchristian homes. As a rule, mediocre

Christian homes do not produce consecrated Christian young people. The reason? Inconsistency. Inconsistency is a form of hypocrisy.[4]

When children notice the injustice of arbitrary spanking, for example, they begin to resent their parents' authority. To be consistent is not an easy task. As an aid in being consistent, you must establish some rules—the fewer, the better—and try to keep them. This will force parents to discipline not on the basis of feelings, but according to some established policies. The parents should let their children know in advance what types of misbehavior they will be punished for, and then follow through consistently. A major obstacle in establishing consistent discipline is disagreement between parents. Lack of agreement between parents is easily detected by children. Children will do everything possible to exploit the situation and they may play you against each other. Lack of agreement also creates confusion as to whom a child should obey. If dad spanks Junior for coloring the walls, but mom allows him to get away with it, Junior will be confused. For the sake of consistency, the parents must be able to unite behind one rule for discipline. It is recommended that you always endeavor to back each other up in front of the children. You may later discuss your differences in private. If you can't agree on the rule, neither of you should apply it.

Lastly, you must be reasonable in disciplining your children. Never make the extreme your standard. Don't expect to raise a perfect child; you are not perfect either. Children do make mistakes and forget things as adults do. They stumble and fall. They break things. That's all part of being children. Kids will be kids. Don't expect too much too soon. We must be able to distinguish between childishness and willful defiance. Remember that discipline is not a goal, but a means to an end. In disciplining children, you must not lose your perspective, which is not perfection, but self-control, high self-esteem, sound character, and obedience to God.

7. *Pray for Them*

Much has already been said about prayer in Chapter 2. However, the task of child rearing is so great that we need to mention prayer here. You need to pray for God's wisdom to raise kids, to understand the struggles your children pass through. You need to pray for your children for God's protection and guidance as they go through life. If you don't pray for them, who will?

The Father's Role and the Mother's Role

In the previous section, the collective roles or duties of parents were explained. Here we examine the unique roles fathers and mothers play in rearing their children. In others words, the previous section covers the parents' joint roles, while this section addresses their individual roles.

In child rearing both parents are better than one. Children need the effective role models of their own sex to emulate and their parents are best suited for these. Dual parents are advantageous not only to children but to the parents themselves, as the weakness of one is compensated by the other. Those who bear the burden alone know this too well.

1. *The Mother*

Mothering is an awesome responsibility, but the influence of a mother on a human life is equally awesome. You are the one who give up sleep, food, and other necessities. You get no praise or recognition for many of your behind-the-scenes duties. You are not often decorated for valor in providing services above and beyond the call of duty. Your role is often conceived of as commonplace. This misconception was well expressed by Henry Bowman when he said:

> *If a woman teaches someone else's children, she is accorded professional status; if she teaches her own children, she is "just a mother." If she studies dietetics and has charge of a large kitchen in a restaurant or institution, she has a profession; but if she applies dietetic facts and principles to the feeding of her husband and children, she is just cooking.*

In spite of her outside responsibilities or interests, to love a home, to live in it, to work in it and for it, to care and be sensitive to the needs of her loved ones, and provide comfort for them is her scripturally recommended duty. Service to the household is the gift and genius of motherhood. This is evident in the Bible's eulogy to a mother:

> *She seeks wool and flax, and works with willing hands. She is like the ships of the merchant, she brings her food from afar. She rises while it is yet night and provides food for her household and tasks for her maidens. She considers a field and buys it; with the fruit of her hands she plants a vineyard. She girds her loins with strength and makes her arms strong. She perceives that her merchandise is profitable.*

Her lamp does not go out at night. She puts her hands to the distaff, and her hands hold the spindle. She opens her hands to the poor, and reaches out her hands to the needy. She is not afraid of snow for her household, for all her household are clothed in scarlet. She looks well to the ways of her household, and does not eat the bread of idleness (Proverbs 31:13-21,27).

The role of mothers in developing character is emphasized in the Scriptures. Greater stress is laid on the character of the mothers of men in power in Kings and Chronicles than in any other part of the Bible. This seems to suggest that if we are to influence the world for good we must begin with the mothers. Your godliness, chastity, charity, diligence, effectiveness, and earnestness will have a lasting influence on your children and an ultimate influence on an entire nation.

Patience, instincts, and spiritual sensitivity are attributes all mothers are equipped with. As a mother, don't be afraid to use these maternal gifts in bringing up your children. Those instincts are created in you by God and are often right. Spiritual sensitivity is etched in the character of the mother of Rufus (Romans 16:13).

One thing a child needs is to have a mom who remains a child herself. To be a child involves being able to laugh with the child, play with the child, have fun with the child, and just be in his/her world. This not only builds love and intimacy, it helps you know your child. Of course, you can't have fun without being creative. Thus to be a child means a creative mothering. Although having fun with your children takes time, the memories you are making with them are worth the effort.

Children need a mother who realizes their potential and believes in their ability. This role of faith is best typified by Eunice, Timothy's mother, of whom Paul spoke so glowingly (2 Timothy 1:5).

2. The Father

It has been well said that there are so many fathers who have children, but so few children who have fathers. There is a growing emphasis on the importance of the bond between fathers and children. Children not only need the support a father provides, but his love as well. Men as well as women need to learn to be parents.

The father's unique contribution is his authoritative role. For boys in particular, fathers are indispensable. Growing up to be a man is never easy; it requires a masculine model to emulate. It is not strange that boys sometimes learn to walk like their fathers. It takes men to build men. Like boys, girls need fathers, with their warm love, courage, kindness, and wisdom. Nobody can show her these facets of a good father nearly as well as you can. The way your daughter perceives you, the most important figure in her youthful days, is the way she will perceive other men, particularly her husband. As a father, your children want you to be the chief executive of the household on some matters. Your children want to see in you a wise, mature man who loves them and can talk to them about important issues of life. To them you are the smartest man in the world and they need your guidance.

Providing religious guidance for children is another important responsibility of a father. Shallow thinking often stamps religion as a woman's interest. Such an idea is unworthy of any informed, thinking man. Of course, women have taken the lead when men have shied away from their responsibilities. The noblest men of history have been devotedly religious persons. From the beginning to the end, the Bible depicts fathers as teachers of their children and guardians of the family's spiritual riches. The father was the one who loved his children (Genesis 37:4), but sometimes had to rebuke them (Genesis 34:30). He instructed them (Proverbs 1:8), guided them (Jeremiah 3:4), exhorted and comforted them (1 Thessalonians 2:11), and tried to give them a proper upbringing (Ephesians 6:4). About Abraham, God said:

> *For I know him, that he will command his children and his household after him, and they shall keep the way of the LORD, to do justice and judgment; that the LORD may bring upon Abraham that which he hath spoken of him* (Genesis 18:19, KJV).

Fathers have traditionally been the priests of the home. This does not mean that other family members should not be introduced to the responsibility of leading in spiritual matters but that fathers are in strategic positions to furnish impetus to learning and living religion. To be firm, to discipline without anger, to admonish without making the child feel inferior require both patience and self-discipline. To counsel youngsters in the midst of their growing pains and problems and provide proper guidance takes the ability to listen to them and be with them every moment you are together, consciously and wholeheartedly.

As a leader, a father can perform no nobler service than to serve as a friendly, practical teacher to his children. While he may instruct them directly in many things, a great deal is taught by example. The total impression of a father's influence and personality will have more to do with what the children become than the words of advice he can offer.

Understanding Your Children

It is not enough to understand your roles and responsibilities as a parent. It is equally essential that you know what your children's needs are and how to meet them. The needs of children are somewhat similar to those of adults explained in Chapter 5. What children need most, besides discipline, which has already been discussed, includes:

- significance,
- love,
- acceptance,
- praise,
- security,
- self-esteem, and
- God.

Everything your child does is directed toward meeting these needs. You cannot travel far on the road to your goal as a good parent until you understand these needs.

1. *Significance*

Like you and every other human being, your child needs to feel he/she is of some value and importance. To help your children build a sense of significance, allow them to help around the house, let them speak for themselves whenever necessary, respect their opinions whenever possible, and spend time with them. Children grow when they are trusted and believed in. They work best when you allow them to exercise their rights as people—to communicate to you what they think and feel. They feel significant when they are given responsibilities in the home. They feel they are part of the team and they are.

Because I teach my daughter, Ann, her lessons, whenever she writes or colors on her own, she brings it to me and says, "Daddy, see!" My respose usually runs like this: "Who did this? Mom or you?" and her response is what you can easily guess: "I did it!" After applauding her, I ask her to show it to her mom. What Ann wants is a sense of importance and appreciation. We all desire appreciation and a sense of significance.

2. *Love*

Deep within each child is the desire to be loved and wanted. No cold gifts will ever replace or fulfill this need. A child who is loved knows that he is wanted and accepted. Love to a child means understanding. The parent who takes the time to understand the child early in life will be able to understand the child later in life. Love means affection. A parent, particularly the father, must be willing to give affection when the child wants it. Love listens when it hurts.

It is true that the best way a father can love his child is to love the child's mom. Few things are more threatening to a child than to see his parents, those he knows best, quarrel continually.

3. *Acceptance*

The need of acceptance is in every child. The way a child is accepted in his/her childhood affects his/her self-esteem. A child who does not feel accepted by his/her parents seeks acceptance somewhere else and becomes vulnerable to destructive outside influences. Only as a child feels accepted by his/her parents does he/she feel accepted by others and by God.

Children feel a lack of acceptance when their parents constantly criticize them, compare them with others, expect them to achieve their unfulfilled dreams, and expect too much too soon. To accept children is to respect their feelings, uniqueness, and personalities while letting them know that wrong behavior can't be tolerated.

To build a sense of acceptance in your child, you must first recognize that the child is as unique as his/her own fingerprints. No two children are the same. To treat them the same way is to invite problems. Allow the child to grow and develop in his/her own unique way. Help the child find satisfaction in achievement. Take pride in the child and show off his/her achievements.

Take time to listen to your child. Listening to your children not only tells them they are important, but it also keeps you in touch with what's happening inside them, how their personality and character are being formed and influenced. Dorothy Law Nolte put it beautifully when she said:

If a child lives with criticism, He learns to condemn.
If a child lives with hostility, He learns to fight.
If a child lives with ridicule, He learns to be shy.

If a child lives with shame, He learns to feel guilty.
If a child lives with tolerance, He learns to be patient.
If a child lives with encouragement, He learns confidence.
If a child lives with praise, He learns to appreciate.
If a child lives with fairness, He learns justice.
If a child lives with security, He learns to have faith.
If a child lives with approval, He learns to like himself.
If a child lives with acceptance and friendship, He learns
    to find love in the world.[5]

4. Praise

Probably nothing encourages a child to seek accomplishments more than sincere praise and honest compliments. When children are told that they have done well, they want to perform better. A child who lives with praise learns to appreciate. When a child does not receive normal praise and appreciation, he/she turns somewhere else to get it, sometimes in hurtful ways. Look for something worthy of praise in your child and learn to praise him/her for that. Give praise for chores well done, for thoughtful acts towards others, for academic performance, for dependability and honesty, for things that can build significance and self-worth, for trying even when success does not follow. Praise should be used to reinforce positive, constructive behavior. As a parent, always look for opportunities to offer genuine, well-deserved praise to your children.

Praise must be a sincere, positive evaluation of a child or an act. Insincere praise is flattery. In the long run, flattery will do your child more harm than good. Sincere praise builds confidence, increases security, stimulates initiative, motivates learning, generates good will, and improves human relations.

5. Security

Children need security. They want to be certain and safe. A child first experiences a sense of security in a strange, new world through the parents' loving care. In order to enjoy security, a child needs some rules for life. Children need to know where the real boundaries are for their lives. Discipline, which we have already discussed, shows that dad and mom care. A child feels secure when there is closeness and unity between the parents, when the child feels a sense of belonging and senses love, trust, and loyalty.

There is no such thing as giving your child too much security, just as you cannot give too much health. A sense of security is a sure sign of emotional health. Security must not be confused with protection. Overprotection makes children feel afraid and uncertain, while security nourishes and strengthens the ego. The child who has inner security can handle life's frustrations and disappointments. A sense of security with his/her parents will largely determine a child's feelings and attitudes toward other people as the child grows up. A secure childhood is the basis of an efficient, satisfying, and happy life.

6. Self-Esteem

All our behavior is guided by our self-esteem or self-image, and children are no exception. The quest for self-worth remains of primary importance for human beings throughout their lives. The problem is that our self-image is built during childhood and resists great changes later in life. A child's feelings about himself or herself, and his/her self-image, will largely determine his/her happiness in life. Your child's life adjustment can be understood in terms of self-esteem. A child who learns to accept himself or herself and his/her abilities, can handle life effectively. If, on the other hand, the child develops a negative self-image, he/she may struggle through life with feelings of inadequacy, inferiority, depression, guilt or anger.

Help! I'm a Parent by Dr. Bruce Narramore[6] with its manual[7] is probably the best book on parenting and I highly recommend it to all parents. In this excellent book, Dr. Narramore discussed three main concepts of self-esteem we must work at to help our children develop proper self-esteem. They are a sense of belonging, a sense of worth, and a sense of confidence.

A child needs a sense of belonging. Self-esteem in a child's eyes is essential to personal survival. In many ways building self-esteem is a family affair. A child develops high self-esteem in a home characterized by democracy and openness, where children are permitted to talk at the dinner table, where boundaries are clearly established, and where children can have fun with their parents. Children with high self-esteem are more loved and appreciated at home than those with low self-esteem.

Every child needs to feel important, needs to feel wanted and cared for. If you give your child the impression that he/she is bad and worthless, he/she will always behave that way. Call a child a rascal and he/she will act like one. You build a sense of worth in your child through discipline and showing respect. We should value children as Jesus did (Matthew 19:14). An undisciplined child becomes self-willed and selfish, useless to himself or herself, to others, and to God. Eli's sons became worthless because of lack of discipline (1 Samuel 3:13).

A child is naturally immature and impulsive, needing parental help to feel secure and confident. You build confidence in your child by promoting individuality and uniqueness, by giving some responsibilities, and by using praise when necessary. In teaching your child responsibility, you must tolerate certain risks. A child will never learn to wash dishes if you are always afraid the child is going to break one of your precious cups. A child stifled through criticism, guilt motivation, unrealistic regulations, and overprotection is programmed for failure and frustration in life. When a child is encouraged, guided, and supported, he/she develops healthy attitudes that last for a lifetime.

Self-esteem is never a permanently established emotional state because each life stage introduces new issues and challanges. A person's self-worth requires constant attention for its formation, development, and maintenance. A supportive, understanding, and loving family can help build and maintain a sound self-image.

7. God

Adults sometimes overlook the spiritual needs of children. We tend to think that religious matters are only for mature minds. This is probably why the disciples rebuked kids who were brought to Jesus (Matthew 19:13,14). Children do need God; otherwise God would not have commanded the Israelites to teach their children godly principles (Deuteronomy 6:6-8). Children have a capacity to understand God, love, mercy, forgiveness, and other spiritual concepts. God has purposely created the family to teach children His nature by using concepts in the physical world to teach truths in the spiritual realm. It is not God's primary aim that the church, the school, or a similar institution train your children in godliness, and you dare not blame such institutions if things go wrong with your children.

A child's concept of God is largely influenced by the relationship with his/her parents. If the parents are loving and kind, children think of God that way. If your influence is to count, you must be everything you expect your child to be. You can't afford to say one thing and do the other. A bad example through inconsistent living is like bringing food to your child with one hand and poison in the other. You must not only show the way, you must go the way.

Understanding Your Teenagers

In the last section, we discussed the needs of your children and how you can meet them as a parent. Although teenagers still have those needs, they have some peculiar problems as well. These peculiar problems deserve our attention in this section.

Your little child of yesterday has grown up and is no longer the same. Your child has entered a world that is almost adult and has left childhood behind. Within, he/she feels new urges, mysterious and beyond his/her own understanding, while on the outside new appeals and stimuli surge upon him/her. Your child now sees things differently. He/she has become an adolescent!

Adolescence (ages twelve to eighteen) brings out many characteristics. Each month witnesses some new attitude, mode of speech or pattern of behavior. One of the signs of adolescence is rapid growth. Pronounced internal and external changes take place. There are changes in weight, height, and appearance, attended by a number of problems. The adolescent awakening brings about an increased consciousness of the opposite sex and interest in sex itself. The romantic tendency asserts itself. The power to think and reason reaches its peak. Bodily coordination and skill come to their best. New social and spiritual qualities come to the fore.

Do parents see and feel the gravity of the problems their teenagers are passing through? Some do, and are doing everything they know to help. Unfortunately, some parents are aware of little more than physical growth or they ignore the difficulties as though they are of little consequence. Most parents are not prepared to handle their teenagers. They often forget that things have changed since they were adolescents twenty or more years ago. With active, concerned, informed parental cooperation and a home environment to match the need, most of these adolescent problems can be handled without too much strain and pain.

To help your teenagers at this point in their life, you must understand what they are going through. Here are some of the problems your teenagers are facing:

- peer pressure,
- outside influences,
- sex,

- a search for reality and identity,
- the availability of many options,
- double standards, and
- economic and societal pressures.

1. *Peer Pressure*

One major problem teenagers face is acceptance. They want to be secure and accepted by others, especially peers. Self-esteem is rooted in the opinions of peers. They either conform or stand alone. Nobody likes to be a loner. As social beings, we all need acceptance and affirmation. To stand against the peer pressure and rejection is not an easy task. Peer pressure has certain consequences.

First, peer pressure is the greatest reason why sex is so popular among teenagers. If a boy has sex, he feels he has conquered. Boys use different phrases to lure other teens into premarital sex:

"Everyone is doing it,"
"You would do it if your really loved me,"
"Since we are going to marry anyway, we just might as well do it now,"
"Sex is no big deal,"
"You don't know what you're missing,"
"Don't be a baby about it,"
"You don't buy a car without testing it, I've got to check her out."

They use these and similar phrases to justify sex and feel comfortable about it. They feel that they love the girls, while in reality they are lusting after them. A girl's situation is different from a boy's. Friends tease and pressure her to the point of humiliating her for not having sex. She is called different names if she insists on being a virgin. She thinks that by saying no to her boyfriend she will lose him. She feels she owes it to him because he paid for the date. If she yields to the pressure, she is considered a slut. If she does not, they call her a prude. Either way, she loses.

Second, teenagers succumb to peer pressure because of fear of rejection or fear of losing by not giving in. They don't want to be labeled "inexperienced" or considered a freak. They don't want others to think they are weird. A boy may have to lie about his experiences just to avoid rejection by his peers. A girl may have to lie even if she is a virgin.

Parents can help to develop value systems against peer pressure. The parents' view of life will play a vital role in the values their teens develop. They can help by building self-esteem and worth. They can help by developing a sense of uniqueness in their teens. When a teen finds encouragement at home and church, he/she can stand the pressure of peers.

2. *Outside Influences*

Outside influences play a major role to weaken a teen's moral stand. Teenagers find it hard to combat the influence of media, contemporary music, cigarette ads, drug pushers, soap operas, dirty jokes, pornography, baneful pictures, sex education, and a host of others. These powerful persuaders are used by the enemy to wage war against their souls. Teenagers pick up wrong attitudes and taste from what they watch, see or read.

One major impact of outside influences on teenagers is in the realm of violence. Recent research shows that the amount and types of violence depicted on television and in movies, books and magazines keep increasing. Violence on TV teaches teenagers that violence is an acceptable way of life. Violence is learned behavior and the media significantly change attitudes toward violent acts. Each program on TV is carefully planned by specialists with the sole purpose of capturing the viewer's attention. Although television can be used for good, it seems that the negative influences on teenagers is alarming.

The second impact of outside influences on teenagers is sinful acts, especially sexual immorality. You can hardly watch a program on TV or read a non-religious magazine without a promotion of sexual activity. It seems the more sexually appealing an ad is, the more dollars it makes. It is not exaggerating to say that those who promote sexual activities through the media are themselves fornicators and adulterers. They brag about their sinful living. They make fun of things pure and good. They despise God's Word.

The third damaging effect of outside influences is the use of alcohol and drugs. Alcohol and drugs influence people in several harmful ways. They sometimes lead to illegal and criminal behavior.

Lastly, outside influences cause teenagers to think less of themselves. Consider pornography, for example. As the reader looks at the sordid material, he identifies with one of the people on the page. Pornographic material causes the reader to degrade other people, including his/her mother.

Christian parents should not keep quiet about the damaging effects of outside influences on the souls of their teenagers.

We must make our stand known from time to time about X-rated movies, the publishing of pornographic magazines, books, pictures, etc.

To help your teenagers combat the outside influences, you must take certain measures. First, you must regulate the use of TV in your home. You must learn to control it rather than becoming a TV slave or addict. Have a policy on the extent your teenagers should watch TV. Second, flood your home with Christian music. Music can be used for good or evil. The right use of music can inspire your teenagers to great heights.

3. Sex

Sex education is now being taught in many schools. Although the information given out clears up misunderstanding students have, experimentation is (perhaps unintentionally) encouraged. What teenagers are not told is how to abstain from sex. Sex education without moral standards is dangerous. Teenagers, out of curiosity, seek innocent ways to check it out. They talk to friends, read pornography, watch movies. Their minds become so filled and poisoned with these things that they just want to do it. After experiencing such a "great" thing, they question why they have been told that it is wrong. And once a sexual relationship starts, it becomes a habit very hard to break.

The ideal situation is for sex knowledge to be taught at home. The parents are in the best position to discuss not only the biological aspects of sex, but the moral and spiritual aspects as well. But in many Christian homes, talk about sex is frowned upon. The best some parents do is to invent weird answers to probing questions asked by their curious children.

When parents turn away from the issue of sex, it makes the teens all the more curious. Even churches spend less time teaching youths that having premarital sex is sin. Some go to the extreme of presenting it as an unnatural act.

Children have only two ways of getting information to satisfy their curiosity—asking questions and exploring. Here is the parents' opportunity. Time is well invested when parents listen to their children's questions and answer biblically. Teenagers have not traveled this road before, but mom and dad have. Teenagers need to hear from their parents and the church that sex is sacred and should be practiced within the confines of marriage. They need to be taught how to use the Word of God to fight and resist the temptation to sin. They need to be informed on the consequences of disobedience in this dimension of their life. Sex education should be taught at an early age; otherwise it may be too late. Parents should initiate small talks on a regular basis about sex as early as fourth or fifth grade or even earlier depending on the child. Some children learn everything about sex as early as the third grade.

Parents should educate their children about the drives of the opposite sex. Girls need to learn that men are aroused sexually by sight. Parents, particularly dad, should make sure that their daughter does not leave home with clothes that would arouse boys. Boys should be taught the significance of touching a woman. Parents should explain the physical and emotional differences between men and women as presented in Chapter 5. A lot of times, girls are not aware of what they are doing to a guy by hugging him, sitting in his lap, moving around with him, or just being nice. Teens must be taught to be careful, to shun immorality, and avoid all appearances of evil. If a boy commits himself never to allow himself to be in a dark spot with a girl alone, he will never have to fight the temptation to have sex with her. Teenagers must be taught self-discipline as a Christian virtue. A person who lacks self-control before marriage will not have it after wedlock. Self-control is a sure prevention for sexual infatuation, the lust of the flesh. Finally, teenagers must be taught the power of choice. They must exercise the will power to say no to temptation.

Parents cannot deliver what they don't have. Therefore, parents must read current books to know what their teenagers are going through and how they can help. In the field of sex education, the market is saturated with well-written books that provide excellent help for parents. Must reading for all parents is *What I Wish My Parents Knew About My Sexuality* by Josh McDowell.[8]

4. A Search for Reality and Identity

Children generally have the impression that their parents know everything. As they grow up, they discover how limited their parents' knowledge is. In search for reality and identity, they ask questions their parents can't answer. Especially in the fields of sex and religion, parents hesitate to give information.

The average teenager is confused and disillusioned. Many teens believe that parents are inconsistent, that ministers are hypocrites, that friends are dishonest. Whom can they trust? They are searching for reality. A large percentage of today's teens come from broken homes. They need someone to guide them and give them rules, boundaries, and restrictions. They want someone who can listen and give advice. When they can't find someone from their home, they go out to find one. Consider, for example, a girl whose needs are not met at home. She finds the "perfect guy," but he too is having the same problems and is searching for identity and security. They both mistake lust for love.

Teenagers wish their parents understood what it is like to be a teenager nowadays. Through proper preparation, parents can provide suitable guidance and forestall the effects of the misrepresentations that reach youngsters from both the inner and outside worlds. They can help them develop a whole-some, positive outlook.

5. *The Availability of Many Options*

Today, children have many options and it is common to choose an easy way out of any problem they face. They see no reason to wait or endure. For example, if a teenager decides to have sex, he/she has many options: birth control pills, condoms, abortion, adoption, and many more. If these options were not available, many teens would think twice before messing around with sex.

6. *Double Standards*

Parents and society sometimes advocate double standards. When a guy loses his virginity, he is considered a winner, but if a girls loses hers before wedlock, she should be ashamed. Society condones it when a boy is involved in premarital sex since he must have experience anyway. But when a girl messes up, we frown on it.

Parents unintentionally teach their girls a double standard when it comes to choosing someone to marry. When you teach your girl not to marry someone just because he is from a poor family, she may get the impression that she should move with boys who can spend money on her. Expressing love through spending and sex often go together. Your teen can't have one without the other.

Another area where parents give a double message is in the realm of maturity. They tell their kids to grow, meaning that they should behave like adults in some ways but not in others. On the one hand, teenagers hear from the media that sex is part of maturity, being a man or a liberated woman. On the other hand, they are told at home not to be sexually active. They get mixed signals. Parents must help confused teens find balance being a teenager in an adult world.

7. *Economic and Societal Pressures*

In this economy, marriage cannot be afforded until a person is in his/her twenties, whereas sexual sensation begins as early as the age of twelve. If premarital sex is to be avoided, one has to wait for more than ten years.

Society has given teenagers, especially girls, the impression that if you don't marry at a particular age, you will never get a man to marry. Parents too often push their teenagers into early dating and weddings. They care so much about the wedding, a moment in their child's life, and care less about the marriage, which is a long-term process. Due to these pressures from society and parents, a girl compromises her moral standards by giving in to premarital sex with the hope of finding a permanent partner in a world where people and things are changing so fast. She does not understand that if she can't keep him now, she wouldn't be able to keep him after she has given in.

Parents should not press their teenagers into mingling. Give your teenagers enough time to develop interests so as to prefer baseball to parties, reading to dancing, fishing to dating, college or career to marrying early. Remember, your duty is to guide and train them the way *they* should go, not the way you want them to go.

Parents can help alleviate the economic pressure in two ways. One way is to save and provide for their children's education so that the children don't have to work to go to school. Through parents' financial support, the children can finish college on time and settle down as married adults. Alternatively, the parents may provide the initial finance for their children to establish a home.

Although parents need to read the best that has been written on parenting from year to year, no amount of reading will take the place of association with their teenagers. They must be involved. If parents are aware of these and other problems their teenagers pass through and are doing all they can to assist them, their teenagers will be better able to cope and not suffer.

Another way parents can help is by allowing their teenagers to be committed to a local church. Of course, the parents too must be committed. Such a religious commitment helps teenagers identify with a group of youths with similar religious beliefs. It helps them discover God's plans and purposes for their lives.

Nothing is more important than establishing your teenagers in fundamental Christian truth. Proper training and rooting in scriptural principles during their formative childhood will help a lot as they grow. This is why Proverbs 22:6 says:

Train up a child in the way he should go, and when he is old he will not depart from it.

The first part of this verse refers to the necessity of training when they are young, while the latter part guarantees their adherence to the training at adolescence or beyond. In a sense the verse summarizes your whole duty as a parent. Finally, remember:

Unless the LORD builds the house, those who build it labor in vain (Psalm 127:1).

A wise man will build his house on a solid foundation (Matthew 7:24-27).

The Rewards of Good Parenting

Being a parent is an awesome task with many ups and downs. But it is one of the most rewarding assignments God has given us. By doing the best we can, our children are better prepared to meet the challenges of the adult world. Good parenting is beneficial to the family, to the society at large, and to God. It pays immediate benefits in increased family harmony. It will bring blessing upon your children and pay them the long-term reward of a happy, fruitful, and fulfilling life. It will pay the lasting dividend of influencing society in a positive way and of an eternal relationship with God.

Children who are raised by good parents are not only useful to themselves, they will be a blessing to society and an honor to God. They have inner peace and fulfillment in life (Isaiah 54:13).

You carry the key to your children's future. Therefore, as Secret Number 10,

> *Train up a child in the way he should go, and when he is old he will not depart from it* (Proverbs 22:6).

Notes

[1] Charles Swindoll, *Growing Wise in Family Life* (Portland, OR: Multnomah Press, 1988), pp. 103, 104.

[2] Patricia H. Rushford, *What Kids Need Most in a Mom* (Old Tappan, NJ: Fleming H. Revell, 1986), p. 81.

[3] Swindoll, p. 102.

[4] Tim LaHaye, *How to Be Happy Though Married* (Wheaton, IL: Living Books, 1968), p. 44.

[5] John M. Drescher, *Seven Things Children Need* (Scottdale, PA: Herald Press, 1976), p. 55.

[6] Bruce Narramore, *Help! I'm a Parent* (Grand Rapids, MI: Zondervan, 1972).

[7] Bruce Narramore, *A Guide to Child Rearing* (Grand Rapids, MI: Zondervan, 1972). A manual to accompany *Help! I'm a Parent.*

[8] Josh McDowell, *"What I Wish My Parents Knew About My Sexuality"* (San Bernardino, CA: Here's Life Publishers, 1987).

CONCLUSION

*If you know these things, blessed and happy and to be envied are you
if you practice them—if you act accordingly and really do them
John 13:17, AB*

We have covered an enormous amount of territory in this book. It may be helpful to summarize what we have discovered. As a professor, students often come to my office to ask, "How do you summarize your book?" My response is, "How much time do you have to listen? One minute, one second?" If you have one minute to listen, here is a list of the "secrets of successful marriages."

1. Unless the LORD builds the house, those who build it labor in vain.
2. Pray with and for your family.
3. Keep your heart with all vigilance, for from it flow the springs of life.
4. The happiest couples are those who talk the most with each other.
5. Understand your spouse's basic needs and be willing to meet them.
6. Above all, love each other deeply, because love covers a multitude of sins.

7. Commitment to your family builds lasting memories and relationships with your spouse and children, the people you are most responsible for.
8. Marriage is a companionship in which each partner helps each other to grow to maturity.
9. The proper use of money is to prosper and profit by its use.
10. Train up a child in the way he should go, and when he is old he will not depart from it.

If you have only one second to listen to the summary of the key thoughts in this book, the three C's of a happy, successful marriage are what you need: Christ, Communication, and Commitment.

Christ is the key to a successful marriage. The chances of making your marriage work apart from Him are very slim. The issue is not an intellectual knowledge of Christianity, but a personal relationship with Him. If you have never committed your life to Christ and received Him into your life as personal Savior, why not do it now? Give your marriage a chance to succeed. Receive Christ as your personal Savior today!

Communication is vital for a marriage to be successful. Good communication just doesn't happen. You make it happen. You spend time with your spouse in conversation. Talk a lot about small, trivial topics as well as the profound, deep issues of life.

Commitment means the family comes first (besides your personal relationship with God). It means a cherished obligation of both partners to make the marriage and the family operate the way it should. Both partners are willing to change and support each other. To them divorce is not a option.

If you need some additional information on marriage and family or you have some problems in your marriage that are not discussed in this book, you have three options. First, you may need to learn more. Being a husband or wife or parent is a long-term educational experience. We can improve in few months or weeks if we are willing to invest the time and effort it takes to learn. The books listed under Notes at the end of each chapter can be helpful for further development of your marital relationship. Second, you may seek professional guidance of your pastor, a marriage counselor, or a psychologist. There is no reason why a person cannot seek professional help. You should take advantage of these available resources. Third, you may seek help from well-established organizations. Two such organizations are:

The Association for Couples in Marriage Enrichment (ACME)
502 North Broad Street
P. O. Box 10596
Winston-Salem, NC 27108
(919) 724-1526, 800-634-8325

International Marriage Encounter (IME)
955 Lake Drive
St. Paul, MN 55120
(612) 454-6434

These organizations help build strong marriages and have chapters all across the country. You may contact them to find the chapters in your area. (The Roman Catholic Churches use IME.) New organizations are developing all the time. For helping organizations in your community, call your local church or local law-enforcement department. Seeking help for family problems can be a strengthening and enriching experience for the partners and for the family. Those who seek help early are the ones who usually find a rich life together.

A successful marriage consists of real people living in the same world as everyone else, so they have difficulties and hard times. Problems, quarrels, and conflicts, however, don't destroy their commitment to each other.

The responsibility for a happy, successful marriage rests initially with the husband. He makes the first move by loving his wife with the total, unselfish, agape love of Jesus Christ. He gets from his wife whatever he invests in her. The rewards, however, for accepting the responsibility God has given us as men are tremendous. The rewards of a joyful heart, a good marriage, a peaceful home, a fulfilled wife, and happy children are worth more than all the money you will ever earn in your life.

The goal of a marriage is not love, communication or maturity, but intimate friendship between each spouse and God and the husband and wife. It is a state you grow into with time and effort. Friendship is the highest level of any human relationship—between a man and his brother or fellow man, between a man and woman. Friendship is the highest level of relationship between a man and God. This becomes evident as we examine the four levels of relationship people had with Jesus Christ: follower (Matthew 4:19; 8:19; 9:9; 19:21), disciple (Luke 11:1; 14:33), servant (John 12:26;

15:15), and friend (John 15:15). Only few believers enter friendship with God in their lifetime. To be a friend of someone is to be able to see things the way he sees things. It is to be the person's associate, someone he can trust and confide in. Such friendship leads to oneness in mind and purpose. The partners become like each other, taking on the other's qualities. No wonder the Bible says, "The two shall become one."

It is your choice to have a happy, successful marriage. To act on what it takes to have a happy, successful marriage involves a decision. Our destiny is determined by our choice, not by chance. If you choose to work hard on your marriage, your spouse will become your best friend if he/she is not already. But many things in life are not free; no pain, no gain. It costs to be a friend and this is why only a few reach this level in the husband-and-wife relationship or man-and-God relationship. Although it is costly, the reward of being the best friend to your spouse is phenomenal. Once a husband and wife have attained this kind of relationship, their marriage will not only last as long as they live, it will become happy and successful.

Yours can be a happy, successful marriage if you will put into practice the principles discussed in this book. Even if only one partner obeys, there will be a tremendous improvement in the marriage. If both partners obey, their home can become a taste of heaven. Remember that

Faith = Belief + Action

If you know these things, blessed and happy and to be envied are you if you practice them—if you act accordingly and really do them (John 13:17, AB).

Settle for nothing less than a happy, successful marriage. None of us will reach perfection, but if we settle for anything less, we end up with mediocrity.

READ YOUR BIBLE THROUGH IN A YEAR

January

1 Gen. 1-2
2 Gen. 3-5
3 Gen. 6-9
4 Gen. 10-11
5 Gen. 12-15
6 Gen. 16-19
7 Gen. 20-22
8 Gen. 23-26
9 Gen. 27-29
10 Gen. 30-32
11 Gen. 33-36
12 Gen. 37-39
13 Gen. 40-42
14 Gen. 43-46
15 Gen. 47-50
16 Ex. 1-4
17 Ex. 5-7
18 Ex. 8-10
19 Ex. 11-13
20 Ex. 14-17
21 Ex. 18-20
22 Ex. 21-24
23 Ex. 25-27
24 Ex. 28-31
25 Ex. 32-34
26 Ex. 35-37
27 Ex. 38-40
28 Lev. 1-4
29 Lev. 5-7
30 Lev. 8-10
31 Lev. 11-13

February

1 Lev. 14-16
2 Lev. 17-19
3 Lev. 20-23
4 Lev. 24-27
5 Num. 1-3
6 Num. 4-6
7 Num. 7-10
8 Num. 11-14
9 Num. 15-17
10 Num. 18-20
11 Num. 21-24
12 Num. 25-27
13 Num. 28-30
14 Num. 31-33
15 Num. 34-36
16 Dt. 1-3
17 Dt. 4-6
18 Dt. 7-9
19 Dt. 10-12
20 Dt. 13-16
21 Dt. 17-19
22 Dt. 20-22
23 Dt. 23-25
24 Dt. 26-28
25 Dt. 29-31
26 Dt. 32-34
27 Josh. 1-3
28 Josh. 4-6

March	April	May
1 Josh. 7-9	1 1 Ki. 8-10	1 2 Chr. 26-29
2 Josh. 10-12	2 1 Ki. 11-13	2 2 Chr. 30-32
3 Josh. 13-15	3 1 Ki. 14-16	3 2 Chr. 33-36
4 Josh. 16-18	4 1 Ki. 17-19	4 Ezra 1-4
5 Josh. 19-21	5 1 Ki. 20-22	5 Ezra 5-7
6 Josh. 22-24	6 2 Ki. 1-3	6 Ezra 8-10
7 Judg. 1-4	7 2 Ki. 4-6	7 Neh. 1-3
8 Judg. 5-8	8 2 Ki. 7-10	8 Neh. 4-6
9 Judg. 9-12	9 2 Ki. 11-14	9 Neh. 7-9
10 Judg. 13-15	10 2 Ki. 15-17	10 Neh. 10-13
11 Judg. 16-18	11 2 Ki. 18-19	11 Esther 1-3
12 Judg. 19-21	12 2 Ki. 20-21	12 Esther 4-7
13 Ruth 1-4	13 2 Ki. 22-25	13 Esther 8-10
14 1 Sam. 1-3	14 1 Chr. 1-3	14 Job 1-4
15 1 Sam. 4-7	15 1 Chr. 4-6	15 Job 5-7
16 1 Sam. 8-10	16 1 Chr. 7-9	16 Job 8-10
17 1 Sam. 11-13	17 1 Chr. 10-13	17 Job 11-13
18 1 Sam. 14-16	18 1 Chr. 14-16	18 Job 14-17
19 1 Sam. 17-20	19 1 Chr. 17-19	19 Job 18-20
20 1 Sam. 21-24	20 1 Chr. 20-23	20 Job 21-24
21 1 Sam. 25-28	21 1 Chr. 24-26	21 Job 25-27
22 1 Sam. 29-31	22 1 Chr. 27-29	22 Job 28-31
23 2 Sam. 1-4	23 2 Chr. 1-3	23 Job 32-34
24 2 Sam. 5-8	24 2 Chr. 4-6	24 Job 35-37
25 2 Sam. 9-12	25 2 Chr. 7-9	25 Job 38-42
26 2 Sam. 13-15	26 2 Chr. 10-13	26 Ps. 1-3
27 2 Sam. 16-18	27 2 Chr. 14-16	27 Ps. 4-6
28 2 Sam. 19-21	28 2 Chr. 17-19	28 Ps. 7-9
29 2 Sam. 22-24	29 2 Chr. 20-22	29 Ps. 10-12
30 1 Ki. 1-4	30 2 Chr. 23-25	30 Ps. 13-15
31 1 Ki. 5-7		31 Ps. 16-18

June	July	August
1 Ps. 19-21	1 Ps. 109-111	1 Isa. 7-9
2 Ps. 22-24	2 Ps. 112-114	2 Isa. 10-12
3 Ps. 25-27	3 Ps. 115-118	3 Isa. 13-15
4 Ps. 28-30	4 Ps. 119	4 Isa. 16-18
5 Ps. 31-33	5 Ps. 120-123	5 Isa. 19-21
6 Ps. 34-36	6 Ps. 124-126	6 Isa. 22-24
7 Ps. 37-39	7 Ps. 127-129	7 Isa. 25-27
8 Ps. 40-42	8 Ps. 130-132	8 Isa. 28-30
9 Ps. 43-45	9 Ps. 133-135	9 Isa. 31-33
10 Ps. 46-48	10 Ps. 136-138	10 Isa. 34-36
11 Ps. 49-51	11 Ps. 139-141	11 Isa. 37-39
12 Ps. 52-54	12 Ps. 142-144	12 Isa. 40-42
13 Ps. 55-57	13 Ps. 145-147	13 Isa. 43-45
14 Ps. 58-60	14 Ps. 148-150	14 Isa. 46-48
15 Ps. 61-63	15 Pr. 1-3	15 Isa. 49-51
16 Ps. 64-66	16 Pr. 4-7	16 Isa. 52-54
17 Ps. 67-69	17 Pr. 8-11	17 Isa. 55-57
18 Ps. 70-72	18 Pr. 12-14	18 Isa. 58-60
19 Ps. 73-75	19 Pr. 15-18	19 Isa. 61-63
20 Ps. 76-78	20 Pr. 19-21	20 Isa. 64-66
21 Ps. 79-81	21 Pr. 22-24	21 Jer. 1-3
22 Ps. 82-84	22 Pr. 25-28	22 Jer. 4-7
23 Ps. 85-87	23 Pr. 29-31	23 Jer. 8-11
24 Ps. 88-90	24 Eccl. 1-3	24 Jer. 12-16
25 Ps. 91-93	25 Eccl. 4-6	25 Jer. 17-19
26 Ps. 94-96	26 Eccl. 7-9	26 Jer. 20-22
27 Ps. 97-99	27 Eccl. 10-12	27 Jer. 23-25
28 Ps. 100-102	28 Song 1-4	28 Jer. 26-29
29 Ps. 103-105	29 Song 5-8	29 Jer. 30-32
30 Ps. 106-108	30 Isa. 1-3	30 Jer. 33-36
	31 Isa. 4-6	31 Jer. 37-39

September	October	November
1 Jer. 40-42	1 Amos 4-6	1 Lk. 18-21
2 Jer. 43-46	2 Amos 7-9	2 Lk. 22-24
3 Jer. 47-49	3 Oba.-Jonah	3 Jn. 1-3
4 Jer. 50-52	4 Mic. 1-4	4 Jn. 4-6
5 Lam. 1-5	5 Mic. 5-7	5 Jn. 7-10
6 Ezek. 1-3	6 Nah. 1-3	6 Jn. 11-13
7 Ezek. 4-7	7 Hab. 1-3	7 Jn. 14-17
8 Ezek. 8-11	8 Zeph. 1-3	8 Jn. 18-21
9 Ezek. 12-14	9 Hag. 1-2	9 Acts 1-2
10 Ezek. 15-18	10 Zech. 1-5	10 Acts 3-5
11 Ezek. 19-21	11 Zech. 6-10	11 Acts 6-9
12 Ezek. 22-24	12 Zech. 11-14	12 Acts 10-12
13 Ezek. 25-27	13 Mal. 1-4	13 Acts 13-14
14 Ezek. 28-30	14 Mt. 1-4	14 Acts 15-18
15 Ezek. 31-33	15 Mt. 5-7	15 Acts 19-20
16 Ezek. 34-36	16 Mt. 8-11	16 Acts 21-22
17 Ezek. 37-39	17 Mt. 12-15	17 Acts 23-25
18 Ezek. 40-42	18 Mt. 16-19	18 Acts 26-28
19 Ezek. 43-45	19 Mt. 20-22	19 Rom. 1-4
20 Ezek. 46-48	20 Mt. 23-25	20 Rom. 5-8
21 Dan. 1-3	21 Mt. 26-28	21 Rom. 9-11
22 Dan. 4-6	22 Mk. 1-3	22 Rom. 12-16
23 Dan. 7-9	23 Mk. 4-6	23 1 Cor. 1-4
24 Dan. 10-12	24 Mk. 7-10	24 1 Cor. 5-8
25 Hos. 1-4	25 Mk. 11-13	25 1 Cor. 9-12
26 Hos. 5-7	26 Mk. 14-16	26 1 Cor. 13-16
27 Hos. 8-10	27 Lk. 1-3	27 2 Cor. 1-3
28 Hos. 11-14	28 Lk. 4-6	28 2 Cor. 4-6
29 Joel 1-3	29 Lk. 7-9	29 2 Cor. 7-9
30 Amos 1-3	30 Lk. 10-13	30 2 Cor. 10-13
	31 Lk. 14-17	

December

	10 1 Tim. 4-6	21 2 Pet. 1-3
	11 2 Tim. 1-4	22 1 Jn. 1-2
1 Gal. 1-3	12 Tit.-Ph'm	23 1 Jn. 3-5
2 Gal. 4-6	13 Heb. 1-4	24 2 Jn., 3 Jn., Jd.
3 Eph. 1-3	14 Heb. 5-7	25 Rev. 1-3
4 Eph. 4-6	15 Heb. 8-10	26 Rev. 4-5
5 Phil. 1-4	16 Heb. 11-13	27 Rev. 6-9
6 Col. 1-4	17 Jas. 1-2	28 Rev. 10-13
7 1 Th. 1-5	18 Jas. 3-5	29 Rev. 14-16
8 2 Th. 1-3	19 1 Pet. 1-2	30 Rev. 17-18
9 1 Tim. 1-3	20 1 Pet. 3-5	31 Rev. 19-22

INDEX